MANAGEMENT THEORY AND PRACTICE
IN
PHYSICAL ACTIVITY EDUCATION
(including
ATHLETICS)

Earle F. Zeigler,

Ph.D., LL.D., D.Sc., FAAKPE
The University of Western Ontario
London, Ontario, Canada

TRAFFORD
2010

1

DEDICATION

This text treating management thought theory, and practice relating to physical activity education (including athletics) is dedicated to all the men and women with whom I worked closely--as thesis advisor, co-author, editor, professor, or on-the-job colleague--at one time or another from 1956 on while employed at The University of Michigan, Ann Arbor; the University of Illinois, U-C; and the University of Western Ontario, London, Canada. Each, in his/her own way, has contributed to the development of this sub–professional area (i.e., management thought, theory, and practice) of physical activity education and made a greater or lesser contribution in furthering the literary and informational material provided in this monograph.

Order this book online at www.trafford.com
or email orders@trafford.com

Most Trafford titles are also available at major online book retailers.

Printed in Victoria, BC, Canada.

ISBN: 978-1-4269-3042-3 (sc)
ISBN: 978-1-4269-3043-0 (dj)

Our mission is to efficiently provide the world's finest, most comprehensive book publishing service, enabling every author to experience success. To find out how to publish your book, your way, and have it available worldwide, visit us online at www.trafford.com

Trafford rev. 04/16/2010

www.trafford.com

North America & international
toll-free: 1 888 232 4444 (USA & Canada)
phone: 250 383 6864 ♦ fax: 812 355 4082

CONCEPTUAL INDEX

5

(e) PERT/CPM (program evaluation and review
technique/critical path method.
(f)) <u>queuing theory</u>

12

PREFACE

A new text in management thought, theory, and practice applied to physical activity education and athletics requires justification. *It should be made clear immediately that this text has been planned primarily for administrators of physical education and athletics at the several levels of educational institutions.* Nevertheless, much has been included here that can be very helpful as well to the sport and physical recreation manager in public and/or commercial sport and physical activity. *In other words, it is the underlying "thought, theory, and practice" that is fundamentally important.* Qualified professional administrators, armed with specialized competency and skill training, should then be able to move back and forth fairly seamlessly between the several branches of this overall field. In which "branch" or "camp" an administrator would "fit best" and "feel more at home" depends completely on the administrator's philosophy.

It has been argued that the 20th century was a transitional one in human history in which the period from 1900-2000 has taken us from one significant era to another. Moving into the 21st century, of course, we started down the path to finding the answer to this assumption. At any rate, changing times are occasioned by the impact of a variety of social forces on society. Additionally, such change has its accompanying, but often unsteady, influence on the professional training of leaders in the large number of fields that make up the society in which such change occurs.

In this instance I am concerned with the development of management education within North American culture primarily, although I appreciate that the idea of management training for the administration of "physical activity education" based on a discipline of "developmental physical activity" (my definitions!) in its various settings has been emerging worldwide with each passing year. More specifically, here I have *primarily* addressed the professional preparation of those men and women who will presumably administer and manage physical activity programs delimited to sport, exercise, play, and expressive movement *within all types of educational institutions at the several levels.*

Unfortunately, what has been called the field of physical education had moved relatively slowly earlier—and, in retrospect, inadequately—to meet the demand for theoretically oriented, well-qualified physical education and athletics *administrators.* Starting in the late 1920s, colleges and universities traditionally offered one course only in physical education and athletics administration. (This basic-course approach–geared to the public educational system only--was typically strengthened only slightly when it subsequently was repeated often quite repetitively in the graduate professional curriculum.) Such a lecture course was usually characterized by a dull "nuts and bolts" approach, often taught by the current (or the former) administrator of the department in which the course was offered.

13

It was just this type of course experience at both the undergraduate and graduate levels that was criticized so devastatingly by Professor Conant in 1962 (on p. 122 of *The education of American teachers*) that the field is still feeling the effects. (In fact, it was the ridicule shown by Dr. Conant of the physical education administration course of that era that can be labeled as *the* critical incident that occasioned much of the rapid action in the direction of a disciplinary, body-of-knowledge approach for the field in the 1960s.)

Inadequacy of Theoretical and Practical Training

To look back before we look ahead: Approximately 50 years ago, I recognized the inadequacy of the theoretical and practical training for management in this field. I was then a young *educator*, a "veteran" of 10 years of teaching and coaching in the field. As a new department head seeking to improve the prevailing situation in professional preparation in the field, I began to experiment with a new approach to the teaching of administration about 1954. In 1959, after finding personal success with it, I introduced the Harvard case-method plan of teaching human relations and administration to the broader field of physical education and athletics (Prentice-Hall, 1959).

This beginning effort was transferred from The University of Western Ontario to the University of Michigan (Ann Arbor) in 1956 where I had the opportunity to teach this subject at both the undergraduate and graduate levels. The beginning of a research endeavor, along with the guidance of several graduate students in thesis investigation, foretold of possibilities for the introduction of a stronger theoretical thrust than had been carried out previously. Then in 1963 a thoroughgoing research orientation to administrative theory and practice was introduced at the University of Illinois (Champaign-Urbana) with direct assistance from King McCristal, Laura Huelster, and David Matthews. This contribution had much to do with the inclusion of this area of scholarly research into the Big Ten Body-of-Knowledge Project begun at that time. Additionally, a substantive group of doctoral and master's theses were completed by outstanding graduate students in this specialized area (e.g., by Marcia Spaeth, Garth Paton, William Penny), a number of which were included later in another innovative publication (Zeigler & Spaeth, Prentice-Hall, 1975). During the mid-1960s, therefore, it became increasing evident throughout the field that the offering of only one, more or less traditional, professional course for undergraduate students was inadequate for both job placement and the demands that were being made of graduates exiting from the many physical education degree programs. This situation changed to a degree in the 1970s when a variety of areas of specialization were being introduced into the basic major program in most colleges and universities on the continent.

Interestingly, and understandably, a demand arose in the United States (and to a lesser extent in Canada) in the 1970s for a specialization that is now almost universally called sport management. Such a training program–one that is geared *almost completely* to sport management in non-educational settings of a public and/or commercial nature–was envisioned by James G. Mason at the University of Miami (FL) presumably at the instigation of Walter O'Malley of the (then) Brooklyn Dodgers in 1956. An undergraduate specialization was started to be followed by a master's program ay Ohio University in 1966. Even though some of our natural-science oriented colleagues find it "deplorable to waste time" on such an option, it can be stated unequivocally that the sport management specialization rapidly became a "success story" starting gradually in the 1970s (e.g., the Univ. of Massachusetts, Amherst, in 1971) and extending into the new millennium. Further, the outlook for the 21st century is bright, although many of these gains are still being consolidated due to the financial stringencies of the 1990s in higher education.

During the 1980s, steady advancement was occurring in management science in both business and educational administration. However, it was apparent to me (and especially to a colleague, Gary Bowie) that little had been done similarly to promote the idea of including laboratory experiences to aid in the development of management competencies and skills in physical education and educational sport management programs. However, we soon discovered that the field was still not ready to take such a progressive step forward. A volume I published that promoted the case method approach to the teaching of human relations and management (Zeigler, 1982), as well as one promoting management competency development in sport and physical education with Professor Bowie (1983), was somehow premature to the thought of most of our colleagues.

Undaunted, I am now reasonably secure in the knowledge that progress in understanding the complexity of professional management training has been made during the 1990s and the early years of the 21st century. And so, looking ahead, I state once again that more attention should undoubtedly be devoted to management thought, theory and practice--not to mention to acquisition of the competencies and skills required to be an effective and efficient manager. In fact, it is my belief that any training program that does not include laboratory experiences with each of its course offerings is inadequate. Hence, those of us "believers" continued to trust blindly that a minority of our colleagues have now become aware of this deficiency too. Also, I thought that those involved with management training would continue to implement positive changes. I believed further that social trends and the job market were forcing professionals in the field to develop sufficiently strong attitudes (psychologically speaking) to bring about this much needed change.

The North American Society for Sport Management

Of course, the inauguration of the North American Society for Sport Management in the mid-1980s with its solid *Journal of Sport Management* (Human Kinetics Publishers) has undoubtedly helped and should continue to be a boon to the field's future development. The recent appearance of the *Sport Management Education Journal is most encouraging as well.*. Also, the blossoming emphasis within the National Association for Sport and Physical Education (within the American Alliance for Health, Physical Education, Recreation, and Dance) looking toward solid sport management curriculum development in cooperation with NASSM has provided a further, much-needed stimulus and leveling effect. The additional, earlier inauguration of the *International Journal of Sport Management* by the American Press of Boston, with Dr. Bill Stier as editor, represents a fine building block for the field worldwide.

Despite the above discussion, the movement toward the almost 100% "scientification" of the overall field of physical education/kinesiology, characterized by the adoption of names like "kinesiology," "human kinetics," and "sport sciences," has undoubtedly mitigated somewhat the effort to improve the burgeoning development of what is called sport management. Obviously, no one should be denigrating any effort to provide a substantive scholarly base for the *overall* field's development. It should be clear to all that the way that people of all ages move should be the paramount emphasis within this scholarly foundation. However, unless men, women, and children understand the background development of the field and the present need for lifelong involvement in developmental physical activity, we will continue to have an inadequate body of knowledge upon which to build our drive toward professional status.

The presence of this inadequacy means that a social science and humanities under–girding is also required along with the natural science emphasis. It also means that the professional aspects of the field's development should be studied concurrently. This is where investigation regarding the theory and practice of programs of developmental physical activity must be included, as well as emphasis on the study of management thought, theory and practice applied to physical activity education, along with accompanying athletics and expressive movement.

For these reasons, therefore, I state once again that I am absolutely convinced that a scholarly social-science approach to management as it relates to physical activity education (including athletics) is more urgently needed than ever before. This is even truer because managers are being challenged as never before in history. In an era of budgetary cutback or management decline, our programs are in many instances being reduced drastically, with some even being eliminated.

16

Managers are increasingly finding, also, that they can no longer make unilateral decisions, despite the continuation of a thrust to a more conservative and traditional attitude toward politics, religion, education, and other pivotal social forces that began in the 1980s. Further, and this takes some explaining, despite the fact that the growth of programs in exercise science has been matched by training programs in the non-educational sport management arena, there has only been nominal movement toward improving the theoretical aspect of management training.

Slice it however you will, colleges and universities are not providing sufficient opportunities for prospective managers to understand the scope of, and to gain experience and achieve competence in, an irreducible battery of theoretically based management skills that ought to be the hallmark of a degree program in physical activity education (and athletics) management. This has been quite largely the approach followed with student teaching internships for those interested in management in educational institutions. This same trend has been followed with students interested in careers in sport management in the public sector. It is not enough simply to farm students out to a mixture of public, semi-public, and private organizations, the assumption being that these typically probably inadequately supervised, and often inadequately planned, experiences will fill the bill.

All of this is highly puzzling, because it must be apparent to our colleagues that change in society, including its seeming rate of acceleration, appears to be increasing. Nevertheless, in most cases we are still "making do" with the approach that was outdated more than a quarter of a century ago! For that matter, all of education is being challenged mightily at present at a time when the purse strings are being ever more tightened. This criticism is not meant to castigate (1) those professors in our field who are relating seriously to ongoing management science; (2) those managers in our field who have developed a unified theory-practice orientation toward their work; and (3) those universities where solid efforts are being made to introduce scholarly management programs as curriculum ventures on the undergraduate level and also on the graduate level up through the doctorate. However, it is also important to note again that people involved in management training are often receiving inadequate support from their colleagues in kinesiology units striving for what they regard as academic respectability.

Need for a Competency-Based Approach to Professional Preparation

In this volume, although the learning of theoretical and applied management knowledge is the primary purpose of this text, we are primarily concerned with the institution of a competency-based approach to professional preparation for management in physical activity education (including athletics). Knowledge achievement and management skill acquisition together, as recommended here represent one more effort to get away from the stereotypical, semi-scholarly book that has been used for decades as the administration text in physical education and athletics. As designed, therefore--even though a type of laboratory experiences is provided at the end of each chapter--this text could well be used with the laboratory manual or workbook designed specifically to promote management competency experiences (Zeigler and Bowie, 2007).

It has never made sense to turn out one more text that largely duplicated five or six other books already in existence. Accordingly, each time I published a new book in this area, I have searched instead for a new and innovative direction within our professional curriculum that might improve the overall offerings available to instructors concerned with professional preparation in our field. (Accordingly, I introduced texts on (1) the case method technique of teaching human relations and administration in physical education and athletics; (2) the theoretical base for administrative theory and practice in the field; and (3) a management competency-development approach in the training of sport and physical education administrators. The latter text and laboratory were created cooperatively with Prof. Gary W. Bowie, University of Lethbridge, AB, Canada.)

In this present circumstance, however, once again no diligent search for "something different" was necessary. I believe that this present offering to the field represents a further step forward. It was planned so as to cover the various aspects of management thought, theory and practice as applied to physical activity education (including athletics). I have deliberated about the present situation in the field from several standpoints. Should this new text for the new century be pointed toward (1) those kinesiology/physical education curricula that still offer one course in management or administration only? (2) those kinesiology/physical education curricula that offer a "minor" including--say--four courses in various aspects of sport/physical activity management? or (3) those sport management curricula where a full-blown program has been, or is being, developed for sport management in other than educational institutions?

My conclusion and response to these three questions is that it would be difficult to attempt to be *all things to all people*! Hence, I decided to "come down in the middle," so to speak. I decided against the first approach (No.1 above)--i.e., writing the one text to cover the waterfront of both physical activity education (including athletics) in public and private education AND sport management in the public sector. (This could only be what we call the "nuts and bolts" approach plus a smattering of theory.) I reasoned that there are other texts like that available. Next I also avoided the third approach

(No.3 above), but only to a degree (an explanation follows immediately below).

In deciding to "straddle" the three alternative presented above to a degree, I felt that what I had to offer would fit reasonably well into a curriculum where a minor (or a truncated major) in physical activity education and athletics management is being offered. Here I envision students electing this approach being required to take something like the following succession of courses or experiences: (1) an introductory, "nuts & bolts," physical activity education (including athletics) management course that covers the entire waterfront, with a smattering of theory; (2) a management theory course; and (3) a management competency development course experience (i.e., a fieldwork experience).

Coordination With a "Laboratory Manual"

After careful consideration, I decided (1) to cover management theory quite fully, (2) to include some "nuts and bolts" material here and there, and (3) to stress management competency development to a degree only. We did this in the hope that what we have offered will provide as sound an under–girding as possible for the young person prior to one or more fieldwork experiences. However, in addition to including questions for discussion at the end of each chapter, we have added one more wrinkle to our approach. We have coordinated our book with a laboratory manual relating to management competency development that has already been made available separately.

This laboratory manual could be used with the one-course approach above (No.1) or with the specialized management competency text approach (No.3). To the best of our knowledge there is no other laboratory workbook such as this available! The manual written by this author and Dr. Gary W. Bowie is titled *Management Competency Development in Sport and Physical Education*. It is available through the Trafford Publishing Company in Bloomington, Indiana www.trafford.com or can be obtained through a link at www.earlezeigler.com It is also available by googling the Stipes Publishing Company and following the links.

When preparing this text, and the laboratory manual mentioned immediately above, I made every effort to be fair to members of both sexes in regard to the use of "he" and "she." After some experimentation with combinations of non-sexist language--that is, he/she, s/he), I found–as have many others–that the structure of the English language does not at present have an adequate solution to this problem. I felt that a solution would have been most helpful to a field in which at least 50% of its members are women. Nevertheless, I was advised that, for clarity and ease of reading, I should typically use the masculine "he" as the general pronoun to conform to the rules of correct grammar and to facilitate the transmission of information.

However, I have made every effort throughout the book to show equal recognition to both sexes. I ask my readers to accept that this decision does not reflect a bias toward or against either sex.) Wherever possible, therefore, I use "plurality" (e.g., persons, managers).

Although much is included in this volume that is basically new to the field, what is still really new and—I truly believe--fundamentally important is the theoretical material AND the strong recommendation to employ an accompanying experiential or laboratory approach. Twenty–five years ago a comprehensive analysis of management science literature indicated the need to introduce a step-by-step plan for management skill or competency attainment (Zeigler & Bowie, 1983). In doing so, we built on Katz's (Harvard) tri-partite categorization of skills and arrived at five subdivisions so as to cover also the personal attributes needed for the professional preparation of the manager, as well as those "conjoined" skills gained through a "combinatorial process" that the individual is required to employ on the job. What Katz calls human skills, I now call interpersonal skills so as to distinguish this category from personal skills (#1 below). These subdivisions or categories have in my work become, therefore, the following:

1. Personal skills (or developing one's own competency)
2. Interpersonal skills (or influencing people positively to work toward accomplishment of organizational goals)
3. Conceptual skills (or formulating ideas and plans while on the job)
4. Technical skills (or managing the various organizational details and techniques)
5. Conjoined skills (or employing the various managerial skills in some combination or proportion to achieve both the immediate and long-range goals)

Granting that Katz' categories of *human* skills, *conceptual* skills, and *technical* skills for the prospective manager, along with our additional subdivisions of so-called *personal* and *conjoined* skills, are not mutually exclusive, the plan enables the teacher and the students to move selectively from theory to practice within each of the five subdivisions or categories described. The method for working toward the achievement of the specific competencies or skills is (1) through the provision of statements describing the theoretic basis of the competencies, (2) by explaining their functions in the management process, and (3) by developing techniques for achieving a degree of success (at least) based on involvement in a variety of problem-solving experiences. After the student comprehends (1) the problem to be met or solved, (2) a questioning process determines (a) what needs to be known, (b) where this information may be obtained, (c) how to organize the actual learning experience, (d) what the probable result will be, and (e) how to evaluate the level of competency attainment.

The teaching and learning process employed by the instructor should of necessity, therefore, include a variety of laboratory experiences in addition to standard lecture and discussion techniques. Other learning devices available include use of the case method, role-playing, independent study, interaction with a personal computer, elementary theory formulation, response to questionnaires and self-testing devices, individual projects, small discussion groups, etc. When the instructor wishes, and class time is available, he or she can introduce action or applied research, based independent investigation (e.g., survey, game theory), debates, internship experiences, panels, forums, and so forth. Basically, a fivefold process recommended by Whetten and Cameron (1991) is implemented that employs five components: (1) skill pre-assessment, (2) skill learning, (3) skill analysis, (4) skill practice, and (5) skill application. Thus, the instructor can assess initial student status, introduce selected experiences to strengthen areas of possible weakness, and subsequently evaluate competency attainment.

The future of the field of physical activity education (including athletics) will depend on the way developmental physical activity programs of a public, semi-public, semiprivate, and private nature are administered in the years ahead. Highly competent managers are needed at all levels to insure that sound fitness and exercise programs are readily available to all concerned that excellent opportunities for highly competitive and recreationally competitive athletics are provided. In addition, special programs of an adapted nature are should be made available for those with remedial or permanent physical handicaps.

Concluding Statement

The caliber of young people recruited into the profession, and the way they are prepared for leadership roles--as managers, teachers, coaches, performers, supervisors, or exercise specialists, is our responsibility. We should carry out this assignment in the best possible manner, in ways that are comparable to those used in the finest professions. The knowledge and theoretical experiences provided in this volume, along with the use of the recommended laboratory workbook for the development of specific management competencies and skills, will–when correctly implemented!—go a long way toward assisting young people to get a "healthy start" as they understand management thought, theory, and practice as applied to developmental physical activity programs for people of all ages and conditions.

Earle F. Zeigler
Richmond, B.C.
Canada
2010

CHAPTER 1

THE PRESENT SITUATION

It has been argued that the 20th century was a transitional one in human history–a period from 1900-2000 that has taken us from one historical era to another. This may be true, but only history in due time will provide the answer. At any rate, changing times are occasioned by the impact of a variety of social forces on society. Such change has its accompanying influence on the professional training of leaders in the many fields that make up the society in which the change is taking place.

In this instance we are concerned with this development within North American culture primarily, although sport and physical activity management training is taking roots in Europe and Japan notably. More specifically we addressed the professional preparation of those men and women who will presumably administer and manage developmental physical activity programs delimited to sport, exercise, play, and expressive movement.

Peter Drucker's advice (1993, Chap. 12) about the idea of "The Educated Person" in Post-Capitalist Society in the 21st century, seems like a good way to begin. He stated that a great transformation has been taking place in the world in regard to (1) a move from capitalism to a knowledge society, (2) a trend from nation-states to megastates, and (3) a shift from a market economy based on traditional market institutions to a market that organizes economic activity around information and knowledge (Chap. 10).

In this "new world," Drucker claims that the direct challenge to our society is the way that we use the new technology in what he calls post-capitalist society--i.e., the knowledge society (Chap. 11, p. 197). If we have the wisdom to shift rapidly and fully to a knowledge society that puts the person in the center of the process, we will be able to remain in the forefront of progress. This post-capitalist society needs leadership groups that "can focus local, particular, separate traditions onto a common and shared commitment to values, a common concept of excellence, and on mutual respect" (p. 212).

However, what is required, Drucker--as a hard-headed businessman–insists, is a new and different kind of educated person than the Deconstructionists, the radical feminists, the anti-Westerners, and the humanists want (p. 212). What is needed, he maintains, is an educated person who has the knowledge and the commitment to cope with the present situation, as well as being prepared for "life in a global world" (p. 214). Leaders in this society under transformation will use sound organizational theory as a tool enabling them to use their specialized knowledge wisely.

Bertram Gross's earlier prediction about the need for an action-theory marriage in management will indeed come to pass (1964, pp. 844-856).

The Mission of Sport and Physical Activity Management

In such a developing world environment, then, what is the mission of a field called sport and physical activity management by some, one that is rapidly catching on all over the world? I believe strongly that our overall field needs to understand its mission much better than appears to be the case at present. Exactly what is its fundamental purpose in society? Further, how does the mission of the overall field relate to the mission of the various professional associations composed primarily of men and women involved in the professional education of future managers? (Keep in mind that the professional sport promoters worldwide live in "another world"!)

In today's world, the outlooks or aims of those people who promote sport competition professionally and that of those who promote such competition educationally appear to be getting closer all the time. (I am referring here to the people involved, for example, in the National Basketball Association or the National Collegiate Athletic Association in the United States, respectively.) Granted that the people in both of these associations are operating on the assumption that the provision of highly competitive sport opportunities in society is a good thing. Also, they appear to believe that promoting ever more opportunity for the masses to watch (and income for such active involvement by the "accelerated few" athletes!) is still better.

Frankly, I believe this has become a dubious premise or principle upon which these promoters and/or educational administrators are operating. I maintain this is so unless they can provide accompanying evidence to substantiate to society that the continuation and enlargement of the present trend is contributing positively to society as a social institution. (All social institutions must have an underlying theory to justify their continuing existence.)

Excesses and Corruption of Competitive Sport Have Increased Steadily

To one who has followed this development down through the 20th century most carefully from both a historical and a philosophical standpoint, I can only report (sadly!) that the excesses and corruption of competitive sport have increased steadily decade by decade. And, even more sadly, the seemingly jaded public (the "fans," if you will) does not seem to realize that sport's status as a desirable social institution is being lowered steadily with each passing year. Competitive sport is forced to stay within the law, but a laudable creed and a workable code of ethics are but vague hopes and dreams for the future.

Paradoxically, this increasingly low professional status is taking place even though ongoing research in kinesiology and physical activity education--and the field's related disciplines--is steadily making the case for regular, developmental physical activity as an essential, if not a vital, social institution. Nevertheless the term "sport," and what it connotes to the average mind, largely overrides the need for the provision of necessary funding of developmental physical activity as a social institution. Such provision for the managing and promoting developmental physical activity in sport, exercise, and physical recreation for people of all ages, be they part of accelerated, normal, or special populations, should be a substantive part of our mission in sport and physical activity management. Yet we find that our professional associations and disciplinary societies are steadily and increasingly becoming more disjointed as they grow farther apart.)

Hence, I believe it is now incumbent upon the field of sport and physical activity management to investigate and then understand what effect sport, however defined and with all of its ramifications, is having on society. Is it more good than bad? Who knows? The professional and semiprofessional sport managers can't answer this basic question. (They wouldn't want to anyhow if it meant a shifting of emphasis.) Therefore it would seem that the world's various professional sport management associations should take a hard look at this steadily growing problem to determine (1) what effect sport is having on society, (2) to what extent the professional associations (e.g., NASSM in North America) may unwittingly be part of the problem, and (3) how professional sport management associations may have the potential to ensure that sport as a whole, and more specifically its many programs at all levels, are moving in the right direction.

Ecology–Oriented Management Practice

We are all quite aware of Tofflers' concepts (1970, 1981, 1994) of 'future shock' and 'third wave world'. Daily there are indications that our external environment is being damaged by one means or another. Such concern has now become worldwide in scope. Accordingly, we must be ready, individually and collectively, for our own personal collision with the future. The world will never be the same again--but, then, it probably never was.

The external environment of the sport and physical activity manager relates typically to the still broader physical and social environment of the public, semipublic, or private agency that the manager is administering within society. It can be argued that all managers should assist the larger community (the external environment) by assuming some direct responsibility for society's welfare over and above his or her own immediate professional task.

I have personally been concerned since about 1970 that the prospective director or manager of sport and physical activity develop an understanding of the concept of 'ecological management' in both the external and internal organizational environments that he or she will face in North America. Such formal education or self-education must take place in the face of the fact that a managerial revolution did indeed occur in the 20th century, the limits of which we today still only envision dimly. Further, the management of change is an ever-present reality.

Assessing society's rate of change that has created an urgent need for sound, adaptive management practice may be literally impossible. Now the world is faced with the additional mandate that such practice be "ecologically sound" as well. However, the onset of so-called post-industrial society has alerted us to the importance of one fact: we must increasingly search for synthesis and consensus because of conflicting demands and trends in our lives. "Second wave civilization placed an extremely heavy emphasis on our ability to dismantle problems into their components; it rewarded us less often for the ability to put the pieces back together again" (Toffler, 1981, pp. 129-30).

What we need now in all aspects of (Third Wave) life is to put all of this in greatly improved, readily apparent context. Today we must do all in our power to "eschew obfuscation" (i.e., to be clear, concise, and precise in what we say and do). We have so much to deal with that is obsolescent, "folklore" that should be viewed simply as excess "cultural baggage." This is nowhere more true than in many of the managerial myths that surface time and again in the immediate, on-the-job environment. (An example of this is the dismal myth that overnight the person who assumes the managerial mantle knows best about everything).

In the management of sport and other developmental physical activity, we urgently need the knowledge from onrushing behavioral theory that will help us to understand the managerial structure in an ever more-insightful manner. Is it too much to hope that search committees recommend men and women for managerial posts who are committed to the employment of sound management theory in accord with ethical practice? Further, it is unreasonable to expect that when mistakes are made in manager selection that people will be prepared to rectify an unproductive situation at the first possible legal and ethical moment?

With a truly scientific--but hopefully still humanistic--approach to management, coupled with an awareness of the unprecedented social influence of "good" or "bad" ecological practice, the managerial team and key associated personnel on the job should seek to develop, employ, and maintain power and influence that lead to the achievement of planned goals imbued with an "ecological ethos." Many people within the organization will be involved in one way or another in assisting with the implementation of the fundamental processes of planning, organizing, staffing, directing, and controlling the operation of the organization. Through such practice. it is imperative that good human relations be employed by all through the use of effective and efficient communication techniques. The successful implementation of these various processes is extremely complex, of course. This is why a top-flight managerial team is becoming increasingly necessary to move a complex organization ahead, a team that is fully aware of the need for "sound ecological-management practices."

For Consideration and Discussion:

As an exercise it is recommended that two students each make a 10-minute presentation, one arguing pro and the other con, as to whether the field is currently making satisfactory progress toward the achievement of its mission. Then a third student should conduct a class discussion on the topic.

CHAPTER 2

PHYSICAL ACTIVITY EDUCATION AND SPORT MANAGEMENT: PAST, PRESENT, FUTURE

One reason for professional people involved with physical activity education and sport management--however described--to assess the enterprise is that highly commercialized physical activity education and sport management is increasingly giving important cultural activities (physical activity education! sport!) an overall "bum rap!" By that I mean that physical activity education sport participation are too important to North America--and the entire world for that matter--to allow them to become anything less than "socially useful servants." These are the functions that they have the capability to fulfill for all people. For example, the "commercialization issue" was raised strongly and clearly–for the umpteenth time actually–in the first article of a series about university athletics turned out by *The New York Times* titled "When the Cash Register Is the Scoreboard" (June 8, 1986). As Michael Goodwin stated,

> Sport has become a big, profitable business on many campuses. A powerful, business-oriented constituency, often unconcerned about the academic side of the university, has sprung up around athletic programs . . . Athletic departments, facing the pressures of bills to pay and expectations to meet, are as bottom-line-oriented as any company on the Fortune 500. Although they are ostensibly part of the universities they represent, many athletic departments operate as separate, autonomous units, raising and spending millions of dollars with little or no university oversight.

If Goodwin had any misgivings in relation to the commercialization of sport in society generally, here his attention to the matter resulted in a devastating analysis of the developing situation throughout the 20th century that has, for these institutions at least, gotten out of hand. The result has been a poor educational situation generally with highly questionable ethical practices emerging on all fronts (pp. 28-29). In addition to these comments about what I am designating as semiprofessional sport in certain universities, the values and norms of all countries involved must continue to prevail through adequate legislation for professional sport as well. At the same time, many of the physical activity education programs in educational institutions were lacking both quantity and quality–or else were not available at all>

A second reason for taking a hard look right now at the background, status, and possible future of sport management is that the complexity of administration or management (terms that I have use almost interchangeably) is well known even to the layperson today. I defined management in a previous text as involving "the execution of managerial acts, including conceptual, technical, human, and conjoined skills, while combining varying degrees of planning, organizing, staff, directing, and controlling within the management process to assist an organization to achieve its goals" (Zeigler and Bowie, 1983). Applied to our field, then--and to the stated purpose of the North American Society for Sport Management--the above description of the management process would apply to an organization that somehow, somewhere in North America is offering at least some aspect of developmental physical activity in sport, exercise, and related expressive movement to some degree to one or more sectors of the population.

In the face of the ever-heightening demands on these professional educators, why people still put their names forward to selection committees for consideration for managerial posts has become somewhat of an enigma to me. Maybe I'm simply getting old, but conversely I must say that they are perhaps unwittingly "asking for it." This seems to be especially true in the field of physical activity education and so-called educational sport. The words of the late Seward Staley (Illinois, UIUC) still ring in my ears: "The best job at the university level is that of a full professor!" Even so he was the dean at Illinois for a long time.

Some "educated guesses" as to why present or potential coach/physical activity educators are willing to move into positions of administrative responsibility can nevertheless be made. First, such positions do typically pay relatively higher salaries, and thus the total amount earned builds up over the years if a person survives the rigors of such a post and continues with it almost indefinitely. In Canadian universities, one gets an administrative stipend of varying amount initially, and this is either removed or you "grow up to it" after the term of office has been completed.

Second, there have been no large rewards for research and scholarly work in physical activity education in the past, nor has such a professor acquired great kudos in intellectual circles. Hence, maybe administration has provided an opportunity for some to receive some prestige on the local, regional, national, and international scenes. Third, it could be argued that present or potential coach/physical educators are better suited constitutionally for managerial roles--i.e., they often have the body type and temperament presumably necessary positively aggressive leadership (whatever that may be).

Fourth, maybe it's a chance to get out of a superfluity of lecture and activity teaching, or perhaps the demanding routine of coaching. Yet, conversely the scholarly productivity of the very large majority of administrator–to quote the late Paul Hunsicker of Michigan–would never

28

"startle the academic world." And yet, oddly, isn't that presumably why we think that people want to get involved at the college or university level in the first place? Finally, and this is not as facetious as it sounds, lately it's about the only way to get an administrative assistant and a secretary!

Thus, any one of a combination of these reasons, and perhaps some others not mentioned, could account for the urge to be selected as dean or director, department chairperson or head, athletic director, supervisor or coordinator of physical education and athletics, or even program chairperson or head coach. Why people choose managerial posts in public recreation, or private agencies, or in commercial fitness enterprises, could also be conjectured upon at length.

Seemingly Little Awareness of the Managerial Revolution

One interesting thing I've observed, even after efforts by many of us for the past 50 years to upgrade management theory and practice applied to our field is that–within educational circles in physical education/kinesiology at least–the new manager or administrator is often still unaware of the managerial revolution that has occurred within the past 50 years at least. This is starkly true, of course, if this person did not prepare specifically for management service either within an educational administration professional preparation program or perhaps in a school of business administration.

Then he or she becomes aware of it when picked for an administrative post, and the difficult and laborious aspects of the management process are usually turned over to someone with training in business practice. This is considerably less true for people who assume managerial posts in recreation and other public, semi-public and private agencies where developmental physical activity happens to be a good part of the organization's program.

But even those in these other groups (i.e., commercial or private agencies--if they have only had one course in administration or management as part of their background preparation--have only a vague understanding of the many aspects and ramifications of the position being undertaken. What's even worse is the fact that even after he or she is on the job, such a person is still not cognizant of the unbelievable complexity of the position! They learn to "do what they do" by trial and error! The typical approach is to work overtime to get control of the new responsibility and to meet the seemingly endless demands of higher administration made by faculty, staff, and students--or the public as consumers or whatever in commercial and private enterprises.

Quite soon one gets the feeling that a treadmill is in operation and that the pitch is getting steeper, thereby creating a situation where one must trot at a brisk pace simply not to fall off the back end! It's an uneasy feeling because the pressure is there constantly; some people end up with duodenal spasms and a subsequent ulcer. Work tends to pile up in enormous quantities when one is absent from the office for just a few short days. Then, too, all the while there is the feeling that he or she is merely doing what is practical and expedient at the moment. The pattern of operation does indeed become one of trial and error, and it seems impossible to take time out for extended future planning.

Finally, because of the many, steadily increasing persistent demands that are made upon his or her office, the administrator reasons that more help is needed--both administrative and secretarial. No matter whether budgetary pressures increase, and so-called management in decline becomes a perennial syndrome, there will probably continue to be an increase in positions of this type now and in the foreseeable future. It's the simple truth that "assistants need assistants of their own!" What is the answer to this dilemma? Here's a concise prescription: "What is needed is an integrated sport management program that proceeds from a systematic approach to management."

Taking this thought to heart, therefore, I will seek to systematize this paper after this introduction by addressing the following topics related to the management of physical activity education (including sport) by responding to a series of questions in sequence: (1) what has been the historical background of sport management? (2) what is its present status? (3) what plan should be followed for the finest sort of progress in the years ahead? and (4) what may we conclude from this presentation?

Historical Background

Before we can discuss what we should be doing right now, as well as how we should be planning for the future in the area of management theory and practice as applied to our field, we would be well advised to review the situation historically. How did this all happen? It happened because the knowledge explosion that has affected almost the entire world has also had its impact on the managing of organizations, and more specifically on the individuals managing these organizations. Management tends to be a dynamic process with steady, almost constant change as a typical pattern of life. The Industrial Revolution of the mid-eighteenth century was the precursor, the effects of which soon spread to all aspects of life including education. Technological change of necessity has been closely related to administrative or managerial change; new methods and techniques of management became part of the technological development itself. With this managerial revolution came more organization and larger-scale organizations. The inevitable result was more bureaucracy and more people serving as administrators.

As North American society within Western culture continued to grow in complexity, amazing social changes occurred. Such change occurs if and when people develop the desire, the physical resources, and the technical know-how to perform the tasks in the most expedient manner possible. Our desires are, of course, closely related to the values and norms of the culture–values that aid in attitude formation so that the leaders can get the support of the people to fulfill the assigned duties and responsibilities.

The continuing industrial revolution, and now what has been called the postindustrial revolution by some because of developing cybernetics, coupled with literally fantastic advances in science and technology, has placed people in a difficult situation in our most developed societies. These factors, along with the exploding population and the resultant development of immense urban and suburban areas, have created a situation in which a certain percentage of the person–power has been forced to concern itself increasingly with the management of the efforts of the large majority of the people in our society. The ability of a relatively few people to master this task to a reasonable degree has meant that the world as we know it could continue to grow and develop, unless adverse ecological factors or human mistakes bring about a steady-state society and culture.

This is not meant to imply that many people have not organized and administered all types of enterprises in the past. The point being made is that most recently an "organizational," "administrative," or "managerial" revolution has taken place, and will continue because of the ever-increasing complexity of our evolving society. It is the more complex thought and the resultant administrative theory that is new in this century. Hence, such theory is now serving us in a similar way to manage our organizations as did earlier, less complex administrative thought and practice enable people of earlier periods to accomplish their goals. Such thought and practice have necessarily been inextricably interwoven with the broad processes of historical evolution.

What we are discovering in North America, of course, is that everything has become big--almost monstrous--and then even bigger still (witness the fate of AT&T!). Thus there is Big Business, Big Government, Big Labor (now getting a bit smaller), Big Science and Technology, Big Agriculture (some problems here too), Big Religion (including the inroads of the fundamentalists in the TV industry), Big Communications Media, Big Education, and now Big Sport and to a relatively small segment of the population: Big Fitness. (Note that a type of physical fitness has always been bestowed on those who must carry out physical labor in subsistence economies!) Of course, as mentioned above, Big Sport within Big Education has now become Big Business too, and this means that fine managers and administrators are needed in all of these enterprises even if we decry much of such overemphasis.

It is still accurate to state that there has been little evidence that managers or administrators in physical activity education (including sport) wherever they may be functioning, either in practice or in administration courses, are concerned with the theoretical aspects of management. In fact, a paradoxical situation arises in physical activity education and athletics at the university level when one is imprudent enough to discuss such a thing as "management theory." The paradox arises because the field seems very definitely to be divided into two groups, neither of which can see the need or importance of such a subject. These groups might be labeled as the "practitioners" and the "scientists." The practitioners don't believe such theory will help them on the job, and the scientist has yet to be convinced of the scientific quality of any such investigation.

This feeling of mistrust must somehow be changed. The great sociologist, Talcott Parsons in mid-20th century (1958) stated: "a formal organization in the present sense is a mechanism by which goals somehow important to the society, or to various subsystems of it, are implemented and to some degree defined." With all of this development as society became increasingly complex, however, there has been a strong trend toward the dehumanization of people. They tended to lose their identities as work tasks became increasingly splintered. The individual became more subordinated to the organization with attendant alienation from other people. A clash of ideological systems is present as well within our increasingly over-organized society. All around us we see examples of inflexibility as totalitarian patterns of management compete with more democratic models. Such models are often subjected to great strain, and the increasing complexity could well be bringing the large modern organization to the point where it will face what might have been the fate of the dinosaur (unless you go along with the interplanetary–theory collision thought ending their existence overnight.

The Marketing Orientation Concept

To avoid the presumed fate of the dinosaur, any organization today must have a stance in regard to what has become known as the *marketing concept*--that business phenomenon that gained such great momentum in the 1940s. Marketing is typically defined as activities that accelerate the movement of goods and services from the manufacturer to the consumer. Thus it is marketing whether one is talking about advertising, distributing, merchandising, product planning, promotion, publicity, and even transportation and warehousing.

32

The development of the marketing concept was a response from business to a society that was steadily acquiring more buying power. The personal income of the average family rose steadily so that life's basic essentials used up a smaller proportion of a person's salary. Along the way the nature of the consumer's demands was also changing along with the rising production levels. All of this brought about a dramatic rise in the demand for services about 1950 and thereafter. As the social environment changed, the business community was affected as well. The variety of demands by the consumer soon brought about the introduction of the concept of "market segmentation." With each segment having its own discrete desires, needs, and preferences, businesses found it necessary to develop and maintain individual market-strategy plans. (In this connection sport and physical activity managers of all types need an ever-improving understanding of marketing orientation so that the needs and interests of the presumed market segment are best served.)

It will not be discussed here at length, but it should be understood that competitive sport in educational institutions, for example, has faced differing marketing environments with each succeeding decade. For example, in the 1960s there was a great need for additional revenue sources as operating costs skyrocketed. This need continued in the 1970s and was further exacerbated by changing social and economic influences (e.g., social values, slower economic growth). Then in the 1980s a need existed more than ever for sport programs to develop individual strategic marketing plans with concurrent evaluation schedules to serve as control mechanisms.

A Formal Organization Defined (Parsons)

Writing in 1958, Parsons explained: "a formal organization in the present sense is a mechanism by which goals somehow important to the society, or to various subsystems of it, are implemented and to some degree defined." With all of this development as society became increasingly complex, however, there has been a strong trend toward the dehumanization of people. They tended to lose their identities as work tasks became increasingly splintered. The individual became more subordinated to the organization with attendant alienation from other people. A clash of ideological systems is present as well within our increasingly over-organized society. All around us we see examples of inflexibility as totalitarian patterns of management compete with more democratic models. Such models are often subjected to great strain, and the increasing complexity could well be bringing the large modern organization to the point where it too will face what might have been the now legendary fate of the early behemoth.

Three Major Eras of Administrative Thought

During the twentieth century an extensive body of literature on administration has developed, also. An initial review of this data suggests three major eras of administrative thought. First, in the early years of the twentieth century, investigation focused on the formal organization itself and job performance within that structure. Frederick Taylor, for example, was one researcher who looked into the question of efficiency. Others concentrated on the formal structure of organizations. All together, these studies constituted what has been called the "scientific management" era of administration (Gross, 1954, p. 38). As a result of such investigation, various scholars formulated several taxonomies and a number of principles that were widely adopted in government, business, and education.

The so-called "human relations era" arose from studies carried out primarily in industry, investigations that were to have an important influence on administrative thought (Gross, pp. 50-51). These studies, carried out at the Western Electric Company's Hawthorne plant between 1925 and 1933, revealed how important the social aspects of job performance are. As a result, the emphasis in administration began to shift more toward the institution of a human relations approach to management. The evidence seemed to indicate that worker satisfaction would result in greater work productivity (Bedeian, 1985, pp. 493-494).

What may be designated as the third major era of administrative thought in the twentieth century has been called the area of administrative science or theory. Chester I. Barnard, writing in business and Herbert A. Simon in public administration were important in strengthening this emphasis that was leading to a general theory of administration that could guide professional practice toward implementation of sound research findings.

A Fourth Stage Is Postulated

Gordon (1966, pp. 6-23), in his assessment of the late nineteenth century and the first half of the twentieth century, traced what he argued were four reasonably distinct, yet overlapping, stages in the history of management thought: the traditional, the behavioral, the decisional, and the ecological. These correspond nicely with the three eras described immediately above, and add a fourth (an "ecological era"). After this, however, it seems impossible to gain historical perspective on what has been occurring during the past two or three decades. Each of the earlier four stages mentioned above were named because some person or group believed in certain generally agreed-upon "truths." Gordon himself was probably on safe ground when he, in conclusion, called for an approach that transcends any one school of management thought.

The mushrooming of the behavioral sciences since has made it literally impossible for a scholar to keep up with the vast quantities of literature in many languages being produced all over the world. As a result those preparing for the profession of management have found themselves facing an impossible task--keeping up with an information overload, as well as retrieving a great deal of knowledge that helps to form a sound human behavior inventory. Also, the conflicting approaches to management (i.e., the different theories as to "how it should be done") that compete for the attention of the manager in the many books, monographs, and journals are very puzzling. Gordon's recommendation of a flexible framework could well be employed as a synthesis of the four approaches enabling the student of administrative theory to build a conceptual framework that provided a much fuller perspective and a "working model" of the management process.

A Situational/Contingency Approach
As A Composite Research Design?

In a 1979 analysis, however, Hodgetts explained that there is one line of thought that envisions three schools of management thought (i.e., the management process school, the quantitative school, and the behavioral school) merging into a *systems* school. A second point of view at this time, however, held that we already had a well-established systems school of thought and that it, along with the three approaches just mentioned, are moving in the direction of an overarching *situational* or *contingency* school. This had been called a *general contingency theory of management* by Luthans and Stewart (1977) in which management problems can be encompassed in a theoretical framework that integrates and synthesizes the various schools of thought into a workable research design that has three dimensions-- management variables, situational variables, and performance criteria variables. The objective is to integrate tenable management theory into a composite system for ongoing study and investigation.

In the mid-1980s, Harold Koontz of UCLA (now deceased), explained that in the mid-1960s he had decided that there was a "management theory jungle out there," a situation in which academic theorists primarily were seeking to explain the nature and theory of management from six different points of view or "schools." However, instead of the situation becoming clarified in the intervening 20 years between and 1985, he stated that "the jungle still exists" (1985, p. 509) and in fact has become more dense and overgrown. Instead of the six approaches indicated above, the number had mushroomed to 11 approaches to the study of management science as follows: (1) the empirical or case approach, (2) the interpersonal behavior approach, (3) the group behavior approach, (4) the cooperative social system approach, (5) the socio–technical systems approach, (6) the decision theory approach, (7) the systems approach, (8) the mathematical or "management science" approach, (9) the contingency or situational approach (see above), (10) the managerial roles approach, and (11) the operational approach. Short Koontz provided short summaries of each of these approaches (pp. 509-513). (Stayed tuned for updates on these and other development; in the meantime, we are urged to promote professional preparation program in universities that stresses an action-theory marriage resulting in basic competency attainment for the prospective manager.)

Finally, the continuing industrial revolution, and what has been called the postindustrial revolution by some because of developing cybernetics, coupled with literally fantastic advances in science and technology, has placed people in a difficult situation even in our most developed societies. These factors, along with the exploding population and the resultant development of immense urban and suburban areas, have created a situation in which a larger percentage of the person–power has been forced to concern itself increasingly with the management of the efforts of the large majority of the people in our society. The ability of a relatively few people to master this task to a reasonable degree has meant that the world as we know it may indeed continue to grow and develop. It is up to us all to do everything that we can to cut down on adverse ecological factors and human mistakes so that we may effect a steady-state society and culture.

Management Literature in Physical Activity Education (including Athletics)

Examination of the early literature physical activity education (including educational sport) in the mid-1960s by Spaeth (1967) indicated that the field was almost completely unaware of the development of administrative theory and research that was taking place in other fields. Subsequently, Baker and Collins (1983) reported that approximately ten per cent of completed thesis research in sport and physical education could be related to administration or management. (The number of theses in the administration area then were exceeded only slightly by those that are "exercise physiological" in nature.) However, despite positive efforts by some (e.g., B. Parkhouse in the U.S.A., P. Chelladurai in Canada), general awareness of the theoretic literature--or any significant contribution to it--has seemingly increased only marginally in the past twenty years.

This evident lack of awareness and concern is troubling since the field has recently begun to appreciate that people should be prepared more carefully and thoroughly for the "assumption of the managerial risk." For example, since opportunities to specialize in streams or areas of concentration within physical education-kinesiology training programs began, the sport management specialization soon appeared to be the most popular program. One is forced to speculate about the intellectual level of these programs early on when the professors and instructors typically such

36

reluctant, unproductive scholars. However, with the inauguration of the North American Society for Sport Management in 1986, the situation has gradually changed for the better.

Professional Status for Managers in Our Field

The phenomena of (1) organized physical activity education within education, (2) organized athletics also within education, and (3) a great variety of public agency, private agency, and commercial programs of developmental physical activity of all types in sport, exercise, dance, and play for all ages and all abilities that have taken place in North America within the past 122 years since the beginning of the first professional association in the field have today blossomed into an unbelievably large and complex enterprise that demands a multitude of wise and skillful managers. The situation is now such that the appointment of a director of physical activity education, or an athletic director, or a manager of a fitness club, or a private agency physical director, or a supervisor of physical recreation, etc. is a very ordinary and expected occurrence. These men and women as they function with their posts are gradually assuming many of the earmarks of a profession.

Having said this, we must keep in mind that a recognized profession needs an organized body of knowledge based on research. A profession that is fully worthy of the name must, of course, meet certain other criteria (e.g., have a code of ethics that is enforced). For now, however, keep the criterion of an organized body of knowledge based on research firmly in mind. Thus the perpetuation of our "species"--the manager of some type of developmental physical activity as it relates to our profession--requires that some effective and efficient organizational structure be developed within educational institutions through which the body of professional knowledge may be transmitted to those who follow.

If we grant the above statements concerning one of the primary criteria of a true profession, as well as the continuing need to prepare new managers professionally through some sort of experience in which this background knowledge is transmitted both theoretically and practically, then let us consider very briefly how administrators and managers at all educational levels and in the business world received their preparation for this demanding position in the past. The answer to this question is immediately obvious: Generally speaking, many, if not all, of these men and women worked their way up through the ranks in some sort of an apprenticeship scheme (no matter how ridiculous some of these schemes may seem when examined in the light of subsequent demands made upon the individual).

One basic prerequisite seems to be that they themselves were interested and active in physical activity and sporting activities. Quite often, as well, they were physical education majors and took several courses of an administrative nature at the undergraduate or master's levels, either within physical education or in educational administration. In some cases, and this was especially true for men, they were (1) not physical education majors at college, but later decided to cast their lots with our field because of successful competitive athletic experience; or (2) they were physical education majors at college, but initially had really not planned to stay with the field. Whatever the case may have been, the fact has been that these people demonstrated many fine personality traits and leadership traits. They knew how to get along with people; they made good appearances; they wanted to get things done; they were willing to work hard; and they believed strongly in the benefits of what they felt was "the right kind" of competitive sport.

Such a method of "preparing" managers or administrators is not unique to this field. A similar circumstance was evident when one examined the professional programs in schools of education, business, public administration, hospital administration, and social work. Still further, the more mature professional schools of medicine, law, and engineering exhibited a similar pattern in earlier stages of their development. This is in contrast, of course, to the recognized academic disciplines, where administrators were picked typically *on the basis of scholarly and research endeavor (and perhaps because they possessed certain desirable personality traits as well)*. In the latter case, this method of selection is still practiced quite generally today, and the very large majority of this group may have never taken even one course in management theory and practice. One is tempted to state facetiously that what has happened in higher education generally over the past several decades shows it, but to this description must be added "the ability to raise money for the institution!"

Despite the inadequacies in professional preparation for management in our field that had existed for decades, it must be confessed that courses in the organization and administration of physical education and athletics have been offered in our field since 1890 (Zeigler, 1951)! By 1927 they were typically included in professional curricula throughout the United States (Elliott). Since that time there has been a proliferation of similar courses relating to administration and supervision at both the undergraduate and graduate levels. In addition, literally thousands of master's theses and doctoral dissertations have been deposited on the shelves of our libraries. Most of these studies involve the descriptive method of research, or some technique thereof, and there is unquestionably a body of knowledge of sorts about practice of an administrative nature. Relatively speaking, however, there is still very little research in management theory. What we have is an endless stream of articles, theses, dissertations, monographs, and texts on the subject-matter area, but what it all adds up to is anybody's guess.

What can be said at the present? If those working in the area are searching for academic respectability, management theory in this field must steadily and increasingly strive for a sound theoretical basis. This is actually happening to a degree now. The fact of the matter is , however, that–even though organization and administration have a long history in our professional preparation programs, investigation into these topics–it still has not achieved the recognition that has been accorded to research in (for example) sport and physical education history. How can we improve this situation? First, the terms and concepts used must be clear, and they must be related to systematic theory. Second, the theory that we are able to develop should be "generalizable" (and therefore abstract). Third, the research endeavor should be as value-free as possible; if we want to introduce values, they should be treated as variables in the investigative methodology. Fourth, such scholarly endeavor will undoubtedly be based on the social (and primarily the behavioral) sciences. Finally, five, correlations are interesting and also significant, but adequate theory should, in the final analysis, clarify processes that will produce quality performance (J. D. Thompson, in Halpin, 1958, pp. 29-33).

A Plan for Progress

We really don't have much choice at the present other than to make all possible efforts to place professional preparation for administrative leadership within our field on an academically sound basis. At present the need for vastly improved leadership comes at us from a number of different directions. We simply do not have enough fine leaders in any field--and our field is no exception to this statement. If we don't have good leadership, an organization or enterprise soon begins to falter and even to stumble. Our field needs fine people who will take charge in the behaviorally oriented work environment of today's world. We've all heard that management involves the accomplishment of an objective through the enlistment of others to work closely with you. However, as Zoffer (1985) stated: "But I would add to that the need to achieve a certain excellence--accomplishing goals efficiently, cost-effectively and imaginatively, while respecting the lives and welfare of the broader community." There is no doubt but that physical activity education including sport has achieved greater recognition within educational circles on this continent than in any other geographical area of the world. Such achievement is an accomplished fact, but we now have to continue in the direction of upgrading professional preparation for administrative or managerial leadership so that the profession of sport and physical education will consolidate those gains made and--like the successful basketball team--continue to "move strongly down court on balance toward the goal" (Rothermel, 1966).

In the area of research, Spaeth (in Zeigler and Spaeth, 1975) recommended strongly that we must strive in future research to examine management as a process or group of processes rather than as an area of content (the old "nuts and bolts" approach, or "this is how you organize a round-robin tournament"). There is nothing wrong with the execution of studies related to the various technical concerns, but we do need to investigate the more fundamental, broader processes of management that might be designated as decision-making, communicating, activating, planning, evaluating, etc.

Similarly, Paton (in Zeigler and Spaeth, 1975, p. 14) suggested a significantly broader approach to the teaching of administration courses in sport and physical education. This is an approach which he and a number of his Canadian colleagues have followed with significant success to that point (e.g., Jackson at Victoria, Soucie, Hansen, Searles, and Chouinard at Ottawa; Moriarty, Olafson, Galasso, and Boucher at Windsor; Chelladurai, Haggerty, and Zeisner at Western Ontario, Daniel at Toronto, Maloney at Dalhousie, Paton at New Brunswick, Park at Bowling Green State University, to name those who have been involved the longest).

This approach is characterized by an emphasis in which the area of content specifically related to physical activity education (including sport) should depend increasingly on a body of knowledge developed through management research and theory in our field. Further, educational institutions provide the setting within which many sport and physical education programs are managed. Current efforts to develop management theory and research on the broad administrative process mentioned above within the educational setting are directly relevant to our field. The fact that management (or administration) is practiced in a specific setting has tended to obscure the fundamental similarities of the managerial process. The study of administration as administration should eventually provide a sounder theoretical base for understanding the management process. Finally, last but not least, underlying all management theory and research are the social sciences (and still more specifically, the behavioral sciences). Concepts and theories related to the behavior of people in organizations (A) have much to offer to an understanding of administration or management.

A Competency-Based Approach to Management Development

I am now convinced that the field of physical activity education (including sport) should be moving as rapidly as possible to introduce a comprehensive management competency development approach as a requirement in all professional preparation programs. (I was originally convinced about this subject when I introduced the case method approach to the teaching of human relations and administration to the field in 1959, the idea being that almost anything represented an improvement over the stereotyped approach in use in the 1950s and earlier.)

I now believe that a true competency development approach should be adopted as soon as possible so that our graduates will be basically equipped to cope with the managerial demands of their positions (whatever those positions may be). There is no question but that bureaucratic forms of organizations are being challenged by the varieties of organizational upheaval that are occurring. We are told that the combined demand for more at faster speeds is working to undermine the great vertical hierarchies that have characterized our public and private institutions in the past. Undoubtedly these emerging patterns and models are bringing about definite changes in managerial practice.

We really don't comprehend fully what these changes will mean to the management of sport and physical education. Interestingly, we do know that by about 60 years ago Snyder and Scott (1954) recommended the implementation of a problem-solving approach in our professional preparation programs. This recommendation has been re-asserted many times since, but a true laboratory-oriented, problem-solving approach still has not been implemented! It would seem that we now have a professional obligation to see to it that our professional preparation programs, as well as our in-service training as it emerges through the work of our professional associations, are so organized that people will be as ready as possible for change when it occurs. This statement has obvious implications for management training.

It was for this reason basically that I became concerned with what might be called the dimensions of management competency as it applied to the management (i.e., administration) of physical activity education and athletics. Concurrently I began to make a solid effort, working with others (like Marcia Spaeth, William Penny, Garth Paton, and John Baker), to pull together from any reliable source available what might be called the body of knowledge on this aspect of our field's endeavor. (King McCristal, David Matthews, and Laura Huelster, all of the University of Illinois, UIUC, were all most helpful and supportive in this endeavor.) In full appreciation of the aphorism "better late than never," I am nevertheless somewhat embarrassed to confess that–probably because of other intervening "challenges and hurdles"–it took me almost 25 years to arrive at the point where a model for a competency-based approach to management development in physical activity education and athletics was offered to the field (Zeigler & Bowie, 1983). Actually, the final steps might not have been taken yet if it were not for Gary Bowie's (Lethbridge) urging in the late 1970s that such was truly needed as soon as possible.

Permit me to retrogress time wise a bit to the late 1960s when the matter of what should be (or what might be) the actual components of physical activity education and sport became clearer as a result of reading, discussion, and reflection. Cyril White, an Irish sport and physical activity

41

education sociologist argued in 1968 that the field had many of the characteristics of a multidiscipline and some of the aspects of what might be called a cross–discipline. He postulated that our future development to so-called interdisciplinary status would require a greater degree of sophisticated research abilities and orientation than the field possess at that time. However, as Phil Sparling (Georgia Tech) pointed out in 1978, the field seemed to be moving in an opposite direction to that postulated by White. White's original idea made sense to me, and it still does today and could become true eventually. This will not occur, however, unless a solid, conscious effort is made by the profession to define what it is that we do, *and then do it*!

In the early 1970s, therefore, I made an effort to help resolve a controversy in the field as to the relationship between what have been called (by some) the sub-disciplinary aspects and those aspects that have been designated as "sub-professional" in nature (e.g., management theory and practice). This analysis resulted in the construction of a taxonomic model for "optimum professional development in a field called 'X'" (Zeigler, 1972). The model included the following five sub-divisions: (1) operational philosophy, (2) a theory embodying assumptions and testable hypotheses, (3) professional preparation, (4) professional practice, and (5) disciplinary research and scholarly endeavor (see Figure 1 below).

The inclusion of operational philosophy (of "X") as an overarching entity in the model is based on the social theory (Parsonian Action System) that the values and norms of the social system will be realized eventually within the society if all goes well. Put simply, this means that decisions regarding the development of a profession are based on the prevailing values and norms over and above any scientific evidence that may be available to create, strengthen, or broaden existing theory. Thus, there is a hierarchy of control and conditioning that operates within the system that exerts pressure downward affecting the society, the social systems, the structure of collectivities, and the structure of roles. Also, we should not forget that such pressure may be exerted upward as well (i.e., that's how gradual change occurs--and even revolutions if the demand for change is strong enough!).

The second phase of the model is theory, or the systematic arrangement of facts or knowledge about a subject or field. From such theory we can also derive assumptions and testable hypotheses that should soon amplify and clarify a developing (and presumably coherent) group of general and specific propositions that can be used as principles of explanation for the phenomena that have been observed. Obviously, any profession must have a sound body of knowledge to serve as under–girding if it hopes to survive with its professional status fully recognized in society.

Figure 1
A Model for Optimum Development of a Field Called "X"

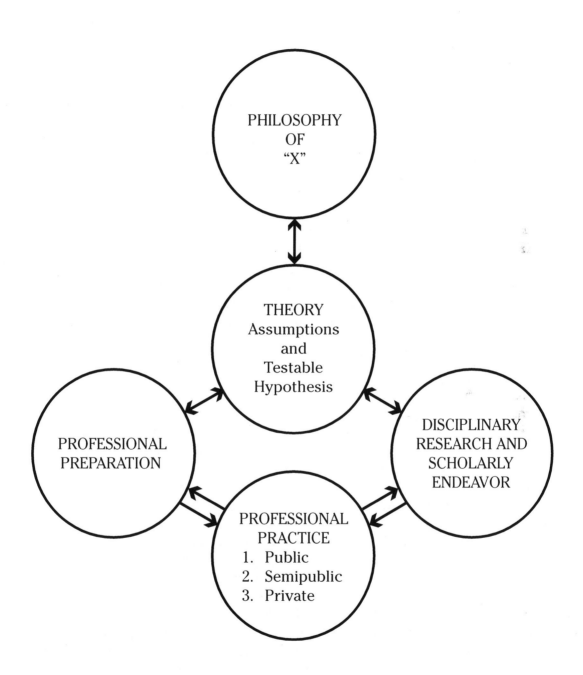

Earle Zeigler, Ph.D.

Professional preparation, the third division of the model, should be designed to educate the practitioner, the teacher of practitioners, the scholar and the researcher, and the administrator. Professional practice, the fourth entity in the model, relates typically to service provided for (1) the public, (2) the semi-public (or semi-private) agency, and (3) the private agency. Disciplinary research and related scholarly endeavor, the fifth division, involves those individuals from the specific profession (or closely related disciplines and/or professions) who contribute in one way or another to the body of knowledge on which the professional practice is based. We have classified such knowledge into sub–disciplinary and sub–professional knowledge (e.g., in sport and physical education, the tenable theory about the functional effects of physical activity and the tenable theory about how best to administer programs of developmental physical activity to be made available to promote the full dissemination of such knowledge, respectively). I believe that this model (i.e., an explanation of "how it works") can be adapted to any profession.

Adaptation of the Model of a Profession: The Competency Development Model

While the model of a profession as it presumably should function was being fashioned, another development was occurring that I did not at first relate to the work I had been doing. To paraphrase what could be described in greater detail, Lloyd E. McCleary, then at Illinois (UIUC) and later at Utah, had worked closely with us at Illinois and helped a number of us to relate what he and his associates were doing in educational administration to our work in sport and physical education administration. As we moved along in the 1970s, it became steadily and increasingly apparent that definite, urgent measures were needed in physical activity education and athletics to prepare people more carefully and thoroughly than previously for the "assumption of the administrative risk" in the years immediately ahead. And so, convinced that positive steps were needed to improve professional preparation for managers in our field, a number of people teaching in this area decided that it was time to introduce a management stream or minor into undergraduate and graduate curricula. To accomplish this for myself personally, I spent a portion of sabbatical-leave time analyzing the literature of management, with special reference to that which applied to the knowledge, competencies, and skills required by the manager. Shortly thereafter, Gary Bowie (Lethbridge) and I united our efforts in the firm belief than an experiential approach to management competency development was indeed urgently needed in physical activity education and athletics (Zeigler and Bowie, 1983). Subsequently we developed the first comprehensive laboratory workbook designed for management competency development (1995). It was updated n 2007 (Zeigler and Bowie).

Figure 2

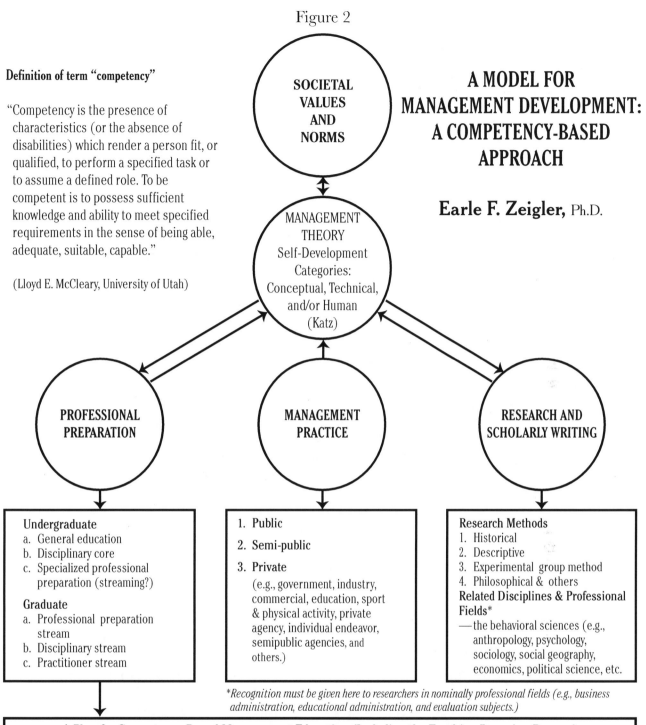

Definition of term "competency"

"Competency is the presence of characteristics (or the absence of disabilities) which render a person fit, or qualified, to perform a specified task or to assume a defined role. To be competent is to possess sufficient knowledge and ability to meet specified requirements in the sense of being able, adequate, suitable, capable."

(Lloyd E. McCleary, University of Utah)

SOCIETAL VALUES AND NORMS

A MODEL FOR MANAGEMENT DEVELOPMENT: A COMPETENCY-BASED APPROACH

Earle F. Zeigler, Ph.D.

MANAGEMENT THEORY Self-Development Categories: Conceptual, Technical, and/or Human (Katz)

PROFESSIONAL PREPARATION

MANAGEMENT PRACTICE

RESEARCH AND SCHOLARLY WRITING

Undergraduate
a. General education
b. Disciplinary core
c. Specialized professional preparation (streaming?)

Graduate
a. Professional preparation stream
b. Disciplinary stream
c. Practitioner stream

1. Public
2. Semi-public
3. Private

(e.g., government, industry, commercial, education, sport & physical activity, private agency, individual endeavor, semipublic agencies, and others.)

Research Methods
1. Historical
2. Descriptive
3. Experimental group method
4. Philosophical & others
Related Disciplines & Professional Fields*
—the behavioral sciences (e.g., anthropology, psychology, sociology, social geography, economics, political science, etc.

Recognition must be given here to researchers in nominally professional fields (e.g., business administration, educational administration, and evaluation subjects.)

A Plan for Competency-Based Management Education (Including the Teaching/Learning Process)

1. Ascertain professional functions & needs.
2. Specify competencies (including self-development and those under conceptual, technical, human, and "conjoined" categories).
3. Determine performance levels.
4. Specify program content & instructional, methodology (involving a problem-solving approach in achievement of performance levels: what needs to be known; where obtained; organization of the learning experience; probable results, and others.
5. Identify and evaluate competency attainment.
6. Validate process periodically.

Teaching/Learning Techniques
(e.g., lecture, discussion, case, role-playing, action research, pure and applied research, independent study, debate, computer-assisted or programmed instruction, internship, game theory, panels, forums, and others—depending upon technique's applicability to learning of a competency)

(Adapted from McCleary & McIntyre 1973)

To assist me with the classification or categorization of more than 100 competencies described in some form or other in the literature, I decided to employ one of the more highly regarded taxonomical models promulgated initially by Robert L. Katz in 1954 and then updated with slight modification20 years later (1974). In addition to Katz's division of the task of management into three basic skills (conceptual, technical, and human), I felt it to be advisable to add a mixed-skill or conjoined category, as well as one in which personal skills could be placed (the total then becoming five).

The next step was to adapt the model for a (any!) profession described above (Figure 1) to the quasi-discipline/profession of management science (or theory). As anticipated, this adaptation was readily accomplished (see Figure 2 above). From this point it became readily apparent that the model for competency-based management education in educational administration developed by McCleary and associates could be merged readily and successfully to my model. My position was reinforced when I discovered that McCleary had also employed Katz's taxonomy (1973). Thus it was possible to adapt the recommendations of McCleary and associates to my own purposes in keeping with the fivefold classification (adapted from Katz). My debt to the work of McCleary and associates (1972) is obvious. The culmination of our work along these lines was the publication of a text for undergraduates in which an experiential approach is featured. Students are provided with an opportunity for self-evaluation in relation to the five aspects of managerial skill through the employment of a series of laboratory experience as part of a formal course.

Managing the Enterprise: Looking Ahead

Up to this point, in addition to some introductory and background material, I have argued essentially (1) that the world is changing and becoming increasingly complex with each passing day, a development that has obvious implications for the field of physical activity education 9ncluding athletics; (2) that the field needs managers who function effectively and efficiently on the basis of tenable management theory to organize and administer its far-flung programs; and (3) that we have done quite poorly in preparing our people to manage, an inadequacy that we should correct as soon as possible by implementing a management competency development program of high quality.

Now let us assume that we can agree on the need for improving the quality of management in the field in the near future. This need is not peculiar to our profession, however, since we are hearing pleas from all over North America about a broader need for a higher quality in managerial performance than may have been present in the past. To meet the challenge to North American industry and business, for example, we were exhorted to consider "Theory Z" as wisdom coming from our Japanese colleagues (Ouchi,

1982)--actually a debatable assumption as it has turned out. Also, about that time there was a spate of books with the world "excellence" in the title. For example, in the book titled Creating Excellence (Hickman and Silva, 1984), we were presented with a list of "new age skills" that management executives should cultivate: (1) creative insight: asking the right questions; (2) sensitivity: doing unto others; (3) vision: creating the future; (4) versatility: anticipating change; (5) focus: implementing change; and (6) patience: living in the long term (pp. 99-246). After mastering these skills, you begin to "walk on water!"

Toward the goal of alerting present and prospective managers of physical activity education and athletics about what they may be facing as they assume the role of "managing the enterprise" in the present societal climate, I will now "freewheel" a bit to offer a variety of opinions, suggestions, and recommendations as to what (prospective) professional leaders might expect to find when they assume a managerial post--and what they might possibly do about any such discoveries or unexpected findings.

An Ever-Changing Society. First, changing social influences have brought about various types of organizational upheaval. As a result our present bureaucratic forms of organization–although often "struggling on doggedly"–seem to need drastic change in both the structure of the operation and in the way managers function within it. We have had our "organization men and women," but are we even today ready for what Toffler called "associative man or woman"--i.e., people who are not immobilized by concern for economic security (1970, pp. 125-134)?

The Matter of Individual Freedom. Second, even within our evolving democracy, we still encounter persistent attempts of some basically domineering (and often at heart fearful because of insecurity) individuals to deny people the freedom they have a right to expect in this culture. As managers we should be asking ourselves to what extent the individual in North American society should be able to choose his or her own goals in life and then have the opportunity and means to attain them to a reasonable degree. How crucial is individual freedom for a person as we all strive to improve the quality of life, or are we inevitably moving toward a social system (somewhat more like present oligarchic communism) that Skinner characterized as "beyond freedom and dignity?" In other words, what is the best or ideal route whereby we may possibly reach a high level of excellence? Do we want a more pyramidal, depersonalized bureau–technocratic society or one that seems to be working for the best interests of individual man and woman (Tesconi & Morris, 1972)? Questions like these are still, in my opinion, especially important for managers functioning in some aspect of physical activity education (including athletics), a group not noted in the past for the implementation of creative models of democratic administration.

Managing by Objectives. Third, one of the areas of concern most neglected by managers has been that of the determination of the organization's objectives. Everyone gives lip service to the need for "managing by objectives" as espoused by Drucker as long ago as 1954, but the moment one tries to pin down a practicing manager in this regard the result is typically an empty recital of words and phrases that displays "the lack of a well-developed language of organizational purpose" (Gross, 1965). One of the best responses to such a deficiency would seem to be a plan based on systems analysis that could quite quickly help an organization to develop a workable general-systems model. One of the great advantages of the "MBO approach", of course, is that it provides middle managers and employees an opportunity to plan together for the achievement of common objectives--objectives for which all will ultimately be responsible. Odiorne (1965) had promoted MBO as strongly as anyone and, according to Filly, House & Kerr (1976), it has subsequently been employed more widely than any other similar technique.

Positive Approach to Management. Fourth, if a person decides to throw his or her hat in the ring by applying for an administrative post and is then selected, the subsequent approach taken to the task should be a highly positive one. This is especially true in academic situations where one is somehow still expected to keep up with scholarly writing and research (and then may make light of the need to make time for solid human relations). Admittedly the dual responsibility is difficult, but it is by no means impossible if a person is willing to work hard and plan carefully. Of course, this is why a limited term of managerial service (e.g., five years) in such situations is highly desirable.

Half-hearted commitment of time to managing clashes sharply with the duties and responsibilities that the managerial revolution has thrust upon us. As Gross (1964) stated, "It provides the people of this planet with their first opportunity of discovering their vast potentials for self-development." Viewed in this light, management is a social skill that will have to be employed wisely to help the inhabitants of this earth work their way out of the predicament into which they have gotten themselves. Transferred to the educational setting, who will not admit that an inadequate administrator of physical activity education and/or athletics can soon bring a department, division, or school down to a level where the program is barely subsisting (i.e., "semi-planned mediocrity")? Thus, considering the importance of the role of manager, and the steadily increasing complexity of the organizational management task, it is my contention that young men and women in the field should be encouraged to prepare themselves adequately for the vital task of managerial leadership. Further, the assumption of this challenge does not mean that the individual must automatically put scholarship and research aside (although it typically has happened that way in the past). The manager should be equipped by word and deed to promote the idea of management as an emerging social science, as one of the sub–professional aspects of our work that demands continued scholarly research.

Need for an Action-Theory Marriage. Fifth, what has just been stated above provides some substantiation for the gradual emergence of management science. Most people say that management thought is too theoretical, and what they need is more practical guidance. This assertion may seem to be true, but I believe it can be said more accurately that really practical administrative thought will simply have to be based on far more tenable knowledge and theory than is yet available. Scholarly investigation on this topic should be carried out to the greatest possible extent on the "observable facts of real-life administration" (Gross, 1964). A manager on the job is typically confronted with a real-life situation to resolve. To resolve the problem effectively and efficiently, something better than trial and error is needed in our increasingly complex social environment. That "something" should be the most tenable theory available. In other words, a research strategy is needed that is characterized by a "theory-research balance" between theoretical and applied investigation.

The Current Theory Debate. Sixth, the mushrooming of the behavioral sciences has made it literally impossible for a scholar to keep up with the vast quantities of literature in many languages being produced all over the world. As a result those preparing for the profession of management have found themselves facing an impossible task–keeping up with an information overload, as well as retrieving a great deal of knowledge that helps to form a sound human behavior inventory. Also, the conflicting approaches to management (i.e., the different theories as to "how it should be done") that compete for the attention of the manager in the many books, monographs, and journals are very puzzling. Forty (plus!) years ago Gordon (1966) defined these historical, actually overlapping approaches as (1) the traditional, (2) the behavioral, (3) the decisional, and (4) the ecological. He concluded by recommending that a flexible framework should be employed as a synthesis of the four approaches enabling the student of management theory to build a conceptual framework that provided a much fuller perspective and a "working model" of the management process.

The idea of such a flexible framework emerged in 1979 from a discussion by Hodgetts in a slightly different manner. He explained that there is one line of thought that envisions three schools of management thought (i.e., the management process school, the quantitative school, and the behavioral school) merging into a systems school. However, a second point of view held that we already have a well-established systems school of thought and that it, and the three approaches just mentioned, are moving in the direction of an overarching situational or contingency school. This was called a general contingency theory of management by Luthans and Stewart (1977) in which management problems can be encompassed in a theoretical

49

framework that integrates and synthesizes the various schools of thought into a workable research design that has three dimensions--management variables, situational variables, and performance criteria variables. The objective is to integrate tenable management theory into a composite system for ongoing study and investigation.

The Complexity of Any Administrative Situation. Seventh, many years of involvement as a manager/administrator, as well as 50 years of experience with the case technique or approach to the teaching of human relations and administration, led me to summarize a few thoughts about the complexity of any administrative situation (Zeigler, 1982). This is so because of the large number of factors that may be involved in any case situation (e.g., past experience, one's present situation, economic incentive, personal attitude). The work situation itself and any changes that are occurring add to the mix. The group code within the organization, which in turn is affected by community standards and societal values and norms, are fundamental factors as well. Management says one thing, but management does another-- this too can have an impact (Hower in Andrews, 1953). In some circumstances certain factors indicated above could be the most important determinants of behavior; in others they might well be relatively insignificant. As the manager analyzes a problem, the task is to gain as much perspective as possible. However, while responding to the facts, half-facts, and opinions seen, heard, and assessed, the manager should keep in mind that each person views a situation differently. Such a realization in itself should often cause managers to hold back at least temporarily before initiating strong, direct action to meet a problem.

Leadership in Organizational Settings. Eighth, in this changing (internal and external) organizational environment that we have been discussing, the interpersonal skills of the leader(s) need further examination and study. Certainly the leader must know himself or herself and know those with whom direct or indirect association is established. I have believed very strongly that the executive needs to establish an open climate. By this is meant that (1) associates can collect information about a problem accurately, (2) bring these data back to the decision-making group, and then (3) take part in the planning and execution of future actions (Bennis & Slater, 1968).

The concept of 'leadership,' however, has been an elusive one down through the years. For a long time what was called "trait theory" was in vogue--that is, we were concerned about the prospective manager's personal characteristics, ones that presumably made him or her a fine leader. In the 1940s, however, trait theory declined because investigations along this line produced no clear-cut results. Thus, even though this approach had, and still has, some descriptive value, it has been supplanted to a large degree by so-called "situational theory." With this approach it is argued (1) that there are situational factors that can be delineated in a finite way and (2) that they vary

50

according to a number of other factors (Filley, House, & Kerr, 1976). Some of these factors, for example, are the leader's age and experience, the size of the group led, the cultural expectations of subordinates, and the time required and allowed for decision-making. Chelladurai (1985), in his discussion of leadership, refers to charismatic leadership and organizational leadership, the latter being "just one of the functions of a manager who is placed in charge of a group and its activities, and is, in turn, guided by superiors and organizational factors" (p. 139).

Further, I should state my personal interest in a leadership spectrum (or perhaps a continuum) in which, as one moves from left to right (i.e., from anarchy to dictatorship), the manager gradually exercises greater authority and the staff members have lesser areas of freedom. I have found through long experience that I have a distinct aversion to one-person, arbitrary, authoritative decisions–especially in educational settings or anywhere else. I have personally eventually walked away from such positions of employment on four occasions. (Of course, I appreciate that in certain lines of work, such as the military or fire-fighting, there typically isn't sufficient time to have a lengthy discussion in an effort to achieve agreement or to take a vote before action is taken.) Nevertheless, I want staff members to be involved in the decision-making process to the greatest possible extent–if they are willing to make serious efforts to be well informed on the matter at hand. Further, once a decision is made democratically by informed members of the group, the organization can and should demand loyal support from all members of the group. (The assumption here is that opportunities will be provided subsequently for people to be convinced in democratic fashion at a not-too-distant future date that a contravening decision should be made.)

Constants and/or Generalizations. Ninth, even though I have been emphasizing that the manager is being faced with a relatively fast-moving social system, a condition from which managers of physical activity education cannot (and probably should not wish to) escape, change for us has somehow not occurred as rapidly as in certain other segments of society. However, managers in our field must now recognize the fact that they too are being put on notice about the fluid nature of their environments. Managers simply must take advantage of every opportunity to prepare themselves to keep ahead (or at least abreast) of their associates intellectually. This is necessary because they must be ready to meet change head-on and make the alterations and modifications necessary so that growth (if desired and/or desirable) and survival will be ensured (the ecological approach, if you will).

The above momentary digression is not meant to imply for an instant that there are not a great many constants and/or generalizations that carry over from yesterday to today and thence to tomorrow which help to maintain the structure and vitality of sport and physical education. This means, for example, that much of what is known about human nature today will be

51

identical or quite similar tomorrow. It forewarns the manager that he or she shouldn't throw the baby out with the bath water just because many changes seem to be taking place. The great problem seems to be the urgent need to both strengthen and focus the body of knowledge available to the management profession so that the literally astounding development in the area of technology is reasonably approximated by the understanding and knowledge available about effective and efficient administrative behavior. While such a balance is being established, the tried-and-true constants or "principles" from the past should be used daily and only discarded or modified when there is ample evidence (scientific or normative) available to warrant any change.

Other Recommendations for Managers. Tenth, I would like to make several final recommendations for managers to consider as they look to the future (as revised from Zeigler & Spaeth, 1975):

1. The manager, in addition to relying on the wisdom of the past, should make it a habit over the years to increase his or her theoretical and practical knowledge. (This is especially true if at any time an area of weakness in managerial knowledge, competencies, or skills is discovered-- e.g., personal computer capability.)

2. The manager should strive to improve his or her communication skills. (Generally speaking, it is reasonable to assume that people will work more enthusiastically with a manager who communicates with them in terms that they can readily understand.)

3. The manager should be prepared to invest himself or herself in the external environment. (Here I take the position that the manager does have a definite community responsibility that, even though in educational situations ours is a strongly service-oriented field to begin with, the manager should still be prepared to "invest himself or herself" in the community at least to a reasonable degree.)

4. The manager should work to strengthen organizational democracy. (With this recommendation, I am reiterating my ongoing concern that managers should continually be aware of both the responsibilities and rights of the people working with them in the achievement of mutually agreed-upon goals. If individual participation and self-development are promoted, the organization itself will be better for having shown such concern.)

5. The manager should recognize that he or she is taking part in the development of a management profession. (This implies that there is an obligation to live up to the various requirements of a true profession--e.g.,

service without undue concern for pecuniary reward, ongoing commitment, mastery of a body of knowledge, adherence to a code of ethics.)

6. The manager should do whatever possible to expand and improve the quality of management education that is available. (The position being taken here is that, despite some improvement, the field of physical activity education including educational sport (not the sport management professional programs!) is still not placing enough emphasis on a reasonable amount of professional preparation for the management task. We are especially vulnerable here from the standpoint of management competency development through laboratory and internship experiences.)

Evaluation of the Modern Era

Throughout my career I have come firmly to the belief that history can serve several fundamental purposes. In regard to management thought, theory, and practice in relation to physical activity education including educational sport, we need "to know where we have been and where we are before we can decide where we ought to go"!

In his outstanding *The History of Management Thought* (2003), Daniel Wren states:

> Within the practice of the past there are the lessons of history for tomorrow; there is a flow of events and ideas that links yesterday, today, and tomorrow in a continuous stream. We occupy but one point in that stream of time; we can see the distant past with a fairly high degree of clarity, but as we approach the present, our perspective becomes less clear. New ideas, subtle shifts in themes, and emerging environmental events will influence evolving management thought. (p. 489).

In Wren's synopsis of the modern era, he traces four approaches that have characterized this period: (1) systems theory (including the development of computers and management information systems), (2) organizational behavior (including human resources management and organization theory), (3) general management theory (including strategic management), and (4) organizations and environment (including cross-cultural management). Based on my longstanding involvement with the field, I feel it is safe, but discouraging to state that we are typically far from the forefront of the pack in any of these categories. However, we can perhaps console ourselves with the thought that we have "plenty of company" within the field of education. The inauguration of the North American Society for Sport Management in 1986 was timely and greatly needed. The *Journal of Sport Management*, and similar publications originated by other management societies worldwide, provides a solid outlet for the reporting of scholarly endeavor and research. However, bringing this endeavor to the point where an "action-theory marriage" is established is the challenge for our managers in the 21st century.

The basic premise of this analysis of the present situation is that the large majority of our dedicated practitioners simply *"don't know what they don't know"* about the best ways to carry out their professional practice! This may sound simplistic and impossible to prove, but it is probably simply an axiomatic statement to make in today's increasingly complex society. Our well-intentioned professionals have been gradually and steadily overwhelmed by available periodical literature, monographs, and books from (1) our own field, (2) from our allied fields, and (3) from our related disciplines. In addition, quite probably, most of our practitioners don't fully appreciate this fact either. "How can this be?" you may ask. It is so–to repeat myself–because the average practitioner simply *"doesn't know what he/she doesn't know!"* Yet, much of this available information could be interesting and highly valuable and useful to the professional practitioner of sport and physical activity management.

It can be argued in rebuttal that such material is often not geared to the interests of professionals who are fulfilling many duties and responsibilities in the various positions they hold. However, this problem is also occurring in sport and physical activity management's allied fields (i.e., recreation management, health education management). Whatever the case may be there, there is undoubtedly much overlapping material emanating from these fields that could be helpful to sport and physical activity management, as well as that emanating from the scholarly production of our related disciplines (e.g., physiology, psychology, history, sociology). Further, much of the available material–when a person by intent or chance happens to discover it—is unintelligible to us, partially understandable, or not available in a condensed, understandable form to the professional in physical activity education and sport. Thus, one can only conjecture in what form such information will be (or unfortunately *won't be*) conveyed to the public on whose behalf the allied professions presumably carry out their work.

To make matters worse, because of provinciality and communication barriers, our field is usually missing out on important findings originally published in some of the leading tongues in which scholarly work relating to our profession is being reported regularly (e.g., German, Russian, Japanese, and Finnish). Further, because of a plethora of rules, regulations, and stipulations, people may not be receiving information about substantive reports of various government agencies at all levels. The essence of much of this information should become part of personal retrieval systems of those carrying out scholarly work in our sub–disciplinary and sub–professional areas of investigation. It is true, of course, that since 1970 Cambridge Scientific Abstracts (CSA) has offered libraries a service for their users called

Physical Education Index that includes abstracts of scholarly articles and research added to monthly. Also, bibliographies of scholarly publications are occasionally made available. However, busy professionals rarely would know how--or take the time--to dig out exactly what they need at the moment.

Still further—and this is really *the* most important point to be made—the field (profession?) simply does not know where it stands *cumulatively* in regard to the steadily developing body of knowledge in the many sub–disciplinary and sub–professional aspects of physical activity education and sport. We do not know what we do not know! Nowhere does the field of sport and physical activity management have an inventory of scholarly, scientific findings arranged as ordered principles or generalizations to help professionals in their work. Hence, I believe it is reasonable to state that we now urgently need something like the law profession's *Lexus-Nexus*, or a variation of that service geared to our needs. (See <www.lexus-nexus.com>.)

This deficiency can—and indeed must—be rectified in the near future. Then the professions (?), AAHPERD, *established as physical education only in 1885!*–should carry such an inventory forward on a yearly or semiannual basis of renewal for all *registered* practitioners to have available on demand. Comprehension of this knowledge in readily available form would be vitally important to the professional practitioner, of course, but the essence of it would ultimately be most important to all people as part of their general education. Initially, however, the profession needs such information to form the basis—the theory, intellectual "underpinning," evidence, body of knowledge—for an evolving professional (practitioner's) loose-leaf handbook that would immediately become an essential component of every person's professional practice in the field of sport and physical activity management. Finally, to execute the proposed development, it would be necessary to gradually implement a systems approach that should result in the rapid development and use of theory and research related to our unique profession.

Along with many other fields, the field of sport and physical activity management has simply not yet appreciated the need to implement a "total system" concept. However, there are many urgent reasons why a holistic view should be held if the profession hopes to merit increased public support in the future. Such an approach would soon concern those involved with implementation of the necessary components of a viable system—input, thru put, output, and subsequent user reaction for corrective purposes.

Concluding Statement

Finally, then, what can be said in brief summary about the ongoing management of the physical activity education (including athletics) enterprise? First, I believe that the field dies indeed have an opportunity to relate significantly to the developing social science of management. I say this with a full understanding that most professional educators in the field are not truly aware of the scientific development that has occurred in the recent 20 years at least. *Second, the vast enterprise that is physical activity education (including sport) for its very survival as a recognizable entity simply must relate more effectively to the urgent need for qualified sport and physical managers.* The North American Society for Sport Management is making a significant contribution to this development. Additionally, such development should be carried out in full cooperation with the National Association for Sport and Physical Education within the AAHPERD and PHE Canada (formerly the Canadian Association for Health, Physical Education, Recreation, and Dance).

Third, each manager has a responsibility for self-examination in an effort to construct a personal philosophy that can be of inestimable assistance in becoming a more effective professional person. In addition to recommending that a manager "look inward" in an effort to develop an explicit personal philosophy, it is also absolutely imperative today that the manager "look outward" at both the immediate and general environments in an ongoing attempt to analyze the social forces that impinge daily on the leader, his or her leadership group, and the organization. The vital importance of human resources management has been made most clear to us in Chelladurai's outstanding work titled *Human Resource Management in Sport and Recreation* (1999). He makes it clear that any attempt at "strategic management must be tailored to be consistent with the type of business that a sport organization undertakes and the types of human resources at its disposal"(p. 272). Sport, exercise, play, and dance have infiltrated our social environment to an enormous extent. Our evolving field–both within education and in society at large cannot succeed without highly qualified, dedicated people to manage this most important cultural enterprise looking to the best interests of all involved..

Note

1. This chapter is intended to be synoptic in nature. Thus what is contained here represents an updated, revised (presumably improved) version of many of the ideas, opinions, and recommendations expressed by me about management theory and practice as applied to physical activity education (including sport) in a variety of publications over a period of approximately 50 years. Prior to a collaborative effort with Gary Bowie (Lethbridge) (1983) designed to introduce a management competency development approach to professional preparation in sport and physical education, I had collaborated also with Marcia Spaeth (SUNY, Cortland) and Garth Paton and Terry Haggerty (now at the University of New Brunswick, but earlier at The University of Western Ontario). Some of this material in this paper had been researched by Professor Spaeth and Professor Paton, respectively, and appeared in Zeigler and Spaeth (1975).

References

Andrews, K. R. (Ed.), *Human relations and administration.* Cambridge, MA: Harvard University Press.

Bennis, W. & Slater, P. E. (1968). *The temporary society.* New York: Harper & Row.

Chelladurai, P. (1985). *Sport management).* London, Canada: Sport Dynamics.

Chelladurai, P. (1999). *Human Resource Management in Sport and Recreation.* Champaign, IL: Human Kinetics.

Drucker, P. F. (1954). *The practice of management.* New York: Harper & Row.

Filley, A. C., House, R. J. & Kerr, S. (1976). *Managerial process and organizational behavior.* (2nd Ed.). Glenview, IL: Scott, Foresman.

Goodwin, M. (1986). When the cash register is the scoreboard. *The New York Times,* June 8, pp. 27-28.

Gordon, P. J. (1966). Transcend the current debate on administrative theory. *Hospital Administration,* 11, 2 (Spring), 6-23.

Gross, B. M. (1964). *The managing of organizations.* New York: The Free Press of Glencoe (Macmillan).

Halpin, A. W. (1958). The development of theory in educational administration. In A.W. Halpin (Ed.), *Administrative theory in education.* New York: Macmillan.

Hickman, C .R. & Silva, M. A. (1984). *Creating excellence.* New York: New American Library.

Hodgetts, R. M. (1979). *Management: Theory, process and practice.* (2nd Ed.). Philadelphia: Saunders.

Luthans, F. & Stewart, T. I. (1977). A general contingency theory of management. *Academy of Management Review,* p. 182 & p. 190.

McCleary, L. E. (1973). Competency-based educational administration and application to related fields. In *Proceedings of the Conference on Administrative Competence.* Tempe, AZ: Bureau of Educational Research, Arizona State University, pp. 26-38.

Odiorne, G. S. (1965). *Management by objectives.* New York: Pitman.

Ouchi, W. G. (1981). *Theory Z.* Reading, MA: Addison-Wesley.

Parsons, T. (1958) Some ingredients of a general theory of formal organization. In Halpin, A.W. (Ed.), *Administrative theory in education.* New York: Macmillan.

Paton, G. A. (with Zeigler, E. F. & Spaeth, M. J.). (1975). Theory and research in the administration of physical education. In Zeigler, E. F. & Spaeth, M. J., *Administrative theory and practice in physical education and athletics).* Englewood Cliffs, NJ: Prentice-Hall.

Rosenberg, J. M. (1978). *Dictionary of business and management.* NY: John Wiley.

Rothermel, B. L. (1966). Conversation with the author, Oct. 3.

Spaeth, M. J. (1967). *An analysis of administrative research in physical education and athletics in relation to a research paradigm.* Doctoral dissertation, University of Illinois, Urbana-Champaign.

Snyder, R. A. & Scott, H. A. (1954). *Professional preparation in health, physical education, and recreation.* New York: McGraw-Hill.

Tesconi, C. A., Jr. & Morris, V. C. (1972). *The anti-man culture.* Urbana, IL: University of Illinois Press.

Thompson, J. D. (1958). Modern approaches to theory in administration. In Halpin, A.W., *Administrative theory in education.* New York: Macmillan.

Toffler, A. (1970). *Future shock.* New York: Random House.

Toffler, A. (1980). *The third wave.* New York: William Morrow.

VanderZwaag, H. J. (1984). *Sport management in schools and college.* NY: John Wiley.

Wren, D. A. (2003). The History of Management Thought (Fifth Edition). Hoboken, NJ: John Wiley & Sons.

Zeigler, E. F. (1951*). A history of professional preparation for physical education in the United States, 1861-1948.* Eugene, OR: Microfiche Publications, University of Oregon.

Zeigler, E. F. (1959). *Administration of physical education and athletics: The case method approach.* Englewood Cliffs, NJ: Prentice-Hall.

Zeigler, E. F. (1972). A model for optimum professional development in a field called "X." In *Proceedings (pp. 16-28) of the First Canadian Symposium on the Philosophy of Sport and Physical Activity.* Ottawa, Canada: Sport Canada Directorate.

Zeigler, E. F. & Spaeth, M. J. (Eds.). (1975). *Administrative theory and practice in physical education and athletics.* Englewood Cliffs, NJ: Prentice-Hall.

Zeigler, E. F. (1982). *Decision-making in physical education and athletics administration.* Champaign, IL: Stipes.

Zeigler, E. F. & Bowie, G. W. (1983). *Management competency development in sport and physical education.* Philadelphia: Lea & Febiger.

Zeigler, E. F. & Campbell, J. (1984). *Strategic market planning: An aid to the evaluation of an athletic/recreation progra*). Champaign, IL: Stipes.

Zeigler, E. F. & Bowie, Gary W. (1995). Management competency development in sport and physical education: A Laboratory Manual. Champaign, IL: Stipes. (This was updated in 2007 with Trafford Publishing, Victoria, BC, Canada.)

Zoffer, H. J. (1985). Training managers to take charge. In Business (Section 3, 2), *The New York Times*, Oct. 20. Introduction

For Consideration and Discussion

As an exercise it is recommended that two students each make a 10-minute presentation, one telling about good administrative practice he/she has encountered and the other explaining what bad administrative practice he/she has experienced. Then a third student should conduct a class discussion on the topic.

CHAPTER 3

UNDERSTANDING THE MANAGERIAL ENVIRONMENT
OF PHYSICAL ACTIVITY EDUCATION AND SPORT

Professionals in the physical activity education and sport need to understand the *general* or *external* managerial environment, as well as that of the *immediate* or *internal* environment that includes the organizational climate, suppliers, controllers, advisers, adversaries, and so-called public with opinions, The need for such understanding is especially true, of course, for those who serve us as our administrators/managers/directors for specified or unspecified terms of office.

The general environment that will be discussed here first is made up typically of (1) the organization's resources, (2) its social organization, (3) the power structure, and (4) the society's structure of values and norms. These terms or components were originally employed by Gross (1964) and then adapted by me to physical activity education and sport settings. Toward the end of this discussion, a comparison will be made of the several analyses that have been presented in this discussion (i.e., those by Gross, Johnson, and Hills, in that order).

Because we are all managers, but to varying degrees, dedicated professionals should continuously show serious concern for the environments of the organizations in which they work. None of us can forget for a moment that there are various social forces in any society strongly impinge on any organization seeking to function within it. Nor can we neglect to work toward a full understanding of the fact that we are dealing with people, human beings who are inescapably unique, and who often exhibit irrational behavior despite the best-laid plans of those who would manage them.

Present Need for an Ecological Approach

Since the late 1960s there has been a steadily increasing emphasis on the subject of ecology. What used to be called "conservation of natural resources" has now been relegated to a subdivision of the larger subject of ecology. Broadly speaking, ecology deals with the mutual relations between organisms and their environment. Here I am suggesting that all of us in the profession should be aware of the need for an ecological approach to what is going on in our field at present. An awareness of the need for such an approach would call our attention more directly to the fact that our basic concern is with people involved with organizations of all types that are functioning in "natural" and culturally influenced environments.

Applying an ecological approach to our allied profession, therefore, means that we as professionals working with our managers have a responsibility to develop and strengthen our particular organization or collectivity so that it will have the capability to adapt successfully to the changing natural and cultural environment in which it is located. If this sounds overly theoretical, keep in mind that fundamental changes in society are continually influencing the professions of sport and physical education or recreation. Out at the practitioner's level, the field of physical activity education in the schools, for example, is as usual embroiled in what seems to be a never-ending struggle for recognition and accompanying status. Is physical and health education curricular, co-curricular, or extra-curricular? The struggle continues with many in the field seemingly ready and willing to accept almost any position within the educational curriculum--so long as it is a position.

The assumption behind an ecological approach is that the organization and its manager--and the people functioning within in--will have opportunities for growth. However, it should be borne in mind that such "growth" does not necessarily mean growth in size. The *adaptive behavior* of those involved in the managerial task (i.e., the chairperson, dean, or director *and* the members of the Executive Committee) should enable the organization to remain viable, to be stronger, to remain competitive, and to be increasingly more effective and efficient in the accomplishment of its aims and objectives.

Keeping a managerial viewpoint in mind, especially in the increasing number of situations where a managerial team is responsible for the direction in which the organization is heading, an ecological approach would be one that is eclectic in nature. This means that it might include, where possible and when desirable, any or all aspects of the traditional, behavior, or decision-making patterns of managerial behavior. Thus the manager may find himself or herself functioning with an amalgam of traditional principles, cooperative behaviorist ideas, and "decisionist" competitive strategies.

Such an "amalgamated approach" may indeed be necessary if the formulation of aims and objectives has occurred democratically. In Western culture people have been increasingly involved in the decision-making process, and failure to prepare people adequately for the introduction of change may cause the achievement of seemingly realizable goals to be thwarted--or at least temporarily blocked--by human conflicts, natural or cultural barriers, or changing circumstances within the immediate (internal) environment. Similar problems or obstacles of varying nature and intensity may arise within the broader general (external) environment. Of course, such situations should serve as challenges to the manager and his or her team, and their approach should be heuristic in nature (i.e., reacting to the ever-present need by adapting or possible adjusting means, behavior, and even ends at some point along the line).

With an ecological approach to management, the managerial team and key associated personnel seek to develop, employ, and maintain power and influence that lead to the achievement of planned goals. Many people within the organization will be involved in one way or another in assisting with the implementation of the fundamental processes of planning, organizing, staffing, directing, and controlling the operation of the organization. Throughout this series of experiences it is imperative that good human relations be employed by all through the use of effective and efficient communication techniques. The successful implementation of these various processes is extremely complex, of course, and this is why a top-flight managerial team is becoming increasingly necessary to move a complex organization ahead.

The General (External) Environment

It is not always possible to state definitively where the immediate (internal) environment leaves off and the general (external) environment begins in a given society. All known societies are open systems, often involving a variety of sub-groups within their geographical boundaries. Careful definition of a particular society is a highly complex task, each one having certain unique qualities while undoubtedly possessing many similarities with other societies. The components of societies are usually described as subsystems (e.g., the economy, the government). In a very real sense these subsystems have developed to "divide up the work," and it is with the interweaving of these systems that the remainder of this paper will be concerned. We must keep in mind here that the larger society, which we will discuss first, is infinitely more complex than any organization that exists within it. However, it is important to be reminded at this point that many of the concepts and group roles of the society can be transferred from one societal level to the other (and vice versa).

General Action System Has Four Subsystems

Before considering a more general discussion of the external environment from the standpoint of resources, the various social organizations, the power structure, and the value structure, there will be a relatively brief presentation of Parsonian "Action Theory." [A significant debt is owed to Professor Harry M. Johnson for his willingness to so freely share so extensively his interpretation of Parsons' material in this article.] This particular (grand) theory has a long tradition in the field of sociology. It has been described by Johnson (1969) as being "a type of empirical system" that actually applies to an extremely wide range of systems from relationships between two people to that of total societies. It cannot be regarded as totally

FIGURE 1

THE FUNCTIONAL PROBLEMS OF SOCIAL SYSTEMS*

Instrumental   Consummatory

	(L) **LATENT** **PATTERN MAINTENANCE** **& TENSION MANAGEMENT**	**(I)** **INTEGRATION**

INTERNAL

(Involves Stability &
Continuity in Relations
Among Units)

(Involves Success &
Satisfaction in Inter-
Unit Relationships)

	(A) **ADAPTATION**	**(G)** **GOAL-ATTAINMENT**

EXTERNAL

(Involves Stability &
Continuity in
Relation to External
Environment)

(Involves Success &
Satisfaction in
Relation to External
Environment)

---

*Adapted from Johnson, H.M. (1994). Modern organizations in the Parsonsian theory of action. In A. Farazmand (Ed.), *Modern organizations: Administrative theory in contemporary society* (p. 59). Westport, CT: Praeger; and Hills, R.J. (1968). *Toward a science of organization* (p. 21). Eugene, OR: Center for Advanced Study of Administration.

concerned with economic theory; it is more "a generalization of economics." It seeks to analyze both structure *and* process.

Initially, to understand this complex social theory, a person should appreciate that the general action system is viewed as being composed of four subsystems: (1) cultural system, (2) social system, (3) psychological system, and (4) behavioral-organic system. What this means, viewed from a different perspective, is that explicit human behavior is comprised of aspects that are cultural, social, psychological, and organic. These four subsystems together compose a hierarchy of control and conditioning that operates in both directions (i.e., both up and down).

The first of the subsystems is "culture," which according to Johnson "provides the figure in the carpet-the structure and, in a sense, the 'programming' for the action system as a whole" (Ibid.). The structure of this type of system is typically geared to the functional problems of that level that arise--and so on down the scale, respectively. Thus it is the subsystem of culture that legitimates and also influences the level below it (the social system). Typically, there is a definite strain toward consistency. However, the influence works both upward and downward within the action system, thereby creating a hierarchy of influence or conditioning (as mentioned above).

Social life being what it has been and is, it is almost inevitable that strain will develop within the system. Johnson explains this as "dissatisfaction with the level of effectiveness on the functioning of the system in which the strain is felt" (p. 47). Such dissatisfaction may, for example, have to do with particular aspects of a social system as follows: (a) the level of effectiveness of resource procurement; (b) the success of goal attainment; (c) the justice or appropriateness of allocation of rewards or facilities; or (d) the degree to which units of the system are committed to realizing (or maintaining) the values of the system.

Strain may arise at the personality or psychological system level, and the resultant pressure could actually change the structure of the system above (the social system). This is not an inevitable process, however, because such strain might well be resolved satisfactorily at its own level (so to speak). Usually the pattern consistency of the action system displays a reasonable degree of flexibility, and this is especially true at the lower levels. For example, strain might be expressed by deviant behavior or in other ways such as by reduced identification with the social system by the person or group concerned.

Thus, it is the hierarchy of control and conditioning that comes into play when the sources of change (e.g., new religious or scientific ideas) begin to cause strain in the larger social systems, whereas the smaller social systems tend to be "strained" by the change that often develops at the personality or psychological system level. In addition, it is quite apparent that social systems are often influenced considerably by contact with other social systems.

Levels of Structure within the Social System

Just as there were four subsystems within *the total action system* defined by Parsons and others, there are also four levels within that subsystem that has been identified as *the social system or structure*. These levels, proceeding from "highest" to "lowest," are (1) values, (2) norms, (3) the structure of collectivities, and (4) the structure of roles. Typically the higher levels are more general than the lower ones, with the latter group giving quite specific guidance to those segments or units of the particular system to which they apply. These "units" or "segments" are either collectivities or individuals in their capacity as role occupants.

Values represent the highest echelon of the social system level of the entire general action system. These values may be categorized into such "entities" as artistic values, educational values, social values, etc. Of course, all types or categories of values must be values <u>of</u> personalities. The social values of a particular social system are those values that are conceived of as representative of the ideal general character that is desired by those who ultimately hold the power in the system being described. The most important social values in North America, for example, have been (1) the rule of law, (2) the socio-structural facilitation of individual achievement, and (c) the equality of opportunity (Ibid.).

Norms are the shared, sanctioned rules which govern the second level of the social structure. The average person finds it difficult to separate in his or her mind the concepts of values and norms. Keeping in mind the examples of values offered immediately above, some examples of norms are (1) the institution of private property, (2) private enterprise, (3) the monogamous, conjugal family, and (4) the separation of church and state.

Collectivities are interaction systems that may be distinguished by their goals, their composition, and their size. A collectivity is characterized by conforming acts and by deviant acts, which are both classes of members' action that relate to the structure of the system. Interestingly (and oddly) enough, each collectivity has a structure that consists of <u>four</u> levels also. In a pluralistic society one finds an extremely large variety of collectivities that are held together to a varying extent by an overlapping membership constituency. Hence, members of one collectivity can and do exert greater or lesser amounts of influence upon the members of the other collectivities to which they belong.

Roles refer to the behavioral organisms (the actual humans) who interact within each collectivity. Each role has a current normative structure specific to it, even though such a role may be gradually changing. (For example, the role of the physical educator/coach or recreation director could be in a transitory state in that certain second-level norms could be changing, and yet each *specific* physical educator/coach (or recreation director) still has definite normative obligations that are possible to delineate more specifically than the more <u>generalized</u> second-level norms, examples of which were offered above.)

Finally, these four levels of social structure themselves also compose a hierarchy of control and conditioning. As Johnson (Ibid., p. 49) explains, the higher levels "legitimate, guide, and control" the lower levels, and pressure of both a direct and indirect nature can be--and generally is--employed when the infraction or violation occurs and is known.

Functional Interchanges

A society is the most nearly self-subsistent type of social system and, interestingly enough again, societies or "live systems or personalities" typically have four basic types of functional problems (each with its appropriate value principle) as follows:

> 1. A pattern-maintenance problem that has to do with the inculcation of the value system and the maintenance of the social system's commitment to it,
> 2. An integration problem that is at work to implement the value of solidarity expressed through norms that accordingly regulate the great variety of processes,
> 3. A goal-attainment problem that implements the value of effectiveness of group or collective action on behalf of the social system toward this aim, and
> 4. An adaptation problem whereby the economy implements the value of utility (i.e., the investment-capitalization unit).

The economy of a society is its adaptive subsystem, while the society's form of government (polity) has become known as its goal-attainment subsystem. The integrative and pattern-maintenance subsystems, which do not have names that can be used in everyday speech easily, consist actually of a set or series of processes by which a society's production factors are related, combined, and transformed with <u>utility</u>-the value principle of the adaptive system-as the interim product. These products "packaged" as various forms of "utility" are employed in and by other functional subsystems of the society.

65

Thus, each subsystem exchanges factors and products, becomes involved as pairs, and engages in what has been called a "double interchange." It is theorized that each subsystem contributes one factor and one product (i.e., one category or aggregate of factors and one category or aggregate of products) to *each* of the other three functional subsystems. Considered from the standpoint of all the pairs possible to be involved in the interchange, there are therefore *six* double-interchange systems. Factors and products are both involved in the transformational processes, each being functional for the larger social system. Factors are *general* and therefore more remote, while products are *specific* and therefore more directly functional. The performance of the functional requirements has been described as a "circular flow of interchanges," with the factors and products being continuously used up and continuously replaced.

An example of interchange process taking place begins to help us see how this complex circular flow of interchanges occurs. Johnson explains how one of the six interchange systems functions typically *to create the political support system in a society*. This is how the functional problem of goal-attainment is resolved through the operation of the society's form of government (polity)--that is, the interchange between the polity and the integrative subsystems. "The political process is the set of structured activities that results in the choice of goals and the mobilization of societal resources for the attainment of these goals" (Ibid., p. 51). First, the integrative system contributes to political accomplishment by achieving a certain degree of consensus and "solidarity." These qualities are "registered" and "delivered" in the form of votes and interest demands. These are, in fact, forms of political support-that is, support from the integrative system <u>to</u> the polity. Conversely, in return, the government (polity) bolsters (integrative) solidarity through political leadership that, in turn, produces binding decisions. Hence, this leadership and the binding decisions can also be considered as "political support"--support from the polity or government to the integrative system (one of the two systems that "produces utility"--i.e., implements one of the four values of which utility is one.)

The Social Significance of Interchange Analysis

As can be readily seen from the example given above, the interchange analysis has tremendous social significance. The interchange of factors and products identifies the *types* of processes that somehow *must* take place in any social system. This scheme specifies also their functional significance and also indicates relations between these processes that are broad but yet important. As was stated earlier, the functional subsystems compose a hierarchy of control and conditioning; thus, the processes involved are influenced, conditioned, and controlled. These same interchange processes must be going on in any functioning social system, but it should be

66

understood that their specific forms vary greatly. The four levels of a particular social system (e.g., collectivities) provide the forms and channels by which any unique social system carries on its functionally necessary processes. Fundamental social *change* means that some basic transformation has taken, or is taking, place in one or more levels of the social system (structure). Obviously, basic change must inevitably affect the operation of the system in some distinct, measurable way.

The social change that may take place within a social system can be viewed as one of three types--i.e., one of three levels of analysis that may be distinguished as follows: (a) the analysis of "circular flow," which explains the pattern of interchange process occurring within a stable social system; (b) the analysis of "growth patterns," which determines the growth or decline of particular attributes or products of the system (e.g., power, wealth); and (c) the analysis of structural change, which is the determination of whether a level or levels of the system undergo any substantive change due to strong lower-level strain.

Critics of Parsonsian theory seem to overlook the fact that it makes definite allowance for equilibrium and change; in fact, radical social change, with or without an actual revolution, does institute a <u>new</u> hierarchy of control and conditioning. This occurs, for example, when the strain at the three lower levels forces a *different* set of priorities in the value subsystem. These new values become resultantly the basic source of legitimation, guidance, and control for the levels below.

Parsons' general action system is then actually an "equilibrium model," but this does not mean that it is necessarily conservative and/or static. As explained above, social systems may, or may not, be in a state of equilibrium, and change is certainly most possible within this theory's framework. This theory is a reasonable, theoretical explanation of how social change can and does take place. Social systems are conceived of as having a normative structure, which may or may not be stable. To understand how to achieve equilibrium within a social system, it is at least theoretically necessary to learn to distinguish between processes that will maintain or change a given social structure. Finally, it is important to understand that sometimes the higher levels of social structure may be maintained (if this is *desired* and *desirable*) by understanding how to change one or more of its lower levels. Quite obviously, this last point is most important to anyone serving in a managerial capacity in any organization within a given social system.

The above brief discussion of some of the basic elements of developing Parsonaian theory of action has necessarily for several reasons avoided the introduction of this information in great detail. For example, the concepts of economic theory involved in the adaptive subsystem of a society (i.e., money,

67

utility, products, and factors of production) were not presented. Such presentation would help the reader to appreciate their close counterparts in the theory of the other three functional problems of social systems (e.g., goal-attainment).

Nor has there been any discussion of the idea, presented by Parsons, that any analysis of the structure of complex societies demands careful differentiation of *four* levels of organizations (not considered as an entity). These levels have been called the *technical, managerial, institutional*, and *societal* levels, and it is clear that these four primary-level outputs are closely related to the four functional problems described above. Technical-level systems involving small groups of people using facilities and making decisions must be coordinated with the managerial level of organizations-- and so on up the scale through the regulation of institutionalized norms until the societal level is reached where the "single focus" of first-order values is brought to bear on the operation. (This differentiation of organizational levels is discussed below under the "application to organizations" section because of its direct relationship to the managerial function.)

Still further, the symbolic media of society have not been introduced (*generalized commitments, influence, power,* and *money*), and they are fundamentally important to the understanding and operation of the four basic types of subsystems within a social system as explained through the functional problems that have been technically identified as pattern-maintenance, integration, goal-attainment, and adaptation.

These actors and others of an even more technical nature would have to be mastered by someone who truly wished to specialize in what might be called the general or external environment, but it was felt that what has been presented is sufficient to introduce managers generally to a basic understanding of the general environment.

Applications to Understanding of Organizations

We in the field of physical activity education are all managers--but to varying degrees--functioning within organizations of one type or another. Thus we should have a fundamental understanding of how developmental physical activity in sport, exercise, and related expressive activities is taught and promoted by a great variety of amateurs, semiprofessionals, and professionals within a multitude of organizations within society generally. Secondly, those of us who function within some formal educational organization, for example, need to have an understanding as to how the elements of a social theory such as that promulgated by Parsons (and his predecessors and successors) are at work continuously within the various levels of the entire educational system.

Organizations, as a type of collectivity, do ascribe primacy to the matter of specific goal-attainment. They seek to exert environmental control through excellent performance so that certain desired goals will be realized on keeping with the organization's value system. Professionals carrying out their duties and tasks within organizations should appreciate that their organization's value system is different, but also is ultimately derived from the prevailing societal value system. Thus, a university, a community recreation program, or a secondary or elementary school, would "tend to select only those goal-attainment, adaptive, and integrative [functional problem] alternatives that contribute to the maintenance of the pattern of its units" (Hills, 1968, p. 65).

As can be readily understood, different organizations within a society have different goals and are typically organized with this purpose in mind. Organizations accordingly presumably have a range of aims (long range) and objectives (realizable in the short range). By this is meant that they have (1) goals that are largely adaptive (related to their economy), (2) goal-attainment-oriented objectives (related to the organization's governance), (3) goals that are integrative (related to the organization's solidarity), and (4) goals that are pattern maintenance-oriented in nature (geared to preservation of organization's value system).

To carry this thought a bit further, some organizations have goals that are primarily related to economic production, whereas others of a governmental nature work primarily toward the achievement of group goals. Similarly, a third type of organization by its very nature or structure is directed or oriented to the function of integration (e.g., legal services which assist in the resolution of conflicts or political parties which organize support for interest groups within the society). A fourth classification of organization correlates primarily with the functional problem of pattern-maintenance and here, as mentioned above, educational institutions may be categorized. Churches, and even the family, can also be placed in this fourth category or classification.

As Hills makes clear (Ibid., p. 65), "any organization may be treated as a functionally differentiated subsystem of a society." The organization is a system directed toward the achievement of its goals. Its value system seeks primarily to continuously legitimate the organization's goals. These goals are typically functions that have a position of greater or lesser importance in aiding the larger social system to achieve its stated values. The system aims to produce and/or market some output that is used by some other viable system within the society. The organization is considered to be successful when the relationship between it and the other systems of the environment becomes a continuing one. This is so because the organization's processes of an internal nature are supported by the external environment.

In theorizing about the hierarchy of complex organizations, Parsons (1960) himself postulated the presence of three managerial levels: the *technical* level, the *management* level, and the *institutional* level. (A fourth *societal* level is mentioned as well with which those managing at the institutional level would necessarily relate.) The production and subsequent distribution of products and/or services occurs at the technical level. Supporting areas are included here as well (e.g., operations research, accounting). The management level--which could well have been given a different name because what we understand as managing must occur at all three levels--has to do with the organizing and administering of the enterprise. At this level there is concern with the inputs, the thruput processes, and what occurs at the output stage. The third or institutional level is directly concerned with the organization's relationship with the general or external environment and all that this would normally entail.

In his comparative analysis of the central administrative agencies of amateur sport and physical recreation in England and Canada, Broom (1971) employed Parsons' theoretical framework as explained above. He pointed out that the institutional system (e.g., the Sports Council and National Advisory Council in Britain and the Canadian Amateur Sports Federation in Canada) was the mediating structure between the managerial level (and, of course, the technical level below it) and the societal level that represents the interests of the citizens of both countries. The professional managers at the managerial level are concerned primarily with the internal affairs of the organization and those working at the technical level who produce the products and the services. Broom continued by explaining that it is at the technical level at which "the primary exigencies to which the sub-organization is oriented as those imposed by the nature of the technical task, such as the 'materials'--physical, cultural, or human--that must be processed, and the kinds of cooperation of different people required to do the task effectively" (Ibid., p. 58). In the agencies that Broom studied, the tasks involved at this level were typically the advisory and technical services made available to organizations and specific individuals and, of course, the ongoing research carried on by the several organizations investigated.

Once the professional members of an organization, and especially its administrators or managers, understand that any organization has both *external* and *internal* functions, they are confronted collectively with the fact that the four functional problems (e.g., goal-attainment) also have both external and internal aspects. We should keep in mind that "since organizations are defined by the primacy of a particular type of goal, the focus of their value systems must be the legitimization of that goal in terms of the functional significance of its attainment for the more inclusive system" (Ibid., p. 67).

Now we should consider what the implications of this social theory are for organizations that face four external problems in relation to their <u>general</u> or external environment. First there is the problem of <u>legitimization</u>, which means simply that the primary goal of the organization must be validated, so to speak, as being consistent with the goals of the society. Second, the *integration* problem presents itself, and it is here that the organization must ensure that its programs and accompanying goals are acceptable to the community-at-large in which it functions.

Third, there is the problem of *goal-attainment* for the organization involved, and this means that the end product must be so produced that the recipients of these services will seek out and accept the products. (It is at this point, for example, that universities at times run into difficulty because of the graduation of larger numbers of men and women in a particular subject-matter area than there is demand for out in the field. This is why it became especially important in recent years for departments, schools, and colleges of physical education/kinesiology to promote the idea of alternative careers-- rather than expecting everybody to somehow end up working in educational circles.)

Fourth, the *adaptation* or adaptive problem of the organization is so fundamental in nature. It is vital, of course, that sufficient resources be procured to guarantee the production of the organization's end product. What is needed here, of course, is money through which the leaders of the organization can bring to bear the necessary physical and human resources to achieve the organization's objectives while moving toward its long range aims or goals. Typically members of our profession need to be reminded by their managers fairly often about the vital importance of this commodity.

Theoretical Comparisons

It is now time to return to a consideration of Gross's approach to the basic components of the external (general) environment in order to make a comparison with Johnson's and Hills' analysis of Parsons' action system in this regard. The similarities are immediately apparent, although the terminology employed is somewhat different. Initially, Gross (1964) refers to *resources* and subdivides his discussion of this topic into (1) output, (2) wealth, and (3) scarcity and abundance. His next category is *social organization*, and he explains how administrators convert human and physical resources into the power to achieve significant results. The managerial revolution had brought with it "more organization, larger organizations, more bureaucracy, and more administrators" (Ibid., p. 439). Third, the *power structure* of the general environment is reviewed. The question of the distribution of power within the system is considered from the standpoint of who makes what decisions at what times. The power dispersion has resulted from the pluralism of interests within a given society, but the increasing size and complexity of societies seems to inevitably bring a variety of "power dispersion patterns."

In this chapter we are primarily concerned with a physical activity education and athletics unit. It is vitally important for the organization whether the manager is attempting to function in a general environment where a dictatorial, semi-dictatorial, or democratic pattern of power dispersion is in operation. How democratic a society is can be quite quickly determined by ascertaining "who participates how deeply in what decisions" (Ibid., p. 451). Hence, in a society where the concept of 'organizational democracy' is not very well developed in the sense that individual members of the organization don't have much to say about their own work and the direction in which the organization is moving, one of the crucial mainstays of a so-called democratic society is lacking. Such a situation can be present in the *immediate* (internal) environment as well as in the *general* (external) environment, and its presence or absence holds great import for professionals and their managerial team in either type of organization.

Finally, Gross treats the *value structure* of the general environment, describing it as "a patterned set of general attitudes concerning what is desirable or undesirable" (Ibid., p. 457). At this level we are reminded that the society in which our organization is functioning subscribes to certain basic human and societal values. Thus, if we and our managers ever ignore the needs and interests of a substantive minority--or of the majority, of course--of the members of our respective organization to work toward the achievement of these basic values, we do so to the detriment of the progress of our organization within the general environment. The situation is that simple, and yet so often it becomes so complex!

Assessment of the value structure of Western culture has been made by many in the past. One continually hears expressed such values as (1) dignity for the individual, (2) equality of opportunity (a concept that is difficult to describe accurately), (3) individual freedom, (4) the rule of law, (5) facilitation of personal achievement, etc. There do seem to be many contradictions, however, and it is with such discrepancies and inconsistencies that we as professionals functioning within our organizations must deal daily both "internally" and "externally." The socio–cultural, "organizational-environments confrontation" takes place continuously and continually. Our motives and our output, for those of us functioning in public educational and other public institutions, must be fully understood by the ultimate decision-makers in a democratic society--the voters. Those of us earning our living as professionals in these fields in some form of developmental physical activity offered by private or commercial agency in the larger society face the fickle public's purchasing decisions. For better or worse, our organizational motives and output--no matter where we serve--

must be reasonably consistent with both the values <u>and</u> norms of the general environment.

Concluding Observations About the General Environment

The major thrust of this chapter is to point out to managers that they can't neglect the general or external environment--or the immediate or internal environment--if they hope to be successful on the job. However, since relatively few physical activity educators or recreation directors have initially undergone extensive management training including field work experience, it was considered advisable to offer managers additionally an approach by which they could obtain a better social perspective in which to place their administrative task, the hope being that increased understanding might make some contribution to improved job performance.

Finally, a manager should plan to assist the larger community (the general environment) by assuming some direct responsibility for society's welfare over and above his or her own immediate professional task. Second, keeping in mind that the general environment relates to the still broader social environment of the educational institution (or of the agency that the manager is administering) within the society typically, there are ever-increasing indications that this general environment has now become worldwide in scope and probably needs its own theoretical subdivisions. We are all quite aware of Toffler's concepts (1970, 1980) of 'future shock' and 'third wave world'--our collision with the future. The world will never be the same again--but, then, it probably never was.

The Immediate (Internal) Environment

At the outset of this second section explaining the *immediate* environment of the sport and physical education manager, we reiterate that a manager must give serious thought to the both "environments" of the organization in which he or she is laboring. This means that the manager must be continually involved in the analysis and understanding of the various external social forces that impinge on the total organization being managed. And yet, moreover, a manager simply is faced daily with a number of human beings at the very core of the managerial process, people whose *purposeful* behavior daily within the organization influences any goal realization that the manager and his immediate associates seek to bring to fruition.

Further, each person within in the organization, as well as each individual outside of the organization with whom contact is made, is inescapably unique and possesses many and varied interests. Additionally, human nature being what it is, conflicts of greater or lesser import are inevitable as all of the participants function and interact in both external and immediate environments. Such a "conflict phenomenon" is true because

73

people by their very nature exhibit behavior that is often characterized by a lack of rationality of one type or another.

The structure of the organization in which human beings function may be explained as a pattern or framework in which individuals and parts or units of the department, school, agency, or company fulfill a variety of roles so that finally the purposes of the enterprise may possibly be achieved. In the process a number of hierarchical and polyarchical relationships are often established that function according to prevailing codes of behavior. It is vital to understand further that there is typically a formal and an <u>informal</u> structure in every organization, both of which exert significant and influential amounts of power on problems and issues that arise.

Now, in this second half of this chapter, there will be a detailed discussion of the manager's *immediate* environment with a concluding brief discussion at the end as to how the manager's "two environments" interrelate. The immediate environment, therefore, includes the organizational climate, suppliers, controllers, controllees, advisers, adversaries, and so-called publics with opinions. The *general* environment, discussed in detail earlier, is made up of the organization's resources, its social organization, the power structure, and the society's structure of values and norms. (These terms or components were used as long ago as 1964 by Gross (Chapter 14), and then adapted by the present author to sport and physical education.)

Physical activity education units , including athletics units (e,g,m departments, divisions, schools, agencies) are human organizations within larger organizations. They are what can be designated as "open" systems, although there is undoubtedly great variation in the "openness" or "closure" of any such systems under consideration. It is extremely difficult, if not impossible, to actually "close" any human organization today.

Typically, four phenomena make organizational systems open to a greater or lesser degree. In the first place, there are usually entries into the unit and exits from it. This means that outsiders may become insiders and vice versa. Secondly, departmental members hold memberships in other organizations, which means that their loyalties may be divided to some degree at least. Thirdly, a type of resource exchange typically exists; the larger community (or general environment) sends students (new members) to the units for the service that is provided. As a result, reciprocal influences take place, and at colleges and universities students are graduated with varying types of diploma and degrees (depending upon the level of education under consideration in this instance). Finally, departmental members and "outsiders" (other faculty, administrators, alumni, representatives from other educational systems, legislators, and the public generally become involved with mutual or reciprocal influence(s).

74

The "visibility" of the many people and/or organizations that interrelate with the department (in this example) varies greatly for many reasons of both a formal and an informal nature. In a sense they help to determine the "texture" of the department. The manager and his/her associates typically develop and employ major and/or minor strategies of an offensive or defensive nature in their relationships with the people and/or organizations that "encircle" the organization described here--the physical education and athletics unit.

The Clients

Within the scope of the educational world, as opposed to the business world, for example, there are some differences but many similarities in regard to the "clients," "customers," or *students* (as is the case here). The clients form a network; basically, they are the receivers of the goods and services of the department. Thus, we might be talking about the graduates of the professional program, or about students studying in other areas who elect courses within the department of physical activity education (or developmental physical activity). Further, we might be referring to those students who are taking part in the intramurals/physical activity program or the program of intercollegiate athletics.

The "internal clients" of a department--to continue the analogy begun above--are those people who make up the rest of the college or university. They might be faculty and non-academic staff members who in some way come in contact with the "products or goods" of the department. They might actually take part in the voluntary physical activity program, or they may have sons and daughters in some phase of the departmental program. Further, they might be faculty or other staff members who attend athletic contests (male or female), or perhaps even their children have (during the academic year or at a summer sports camp) expressed needs or interests in physical activity in sport, dance, play, or exercise.

The "less visible clients" of physical education and athletics are a relatively large, amorphous, unorganized, and non-vocal group typically, but they can become extremely vocal on seemingly short notice if a problem or inconvenience arises. These are people in the community who have had good, bad, or so-so experiences with sport and physical education in the past (taxpayers, merchants, professional people, legislators at all levels, etc.). We often don't know how to reach these people--or at least we don't usually give much thought to the matter--until all of a sudden they begin to "come out of the woodwork" with attacks against us in times of crisis when problems and issues of varying nature develop.

For example, many educational institutions, and notably those at the college and university level, often encounter negative criticisms of varying intensity because of sharply rising costs, the "lack of rigor" in their offerings, the impracticality of many courses and programs, the on- or off-campus behavior of students, and the presumably radical ideas of some faculty members. Unfortunately, administrators and professors have practically no "political clout" and are therefore vulnerable to both criticism and subsequent budgetary cutbacks or restraint. Whose fault this is, and whether anything can or should be done about it, is an open question.

The "number of clients" aspect of the immediate environment of the sport and physical education profession brings further highly interesting questions to mind. For years the profession has been working toward 100% involvement of all children and young people at all educational levels up to some point within the college or university experience. This does make possible a great many opportunities for creativity and initiative, but it does also nevertheless place a tremendous burden upon the allied professions to care for all children and young people adequately according to their needs in health and safety education, physical activity education (including athletics), recreation and park administration, and dance.

However, we should not forget that the profession (and our allied professions too) has a responsibility to function and serve throughout the entire lives of people--not just while they are at some level of the educational system. Thus, our responsibility extends to all people--whatever age they may be, and no matter whether they are "special," "normal," or "accelerated." Such programming can be carried out for pre-school children and for adults throughout life by the efforts of public, private, and commercial agencies, as well as by families and individuals in their own ways. Broadening our outlook and efforts in this way would permit the field to enlarge its scope from the standpoint of both breadth and depth.

In the past, businesses have been concerned with "the stability of client demand." In physical education and athletics the problem is similar but far from identical. The profession developed its position over the past hundred years, and has now reached the point where physical education, or some variation thereof, is included in the curriculum of the schools (to a greater or lesser extent from the standpoint of time involvement). The idea of a requirement at the college and university has met severe challenges. It could well be that in time, as programs at the lower levels improve, the requirement will cease typically at the completion of grade ten (for example).

As far as athletics is concerned, historically games and sports were tolerated at first by faculty and administration; then permitted to make great strides while flagrant abuses developed; and finally were brought under control to a degree--and have generally been regarded as extracurricular ever since. So "client demand," of one type or another, with varying degrees of "quality and quantity," seem to be present; and it seems strongly probable that sport, dance, and exercise are "here to stay." The extent of the requirement in the schools will probably be lessened in the years immediately ahead.

The Suppliers

Physical activity education and athletics units do not operate in a vacuum. They need assistance in the form of resources, associates, and supporters in a similar way to that typically received by business organizations. In some ways their lot is not as difficult as is the case with private enterprise.. For example, the taxpayers pay money into governmental coffers through different types of taxation (not to mention the approximately 30% of overall resources funded by student tuition), and through this source of supply the department receives funds that enable it to purchase the services of faculty and staff *and* the expendable, semi-expendable, and capital goods needed to carry out the department's various functions. On the other hand, that arrangement can cause severe handicaps to develop if, say, athletics are regarded as extra-curricular or ancillary and thereby placed in a position whereby this phase of the program must sell itself to the public on the basis of a win-loss record. (One can't resist inquiring what would happen to many aspects of the so-called regular curriculum, including some required physical education classes that are offered, if they were forced to function in such a profit-or-loss manner.)

One type of "associate' as mentioned above would be that individual or department within the school or university which gives help directly in the "processing of the product"--the male or female student moving up the educational ladder. Such an associate would be the educational counselor or a similar person in the office of the dean of students. Other examples of "associates" would be teachers of other subjects or members of the administrative staff (including those who maintain the buildings and grounds). "Supporters" are considered part of the category of suppliers would be alumni, legislators, "friends," of the school or university, etc. In a business organization they might be the investors or those who lend money to the enterprise.

The Advisers

All organizations have advisers, and physical education and athletics departments are no exception. In fact, they have probably had more advice given to them over the years than most other departments within the institution. This has been especially true in the area of interscholastic and intercollegiate athletics, but it is to be hoped that the need for such continuing advice will decrease in the future (as further "professionalization" occurs, and at such time as (we hope) a greater degree of sanity emerges within the programs within their internal and external environments). Even those operating the gymnasium, swimming pool, or classroom have received plenty of advice as well. Often this has been from administrative and supervisory personnel who in a large number of cases had "graduated" from the physical education or coaching ranks into such positions.

Physical activity educator/coaches should not be ungrateful for the advice they have received in the past, or for that which they will continue to receive--perhaps to a somewhat lesser extent--in the future. It is inherently difficult for people to bring themselves to the point where they truly want to ask for advice from the "outside." Even if such advice is sought, quite often there is an immediate resistance to the counsel once it is given, unless it agrees quite completely with the plans which were submitted or presented to the adviser for review. There are various motives that underlie the employment of advisers. One often has the feeling (when serving as an adviser) that he/she is being used by administrators who wish their own thoughts and ideas echoed, or who have been requested by their own superiors to seek such counsel. There is no doubt but that the presence of an outsider may tend to create an adversary relationship.

The above comments are not meant to imply for a moment, however, the idea that the various types of advice offered are usually worthless or never used if they don't conform to the predetermined plans of the administrator seeking such help. Such assistance can be of inestimable value as the manager seeks to weigh the alternative courses of action open. Sometimes it is simply a case of engaging someone to process information in a variety of ways, and it would be difficult for anyone to resent such information being made available for subsequent use in the decision-making process.

Often the question may arise as to the "detachment" of the "involvement" of the adviser. This is especially true if such advice proceeds beyond the stage of information provision and moves into the realm of the making of one or more recommendations for immediate or delayed action on the part of the department or program.

All things considered, the adviser should be viewed as a relatively senior person at least with a successful experience that would tend to lend credence to the "quiet wisdom" which he or she is transmitting in a variety of ways to those seeking help. The adviser concerned needs to have the benefit of the confidence and friendliness of those from whom information is being sought. If the adviser is viewed either as a threat or an ally, it may not be possible to offer detached and sound advice.

The Controllers

Departments or schools of physical activity education and athletics encounter regularly those who officially or unofficially exert a controlling function through their influence. The department head or director undoubtedly has an advisory committee or an executive committee. He or she will probably be guided or directed also by various boards of control or directorates, not to mention the dean, superintendent, academic vice-president, and others. These are the people or groups who fit at some point into the hierarchical pattern of the organization's formal structure, while here it is more the intention to enumerate briefly those individuals, groups, agencies, or governmental units that exert a greater or lesser amount of control on different occasions and at different times.

An example of such a "controller" of physical activity education and athletics on the North American continent would be a state or provincial professional association whose members might agree on a recommended curriculum or type of program. This professional body would not have the power at the present time to actually enforce its recommendation upon any one high school, junior or community college, or university, but it could well cause embarrassment to the physical education unit of any one institution if that department didn't seem to be moving in the direction in which the professional association was presumably pointing its membership. This would be the case also at the national level, although the influence might typically be considerably less.

Accrediting agencies represent another example of a controller, only in this instance there is no question as to the strength of the influence. Schools and universities will go to great lengths to avoid being put on probation or actually having their accreditation revoked until certain standards are met. Of course, on some occasions accrediting agencies are loathe to invoke restrictions or penalties on prestigious members because the prestige of the agency itself might be weakened. The field of physical activity education and athletics has had its share of such controllers over the decades, and the administrator resists or ignores them at his or her peril. These controllers find representation either formally or informally "at the court" of physical activity education and athletics. This means that the wise administrator can display foresight by recognizing these influences (or potential influences), and by being ready to employ or deploy them to the unit's (e.g., department's) best advantage.

The Adversaries.

Adversaries confront managers on a regular basis, although even in the area of interscholastic and intercollegiate athletics the competition is rarely so cutthroat as it might typically be in business where democratic capitalism prevails as a determining influence on the state of the economy. Those who compete with us for students at the college and university level are, of course, our adversaries, and this is especially true in those states or provinces where public universities are reimbursed by the government on a per capita basis. When enrollment projections do not hold up in these situations, university recruitment policies and procedures are stepped up sharply and begin to resemble the recruitment practices often attributed to representatives of university athletic programs.

Careful delineation of the specific meanings of such terms as recruitment, subsidization, and proselytizing are needed to lessen the opprobrium of universities and colleges regarding each other strictly as adversaries in the strongest sense. This problem does not arise in the same way at the secondary school level, except when occasionally parents are encouraged to move from one school district or city to another so that their child may play for such-and-such a school or coach--a practice that has been more strictly regulated in recent years. Departments or schools of physical education rarely if ever have competed for students with high academic ability; in fact, it is sad to relate that the idea of such competition--at least to a reasonable extent--tends to make one smile because the very idea is definitely anachronistic.

Gross distinguishes among competitors, rivals, and opponents or enemies--as sub-categories under the main heading of "adversaries" (1964, pp. 427-29). Because they tend to overlap in their meanings, it is difficult to maintain the distinctions as explained. Competitors "produce the same or similar products." Rivals "produce entirely different products but compete for resources, assistance or support," while opponents are "external individuals or organizations who, although not necessarily competitors or rivals, nevertheless impede the operation or progress of an organization." Finally, "enemies are opponents whose opposition carried them into the more bitter forms of conflict."

Several analogies from physical activity education and athletics will help to place these adversaries in perspective. Another institution with whom you compete in a sport would be a *competitor* in this context, whereas a *rival* would be, say, the English department that wants to use the athlete for a dramatic performance during the basketball season--while at the same time requesting extra money for this program from a limited school budget. An *opponent* would be the municipal recreation program with so many basketball leagues in operation that they are threatening to encroach on the gymnasium time requested for the varsity, junior varsity, and freshman basketball teams. An *enemy*--to choose perhaps a "far-out' example--might be a community recreation league coach seeking to lure high school athletes into his basketball program because he wants to win an intercity league championship. As we consider these very fine distinctions, we recognize

80

them, but the terminology employed by Gross has overlapping meanings for us.

Publics with Opinions

Physical activity education and athletics, because of the high degree of visibility of its activities, encounters many different types of "publics with opinions." Of course, this has both good and bad implications for the success of the total program. If a star athlete breaks a wrist taking part in gymnastics in a required physical education program, all sorts of repercussions may develop based on the opinions and actions of people who don't fully understand the situation. (This actually happened in a mid-western state, and the young man's father--who was a member of the state legislature--tried to have physical education eliminated as a requirement in that state!)

Occasionally an instructor is deemed to be negligent, and this behavior reflects on both the individual concerned and on other personnel within the department and school. Basically all programs operate within the values and norms of the society or culture in which they function, and the instructor defies these strictures at his or her peril. Although times are changing, there are still many communities in which explicit sex education and possible subsequent discussion in a coeducational health education class would cause certain factions within the community to rapidly become a "public with negative opinions" about the school in general and the department of physical and health education in particular.

Obviously, there will always be diversity of opinion on any controversial subject in an evolving democracy where pluralistic philosophies of education are permitted to exist side by side. If problems develop, they will typically come from adverse opinions on the part of those within the immediate environment mentioned earlier in this paper. The manager cannot put out of mind other quarters where possibilities for adverse opinions might surface at any given moment. These bad (or good) opinions might originate with organizations or individuals that might wish to engage physical education "services" in the future--or even might never wish to establish a connection. Nevertheless, they help to create a climate within the environment which would have a deleterious effect on the status of physical education and athletics. An example of this latter point might occur if a community leader were to publicly deplore the poor leadership and behavior exhibited by a hockey coach over the course of a season's play. Such "adverse opinion" can be designated as intangible, but might well influence decision-makers in regard to the size of the upcoming (or future) physical education and athletics budget.

Thus, the administrator should appreciate the complexity of obtaining an accurate measure of public opinion within the immediate environment. Descriptive research involving the sampling of opinion can be most helpful if carried out in a mature and sophisticated manner. In addition to discovering what "most people" think about the way things are going and discovering what they feel their future needs and interests may be, it is highly important further to keep in touch with what the leaders of the various groups and/or factions are thinking. Such analysis is difficult to carry out even for professionals. What often happens is that the obtaining of such information is typically left to amateurs or chance within their own departments. Obviously, there is great room for improvement insofar as development of true understanding about what the "public" thinks or feels concerning the many aspects of a total physical education and athletics program.

Observations and Conclusions

Several points need to be made to conclude this discussion of the "immediate environment" of the manager/administrator. This discussion has been purposely narrow in that the general environment of the manager has deliberately not been included. Nevertheless a few observations pointing in an "external direction" should be made in this concluding section.

In the first place, a manager should plan to assist the larger community (the general environment) by assuming some direct responsibility for society's welfare over and above his or her own immediate professional task. Second, keeping in mind that the general environment relates to the still broader social environment of the educational institutions within the society typically, at present there are strong indications that this general environment has now become worldwide in scope (and probably needs its own theoretical subdivisions). Finally, we are all quite aware of Toffler's concept of 'future shock'--our collision with the future--that everyone needs to understand as thoroughly as possible.

Community Responsibility. If organizations functioning in a society hope to prosper at the same time as society itself is moving forward substantively and qualitatively, the manager as a leader must assume some responsibility for the welfare of the external (general) environment. One should not expect that a manager, his or her associates, and those who sponsor the organization that is being administered will reap the benefits of the society in which they operate and not offer something of themselves in return. Obviously, community service by any one individual can be overdone and could truly negate one's job effectiveness. On the other hand, society cannot hope to progress and to solve its pressing problems if organizational leaders and managers do not do more than just carry out their *(immediate environmental)* professional duties responsibly and pay taxes.

Flory (1965, pp. 200-01) stressed three conditions that must be met by the mature member of a society in this regard. First, a person "must accept the fact of his or her existence in the world at this time." Second, the mature person "has to accept the fact of individuality." By this he means that each member of the manager's organization, including the manager, is unique both physically and psychologically, and this means that the manager should appreciate, not denigrate, how and what unique individuals can contribute to the organization's growth and development--and that of the larger community as well. Third, the mature individual "must recognize that no adult can be loved, or even liked, by every worthy citizen of his or her own community."

If an administrator or manager decides to accept some responsibility for the development of the community at the local, regional, national, or international levels, it is obviously required that an effort be made to understand as fully as possible the structure and function of the larger society--his or her general environment. The executive should not assume this responsibility because he or she thinks that the organization represented will necessarily be more highly regarded or make more money. One should help the community to progress and solve its problems because such assistance is needed, because a manager sees a spot where he or she can be of help by virtue of some personal or professional qualifications. Therefore, he or she wouldn't feel right about not helping out in some positive way.

Recurrent Themes in the 'World Family'. What Kaplan (1961, pp. 7-10) called the 'family of man,' we should probably call the 'world family' today-- and (as a colleague quipped) that term includes the non-human living creatures too (a good point!). At any rate, as mentioned above, a manager can no longer think that the organization's general environment is limited to local and regional boundaries. The recurrent themes that he discovered in the various world philosophies merit the consideration of managers who would truly understand the ramifications of the extension of their general environment that has taken place.

First, he delineated a theme of *rationality*--the idea that the world is regarded as a systematic unity. Second, he discovered a theme of *activism*-- the thought that increased understanding should serve us as a guide for positive action. Third, he found a theme of *humanism*--a position that humans are what are central in most philosophies and probably in the world itself, a world that is characterized by continuity between humans and nature. Finally, he discerned an increasing concern about values--the view that the lives of people should be strongly related to moral values in the fulfillment of their highest aspirations.

Thus, as administrators and managers explain and compare their programs of physical activity education and athletics, they should not expect

83

that these programs would ever become identical. The need for preservation of indigenous games and activities can certainly be appreciated. Yet there is reason to expect that 'family resemblances' will be found because these recurring themes do run through the basic value systems and philosophies-- and hence through societies and cultures--*including their educational systems and sports and games.* In their work with colleagues abroad, therefore, managers should seek to share, explain, and--most of all-understand. Internationalism in sport and developmental physical activity is truly one of the highest of goals for which managers should strive.

The Environments, Future Shock, and Third World Emphases. Up to this point, a case has been made for the position that, to the best of their ability and comprehension, managers should seek to understand both the internal and the external environments of their organizations. Interestingly, these environmental subdivisions have their own breakdowns that may be considered "natural" and "cultural," so to speak. The natural environment of an organization has to do with geographic locale, for example, which can influence operation and results greatly. The cultural environment, conversely, relates more to the findings of behavioral science with which a manager must be knowledgeable.

After all of this, therefore, the discussion can be brought to a close with a firm reminder that a managerial revolution is indeed occurring, the limits of which we today are only dimly aware (Zeigler, 1984, pp. 34-45). Assessing the society's rate of change may be impossible, but we must increasingly search for synthesis and consensus as we face conflicting demands and trends in our lives. "Second wave civilization placed an extremely heavy emphasis on our ability to dismantle problems into their components; it rewarded us less often for the ability to put the pieces back together again (Toffler, 1980, pp. 129-30).

What we need now in all aspects of (Third Wave) life is to put all of this in greatly improved and apparent context. Today we must do all in our power to "eschew obfuscation" (i.e., to be clear, concise, and precise in what we say and do). We have so much to deal with that is obsolescent, that should be viewed simply as "excess cultural baggage." This is nowhere more true than in many of the managerial myths that surface time and again in the immediate, on-the-job environment. (An example of this is the dismal myth that the person who assumes the managerial mantle knows best about everything; see Hunt, 1979, p. 19).

In the management of physical activity education and athletics, we urgently need the knowledge from onrushing behavioral theory that will help us to understand the managerial environment in an ever-improving manner. It is too much to hope that search committees will recommend men and women who are committed to the employment of sound management theory in accord with ethical practice? Finally, it is too much to expect that when mistakes are made in manager selection that people will be prepared to rectify an unproductive situation?

References and Bibliography

Broom, E. F. (1971). *A comparative analysis of the central administrative agencies of amateur sport and physical recreation in England and Canada* Doctoral dissertation, University of Illinois, UIUC.

Flory, C. D., ed. *Managers for tomorrow*, New York: New American Library, Inc., 1965.

Gross, B. M. *The managing of organizations*, 2 vols., New York: The Free Press of Glencoe, 1964.

Hills, R. J. (1968). *Toward a science of organization.* Eugene, OR: Center for the Advanced Study of Educational Administration.

Hunt, P. Fallacy of the one big brain, in *Harvard Business Review on human relations*, New York; Harper & Row Publishers, 1979, pp. 19-29.

Johnson, H. M. (1969). The relevance of the theory of action to historians. *Social Science Quarterly*, No. 2, 46-58.

Kaplan, A. *The new world of philosophy.* New York: Random House, 1961.

Parsons, T. (1960). *Structure and process in modern societies.* New York: The Free Press.

Toffler, A. *Future shock*, New York: Random House, 1970.

Toffler, A. *The third wave*, New York: Bantam Book, 1981.

Zeigler, E. F. (1982), *Decision-making in physical education and athletics*, Champaign, IL: Stipes Publishing Company.

Zeigler, E. F., and Bowie, G. W. (1984). *Developing management competency in sport and physical education,* Philadelphia: Lea & Febiger.

Zeigler, E. F. & Spaeth, M. J. (1975*). Administrative theory and practice in physical education and athletics.* Englewood Cliffs, NJ: Prentice-Hall.

For Consideration and Discussion:

As an exercise, it is recommended that two students each make a 10-minute presentation, one describing an organization's general environment, while the other explains that which is deemed to characterize the internal environment. Then a third student should conduct a class discussion about how these descriptions be applying to the institution where this course is being conducted.

CHAPTER 4

CURRENTLY USEFUL GENERALIZATIONS
for
PHYSICAL ACTIVITY EDUCATION
(including ATHLETICS)

The words "currently useful generalizations" may sound "anemic" in the description of what our program is all about within education at all levels. However, it seems much more practical and realistic to describe here what we generally accept as "our" responsibility" within the overall educational program. Hence, you will find concise summaries (i.e., "currently useful generalizations") concerning the management/administration of physical activity education (including athletics).

If this material seems reasonable, generally speaking, the credit should go to many of the administrators working in this area whose experience and insight has enabled them to gather and report a significant body of knowledge. Any deficiencies that may seem apparent when you attempt to apply these "generalizations" to specific problems may be caused by this author's inability to reflect correctly what many leaders have said and written, or by the peculiarities of the particular situation to which you are trying to apply them. The following statements may sound authoritative and definitive, but they must be challenged by you as you strive to apply them subsequently.

Consider the total physical education, and recreation program. You may be able to suggest several additional categories, or to combine or eliminate some of the following areas that are recommended as a point of departure:

Aims and Objectives
Health and Safety Education (related)
Physical Education Classification
  or Proficiency Tests
The Required Program
Intramural Athletics
Interscholastic or Intercollegiate
  Athletics
Voluntary Physical Recreation
The Individual or Adaptive Program
Facilities and Equipment
Public Relations
General Administration
Evaluation

Aims and Objectives

The determination of aims and objectives seems basic. A philosophy of life should coincide with a philosophy of education. Thinking should be logical and consistent, and these beliefs should not conflict too much with practice in physical activity education (including athletics). Professional educators in this area should be operating on the basis of the "currently useful generalizations" for which they stand. If one calls principles "generalizations," this does not mean that he does not believe anything. It does mean that he/she will base actions taken according to what appears to be best at the moment.

> (Note: for the remainder of this chapter to avoid awkwardness, I will use "he" instead of "she", but I trust the reader will understand that I am not thereby "downgrading" in doing so.)

It is most often practical to work from specific objectives toward general aims. Expediency may cause a physical activity educator to sidetrack some of his beliefs, but this does not mean that he must perforce lose sight of what he believes to be ultimately right. It is difficult for those in the field to agree on one basic philosophy. Obviously, there will always be at least several schools of thought. Although various beliefs should be expressed in a substantial way, truly definitive philosophies physical activity education (including athletics) are rare.

Although physical activity education has made a solid effort to achieve a stronger scientific base, science and philosophy have *complementary* roles to play in aiding the field to find its proper place in the educational system. Philosophy considers the *basic* problems of physical activity education (including athletics) in a systematic fashion. Philosophical thinking enables the professional worker to view his field as a whole. He will not see himself merely as an athletic coach, a physical conditioner, an organizer of intramural sports, or an athletic director.

Philosophy helps the professional to fashion a mental image of what his field should be. It is prospective in the sense that it forms a vanguard; it should lead actual practice. A philosophy, of course, must be practical, or it would be worthless. An instrumental philosophy would necessarily imitate science in part, but only as it serves as a plan for action. Science describes a field as it exists; philosophy pictures it as it should be. Philosophy is an excellent complement to science; it reaches and points toward the world of tomorrow.

A philosophy of physical activity education, typically as a part of an over-all educational philosophy, has a relation to the general field of

87

philosophy. A prevalent view is that which holds a philosophy of life basic to a philosophy of education. To the former is assigned the establishment of fundamental beliefs; to the latter, their application to a specific field. A basic philosophy outlining specific aims and objectives could help physical activity education greatly and in many ways. This is true because there are now many serious conflicts dangerously splitting the field within education and "outside" in society at large. Yet all factions might readily agree that it is important for the administrator of physical activity education to strive to form a sound philosophy.

Health and Safety Education (Relationship to)

Physical activity education by its very nature is intimately related to the health and safety education program of an educational institution. Typically there are three aspects to the latter as follows:

Health Services. Health service today implies determining the student's health status, informing parents of any defects that exist, educating parents and offspring in the prevention of common defects, aiding the teacher to detect symptoms of illness, and helping to correct defects which are remediable.

It took many years for boards of education to realize that schools must be concerned with more than illiteracy. The new educational era demands that the school take unto itself practically all of the child's problems. Today, if conditions are ideal, the physician, medical specialist, nurse, dentist, psychologist, psychiatrist, nutrition expert, janitor, and teacher all have a part in the over-all job of keeping the child healthy.

Boards of education are increasingly taking the responsibility for health services. There are, however, many civic leaders who favor board of health control in this area. Cooperation between the two boards seems advisable on many occasions, but such an arrangement usually has its weaknesses. The fact that it is quite difficult for either agency to set policy which encroaches on the other's sphere of operation indicates that the responsibility for the health of the child should not be divided at this level.

"Medical inspection" was the now-archaic term formerly used for the medical examination of today. What is the school's responsibility for health appraisal? What type of medical examination should there be? Who should look after the correction of remediable defects? What is the relation of psychological services to the school health program? Who should maintain the health and accident records? What is the best plan for emergency care?

The medical examination itself serves more functions than is generally realized. In addition to diagnosis of defects and subsequent notification of parents, the school health authorities should strive to secure correction of remediable defects by careful guidance of the children involved. Each child must be helped to develop a scientific attitude toward bodily ailments. Having established the importance of the medical examination, ask your some questions about the actual examination the children receive. Is the parent invited to be present so that the physician can explain the results? Is the teacher present to learn more about the child for future guidance? Is the examination sufficiently complete and detailed? Too often, physicians are so rushed in the performance of their duties that the child receives only a more-or less perfunctory check-up.

It cannot be argued that a carefully maintained health record is superfluous in the development of a child. To be sure, limited budgets may restrict the adequacy of any such record. On the other hand, it is extremely important that the child receive the services of various educational experts. To get a complete picture of the child, youth, or young adult many things must be known about his environment, disease record, scholastic ability, social adjustment, and health practices. Health services should be involved with the appraisal, correction, and protection of children and youth throughout their years in the educational system.

Health Instruction. Health instruction is the second of three subdivisions of health and safety education. There are many questions to be answered here. Should health instruction classes be scheduled separately? What should a course in health include? What about the introduction of controversial subjects such as sex education? What should be the role of the physical educator in the field of safety education? Should driver education be included? Who should teach health-the physical educator, the health education specialist, a physician, or the science teacher? What attention should be given to mental health? Is a health coordinator necessary in a school?

The health instruction class has been a perennial problem. Facts about health have become a considerable part of the knowledge of how to live. Most important, of course, is that health education should be an influence in favor of "clean living." Although people know that regular medical checkups are advisable, they usually maintain their bodies in much poorer condition than they do their cars. Most people have their cars' oil changed regularly; yet, they insist upon waiting for pain before going to the physician.

Down through the years, health instruction has generally been taught somewhat poorly. Just as in the case of earlier "physical training," parents realized that health courses were, in many instances, next to useless. Even today they must still be convinced that most physical activity education teachers are anxious to incorporate the modem problem-solving approach into the teaching of health. Here is one area where the case method of instruction might be employed to advantage. Health instruction is more than just the teaching of principles and facts of healthful living; it is more than merely drawing the various systems of the body on the blackboard and explaining them superficially. Health education should have as its goal the integration of this book-knowledge with actual living achievement. This is no mean task-to motivate children and youth to use the facts to help them live at their best in order to be able subsequently to serve most.

Healthful School Living. Healthful school living itself can be subdivided into three categories: the conditions of the school environment, the conditions of the classroom experience, and the conditions of school organization. With so much school construction in all stages of development, the school building itself demands serious consideration. The taxpayer and parent must be shown that the demands of health and those of architectural beauty do not inevitably clash. And if they do, the students themselves should have first priority. The school plant must be *both* hygienic *and* beautiful if the student is to have the best educational opportunities. Although plans should be made for schools to be close to the geographical center of population, due thought should also be given to adequate size of building and surrounding area as well as to hygienic environment and the student's safety.

Conditions of the classroom experience are important, also. And what about the problem of discipline? Should the teacher dominate the students by sheer will power, or should the children be helped to develop their own standards of behavior? The end of all discipline would seem to be intelligent self-direction. Should such factors as undue fatigue, success and failure, noise and excitement, "sedentariness", the hygiene of reading, and individual differences be considered?

90

The actual conditions of school organization play an important role in healthful school living. Is there a proper balance in the school among work, play, rest, and the taking of nourishment? For example, do we realize the educational potentialities of the school lunch by considering the adequacy of the cafeteria, time allowed for eating, economics of the project, student participation in conduct rules, and health supervision of the lunchroom employees?

Is the course curriculum properly divided, keeping in mind that the students are more efficient mentally in the morning? What supervision is there over the health of the individual teacher? Should the general tone of the child's day be "hurry"? Modem society is so rushed that a conscious effort should be made to slow down the daily tempo of the school program.

Physical Education Classification (or Proficiency Tests)

After the examining physician has informed the physical activity education teacher if the child is healthy, almost healthy, in need of adaptive work, or fit for only passive exercise, the teacher should test and classify the *normal* individual according to the objectives of the school's program. Testing and measuring are necessary in order to prove to administrators, supervisors, students, and the public that many students are physically and recreationally "illiterate." These tests provide classifications for the following purposes:

(1) To serve their individual needs.
(2) To promote fair competition between individuals and groups.
(3) To facilitate instruction.
(4) To assemble individuals of like interests as well as of like abilities.
(5) To insure continuity in the program from year to year.

A battery of physical education classification tests should include items that the department considers that most students should be able to pass within the time allotted by the school to physical education requirements. Every effort should be made to hold the tests used to the desirable standards of validity, reliability, objectivity, simplicity, standardization of procedure, duplicate forms, and "worthwhileness". Certain test items are often considered to be of greater importance to the development of the individual than others. If the student fails any part or all of the battery, he might be required to select activity in the order that the department feels is best for him. For example, if a young man failed tests in swimming, body mechanics, motor fitness, leisure skills, and self-defense, he might be required to correct these deficiencies in the order that the department of physical activity education deems best. A similar battery of tests with differing emphases should be constructed for girls and women with priorities determined according to the department's stated philosophy. It is recommended that this philosophy should reflect the thinking of the best leadership in the field, educational administration, the staff of the physical activity education department, the parents, and the students themselves.

It might be wise to permit the incoming student to begin with some form of physical recreational activity, so that he will develop good attitudes concerning the continuing value of this type of activity. It is suggested that the activity he chooses coincide with some deficiency demonstrated by the classification tests.

The department should consider classification and proficiency tests in the following categories:

  (1) Cardio-vascular efficiency.
  (2) Age-height-weight.
  (3) Motor fitness.
  (4) Body mechanics.
  (5) Self-defense
  (6) Aquatics & life saving
  (7) Dance
  (5) Skills and appreciations.
  (6) Health and sports knowledge.

Obviously, the work of the administrator/manager of physical activity education has only begun when tests have been selected and administered. When the tests have been carefully scored, rated, and appraised, the program needs of all the students can be evaluated. Testing can also aid in measuring the progress of the students and in grading.

The Basic Required Program

The conditioning program. If the student has not met the standards of the cardio-vascular and motor fitness tests, it is necessary to raise the general level of condition. Forcing an individual to follow a long, conditioning program, including such exercises as calisthenics, pulley-weight manipulation, rope climbing, and running, may frighten him away from physical activity education for many years to come. On the other hand, allowing the student to engage in any sport he desires may result in a continuation of the ineffectiveness displayed in the classification tests. It would seem logical to follow the middle road by selecting a combination of activities from each of these categories. The emphasis should be placed on motivating the student to participate with interest in all the phases of a complete physical activity education program based on sound health and safety education principles.

The student's needs may be met best through the following activities:

(1) General body-conditioning: through exercises, weight training, jogging, and swimming, and a course in body mechanics (if needed).
(2) Aquatic activities stressing the development of an all-round ability in the water, including distance swimming, life-saving, water safety, stunts and skills, and water wrestling.
(3) Tumbling and stunts.
(4) Wrestling and self-defense instruction.
(5) Sports participation of an individual, dual, and team nature stressing the acquisition of individual skills.

A conditioning program for a definite period of, say, six to twelve weeks might include activity in at least three phases of the above.

The sports instructional program. A student showing a fair level of conditioning in the cardio-vascular and motor fitness tests might be referred immediately to sports instruction, but only for, perhaps, the first six weeks of the school year. With excellent instruction, interest can be aroused. In subsequent units, sports instruction can be coordinated with the other areas of instruction in which the student may have been shown to be deficient.

In the sports instructional program it is wise to schedule a yearly plan for all the various individual, dual, and team sports to be offered. A unit in a sports activity should be a planned sequence of learning and should take from twelve to thirty lessons for completion, depending on the difficulty of the activity. In planning a teaching unit, consideration should be given to (a) objectives, (b) learning experiences, (c) subject matter, (d) instructional methods, (e) a list of equipment and facilities needed, and (f) adequate means of evaluation.

3. *The elective program.* The elective program is actually a part of the physical activity education *requirement*. In this way it differs from the voluntary physical recreation program. "Elective" means that a student who has met all the standards set for the required program is permitted at some stage of the academic year (or perhaps for his total course) to select from suggested activities a physical education plan to suit best

his needs and interests. Credit should be given for this activity, and definite instruction, supervision, and guidance should be offered, if it is to be considered a regular part of the course of study. If possible, the student should meet with an adviser to help determine the objectives of his program.

Note: A department should give consideration to the question of a student maintaining proficiency in certain phases of the entire required program over the years (e.g., maintaining a minimum level of cardio-vascular conditioning).

Intramural Athletics/Extramural Competition

A fine intramural athletics program is most important in the achievement of a balanced overall program in physical activity education. Intramural athletics has improved significantly at the college and university level over the years. However, at the high school level the surface has barely been scratched. More help is needed in this area to fulfill the educational responsibility adequately. If the average student has a sound experience in competitive sports, he is likely to have a favorable "image" of physical activity education. High school boys and girls are the "public of tomorrow" that will decide whether physical activity education is worthy of financial backing at all levels of the educational system.
Accepting as a premise the fact that competitive athletics is a desirable part of the total program, the intramural program provides recreational opportunity for leisure as well as another chance for the student to develop social contacts and group loyalties. As a result, the student should develop an appreciation of, and a lasting interest in, physical recreation. Healthful exercise and organic development must be considered as specific objectives.

> Note: Program administrators should keep in mind that "extramural athletic competition" may be desirable on selected occasions within the aegis of the Intramural Program. This would be separate and distinct from the varsity program.

Interscholastic and Intercollegiate athletics

Interscholastic and intercollegiate athletics, along with intramural athletics, are integral to the total program. Under ideal conditions, participation provides the opportunity for fine educational experiences. The chairman or head of the department should be responsible for the program that should be financed by institutional funds. It is recommended that all gate receipts be placed into the general school or college fund. Unfortunately, there have been many problems in this aspect of the program to harass the administrator/manager. What is the present status of the interschool program? Are more stringent controls needed? What should be the principal's or dean's relationship to athletics? Are the health and safety of the participants being fully considered? Is insurance coverage adequate for any emergency? How should athletics be financed? What about the use of radio and television in athletics? What purpose do tournaments serve? Should a student be declared ineligible for competition because of poor grades in school work? Should more extensive athletic competition be encouraged for girls and young women? To what extent should interschool competition be encouraged at the elementary and junior high levels? What about professionalism, gambling, and the role of alumni? How should the program be evaluated? These are but a few of the questions that must be answered.

Because participation in athletics is entirely on an elective basis, it is a part of the program of voluntary recreation. Class credit in physical education should be given for team participation, however, but this should not take the place of the existing requirement. Team participation should never take the place of body mechanics instruction, self-defense instruction, aquatics, etc., unless duplication is involved (e.g., a member of the swimming team should not be required to take aquatics).

A student who falls below the normally acceptable academic standards of the institution might be asked to discontinue athletics just as he might be asked to discontinue other "extracurricular" activities. Each student's case should be considered individually.
All sports are *major* sports. Each sport should have a varsity team with sound coaching. In colleges and universities, freshman teams should be operated with limited schedules involving very little traveling. This recommendation is based on the orientation needs of the freshman year.

Organized practice should be held only during the season in which the sport is played. However, for reasons of expediency and because football is a "unique phenomenon," spring practices in that sport may be held on the college/university level. However, they should be limited to a maximum of twenty sessions.

Coaches should be regular members of the school, college, or university faculty, with salaries and tenure similar to those of other teachers. Because of their ability as teachers in the sports they coach, the coach in higher education should be used as an instructor for these sports in the major program of the physical activity education department.

95

Voluntary Physical Recreation

This is the area in which the department can make a most lasting contribution. "Recreation assists man to become an artist in living." Physical recreation is that facet of the total recreational offering that relates primarily to the department of physical activity education and is so popular with children and young people. Physical activity educators have a responsibility to encourage students to develop healthy attitudes toward other areas of recreation-social recreational interests communicative recreational interests, aesthetic and creative recreational interests, and "learning" recreational interests. Often the "motor moron" is ridiculed, although he may be the class "brain" and an accomplished musician to boot. However, this individual is no more to be ridiculed than the proficient athlete who may be tongue-tied or confused when he is addressing a group. Both of these types are "more to be pitied than censured." Young people such as those described have both been exploited to a degree by either over-zealous, protective parents or thoughtless coaches. If "intelligent self-direction" is the aim of education, how truly uncultured both these young people are!

This judgment may seem a bit harsh, and it is possible that young people may not be happy at first exploring other facets of the recreational kaleidoscope. They can be helped to widen their activities, however, by example as well as by precept. When the athlete sees the coach enjoying himself in another sport or attending an art exhibit or a concert, he is likely to follow suit. However, teachers are often so busy providing recreational opportunities for others that they don't take time to enjoy recreation themselves.

How should recreation education (i.e., preparation for future leisure involvement) be interpreted? Is recreation entertainment or part of the educational curriculum? What type of planning is needed to adapt school facilities for recreational purposes?

The Individual or Adaptive Program (Special Exercise Prescription)

This phase of physical activity education is perhaps the most neglected. There is a definite need for this type of remedial work, although those who "control the purse strings" and/or administrators often do not feel it is important enough to merit a sufficient appropriation. This activity was once called *medical gymnastics,* and subsequently *corrective exercise.* The latter was shortened to *correctives.* This specialized area of physical activity education may well be called *the individual program, the adapted program, adaptive physical education,* or *special physical education.*

Earlier studies show a very low percentage of normal posture among students. A very large percentage have rounding of the shoulders, while more than half of them have increased antero-posterior spinal curvature. There is an ongoing need for body mechanics instruction and corrective exercise. If physical activity educators do not help this situation in the formative years, the situation becomes almost hopeless toward the end of the high school experience. Obviously, this task is a matter that should be handled in a cooperative manner by physicians and physical activity educators.

Directors' ideas of health and correction are frequently very limited. Nevertheless, every administrator should recognize definitely what movements, techniques, and skills in their departments may have deleterious effects. They should remember that upwards of 75 percent of their students have faults in posture and consequently are using "bodily machines" that are out of correct alignment. The result is slow injury to joints, ligaments, and muscles. Hence, a basic need arises for fundamental corrective positions for all activities.

Even the posture of athletes is bad. Coaches and teachers should explain to athletes that their performance can be improved through normal joint alignment. This is, of course, most important at the elementary school level, where such rapid growth and "excessive discrepancies" in structural relationships occur. It should also be stressed that in addition to the possible benefits in health and physical efficiency, one's appearance will also be improved through normal joint alignment. From what has been said, it should be evident that the field of physical activity education must either do something about body mechanics and adaptive work or inform educational administrators and the public that it cannot do anything, or hasn't been allowed, or hasn't the facilities, or isn't interested in this phase of the work.

Facilities and Equipment

The question of adequate facilities and equipment for physical activity education is often a vexing one. Recommendations made in the past were often overlooked or modified to the point where the resultant facilities are not adequate for the task. Physical activity educators do not know all the answers about facilities and equipment. They could not possibly understand all of the engineering and architectural problems involved. They do understand, however, the problems they are likely to encounter after the gymnasium or the pool has been in use for some time. The task seems to be one of developing ways of forwarding such information to the attention of the architects involved in the planning.

Communities face almost insuperable odds in their attempts to finance education. This means that physical activity educators should be careful to avoid demands for unreasonable size in new gymnasia, locker rooms, and other facilities. With the tremendous growth in the school population, however, the needs cannot be underestimated, as these essential parts of a school building are going to be in use for a long time. Careful study and close coordination are necessary to insure that the public's money is spent to best advantage. When communities are short of classroom space, swimming pools that are going to be called "lakes" or gymnasia the size of airplane hangars are out of the question. Economy and adequacy are two words that may cause conflict unless the needs of physical activity education (including athletics) are made known in such a way that all concerned will appreciate the problems.

The question of combining an auditorium and a gymnasium is a perplexing issue. "Gymtoria" are certainly better than nothing, but in the final analysis they do not appear to be completely practical. Why the physical activity education program, on the one hand, or that generally carried on in the auditorium on the other, should suffer from interruption is a question that is difficult to answer. Supplying both facilities costs a great deal of money, but formal education should not have to get along with inadequate facilities. If physical activity educators work constantly to make their programs truly worthwhile, and sound public relations are carried out, the public is given a better idea of what the field is trying to accomplish. Under such circumstances, the money necessary to do the job should be forthcoming sooner or later.

Greater care seems to be needed in purchase and care of equipment. Money is easily wasted in poor planning and improper care of equipment. Equipment should be purchased locally to the greatest extent possible with the business being shared among the sporting goods stores in the locality. Asking for the submission of "tenders" is time-consuming, but such an effort to standardize equipment purchasing is highly desirable. A program should use quality equipment; yet, dealers should not be asked to forego a fair mark-up when they solicit school business. *Professional* physical activity educators should not expect "hand-outs" or prejudicial treatment simply because they control large equipment purchases.

A good equipment man is invaluable to a high school, college, or university. Careful storage of equipment is nothing more than common sense and good business. Proper procedures for the control and issuance of expensive equipment are highly desirable.

Public Relations

If this is an era of "new conservatism" because of the overall economic situation, physical educators must redouble their efforts to improve relations with the public. People are influenced more by actions than by what a group *says* it is trying to accomplish. Physical activity educators must be able to prove that children and young people are being helped to lead more effective lives through their participation in physical activity education. Although equipment and facilities in this area are at least as costly as those for any other subject area, the public will not complain if it is given full value for its tax dollar.

Although teachers and coaches are busy with their many duties, they should take the time to concern themselves with public relations. Very few people are aware of the aims of modern physical activity education. Physical activity educators (including coaches) still face the "aristocratic irresponsibility" of the traditionalists who would relegate them to the "frill" category. The public should know how much money is spent on intramural athletics for the *many,* as opposed to how much goes for interschool and/or intercollegiate athletics for the few. At the same time, the gate receipts of major sports should not be slighted. This money is a great help and is often used to finance intramural programs.

Continuous, reliable, responsible public relations will develop an informed public that will not mutter about "fads" and "frills." The administrator/manager of the physical activity education program should know what is news in his area and then make certain that it is presented to the various media in an interesting manner. Sports writers are allies in this venture; their influence is very great. The coach must be willing to devote some of his time to public speaking and must be adequately prepared when he speaks. A few basic talks about the various phases of the overall physical activity education program, including athletics, can be made to stretch a long way, but they must be developed with an eye to presenting the content of the message in the most entertaining manner.

Exhibitions and demonstrations of physical prowess and skill have been used often as public relations devices. Generally, these techniques are excellent, but they can be artificial and quite formal. To some, children must move like robots to show parents and the public that something is being accomplished in physical education periods. When this type of presentation takes place even some physical activity educators lose their sense of perspective. Rather than giving such stylized demonstrations, they might well present the actual teaching of the techniques that lead to proficient performance. This is most interesting to parents, since it informs them of what happens in daily classes. Despite the various devices that are employed to further public relations, perhaps the best means of satisfying parents is to show them that their children are receiving as much individual attention as possible, and that they are progressing. A satisfied, happy student is the best "broadcasting station" that has yet been encountered.

Professional Preparation of the Physical Activity Educator/Coach

This topic, of course, is the primary task of the university teacher, but elementary and secondary school teachers and administrators are experiencing the results of the product that is being produced by the professional courses at the college or university. When deciding upon course changes, university professional educators may take a narrow approach. It is necessary to study (1) the past development, (2) the actual job situation teachers are going to face, and (3) the society in which teachers will live in order to get the realistic picture necessary to the development of sound curricula.

What is a physical activity educator? In undergraduate and graduate work there has appeared to be some confusion. In many facets of professional preparation, however, physical activity education is setting a desirable pattern for teachers in other subjects to follow. Many areas still need attention, however.

First, the status of the major student in physical activity education/kinesiology must be raised in the minds of the public and other teachers. By and large, physical activity education majors will need a broader educational background. This deficiency shows up in many ways. This problem has developed partially because there is too much knowledge and skill to be mastered within four undergraduate years.

Second, ways must be discovered to bring the people involved in various specialties within the field into a closer relationship. "A house divided against itself cannot stand." All professionals can help this situation by working to promote greater unity within the profession.

A third problem is that of "passing courses" just to graduate. The traditional subject-matter approach to learning has sometimes stifled initiative. The professional student takes a set number of courses and goes to college for a required number of years. Upon graduation, the "teacher" is presumably sufficiently educated and competent to engage in his profession. A "competency approach" would help to eliminate the ineffectual, repetitive teaching that standard professional courses have been charged with offering. It is important to develop a more effective way to measure teaching ability as determined by specific competencies. These competencies should be developed through selected experiences with subject-matters as resource areas.

Because of the complexity of the total field, many relationships within the field are unclear. What is the relationship between physical activity education and school recreation? Must physical activity education leave correctives and adaptive physical education to the field of physical therapy? Where does school school health and safety education fit in? Health education is too important to leave in the hands of the busy physical activity educator/coach. What about safety education and driver education? Should there be recreation specialists in the school systems to supervise all the so-called extra-curricular activities? Where do athletics belong anyhow? Why should the department of physical activity education below university level make decisions about athletic matters when the entire school is concerned? What about the use of coaches who aren't qualified physical activity educators? Can one person meet all of the foregoing responsibilities and many more within the school, college, and university, or should there be continuing efforts to promote even further specialization?

A "common sense approach to evaluation" has been accepted by many physical activity educators who feel that their field is still an arts (or humanities) subject. In such a circumstance, it is not open to an experimental approach. The public seems to believe that anyone with a good personality, a fair educational background, and some excellent sports skill can teach physical activity education. There is no real need for him or her to study in the areas of anatomy, physiology, kinesiology, physiology of exercise, psychology, tests and measurements, and corrective exercise. The teacher should simply keep them busy, have some progression, and develop a "smart-looking" class. Physical activity educators simply must decide if such a slipshod approach will yield the increased status many seem to want.

The field of education still tends to take a "don't you know your place" approach to students. One of the best ways of improving the various teacher education programs may be missed when students are not used as *critical* evaluators of their own progress and the worth of the various aspects of the curriculum.

Lastly, there needs to be a fuller understanding of "democratic administration." What departmental decisions should be shared? Should a department head go along with decisions of the total staff? Can administrators superimpose their will upon others and achieve optimum results? Staff members who have been allowed to grow and develop in an atmosphere where democratic spirit prevails have an *esprit de corps* which professional students will find contagious. People are great imitators, and physical activity education graduates tend to follow the prevailing pattern of their undergraduate institutions.

General Administration

General administration is a sketchy area-a catch-all for problems that do not fit logically into any of the other subdivisions in this chapter. Administration or management of any educational program is the leadership of the personnel involved in conducting the program, and in that larger community of persons who are interested in, provide support for, and ultimately approve or disapprove of, the program itself.

Depending on how the task of an administrator is conceived, it can be simple or complex. If an administrator or manager is "the boss," matters will be quickly expedited. However, there may be a significant staff turn–over. On the other hand, if staff members are regarded as co-workers, much time may be consumed in discussing this or that phase of the program. However, in the latter situation the staff will be happier and may thus do a better job. On balance, there appears to be a logical middle path between dictatorship and anarchy that will result in optimum staff growth.

Relationship to the Teaching and Recreation Professions

Most people feel unable to devote sufficient time to carrying out their responsibilities in the many professional organizations whose functions often· appear to overlap. Many teachers have failed to fulfill their obligations here, thus making the burden heavier on those who are more conscientious. Professionals in the field physical activity education (including athletics) must take care not to forget their fundamental responsibility to the teaching profession as a whole. Allegiance is owed to the National Education Association, as well as to the American Association for Health, Physical Education, Recreation, and Dance. To promote the goals of general education, as well as to secure higher status for physical activity education, a much greater effort must be made in this area of professional service.

What about the relationship between physical activity education and the recreation profession? Cooperation among the various areas of recreation, parks, physical activity education, and athletics is highly desirable. The strength that can be gained from unity is enormous. Yet, often these groups appear to be "fighting for the use of the same bodies." The physical activity educator has no right to practice anything in the recreation profession but physical recreation, unless he has specific preparation in recreation education. The recreation director should not attempt to administer parks unless, through experience or training, he is prepared to cope with such a task. The reverse of this is just as true.

If there are sharp differences between the position of physical activity educator and that of recreation superintendent, an effort to determine a working relationship can be mutually beneficial. And what about the concept of the community school? This and many other questions wait to be answered through cooperative effort. The following analogy may help to clarify the entire problem. Both professionals are playing on the same team! The physical activity educator takes his turn as the pitcher quite early in the game, but not before the recreation director "pitches" to the preschool child. Sometimes the physical educator is batted out of the box very soon, and in many elementary schools he never gets beyond the warm-up stage. Under normal circumstances, the recreation director must pitch from the fourth inning on in this game that includes each player's entire life. Neither physical activity educator nor recreation director can forget that there are eight representatives of other fields on this ball club-adult education, commercial recreation, private agencies, and others. Look to them for support and guidance. The status of the two professions, the physical activity educator as a professional educator, and the recreation director as a professional person, will grow as the worth of the overall program increases.

Evaluation

Many respected educators still say that there "is so little for the mind" in modern education, because they believe that misguided Deweyites hold the fort. Careful scrutiny of school programs might give the opposite impression: "There is 'far less for the body' in schools, colleges, and universities. Every year classification and proficiency tests indicate that students generally are woefully weak, misshapen, and uncoordinated.
Evaluation is the subject matter of physical activity education is where many professionals falter. What is there to measure? If measurements were taken, whom would it influence? Only in relatively few schools are physical activity education grades figured in with "academic" averages.

Is physical activity education an art, a social science, or a pure science? At present, it doesn't fit neatly into any category. The field was once one of the liberal arts, but in the Middle Ages it was torn from this lofty perch. Physical activity education appears to have deep roots in all three of the above areas depending on the angle from which it is viewed. One group stresses that it belongs to the humanities, because the aim is to help young people achieve certain attitudes and appreciations that will enable them to lead richer, fuller lives.

A second faction will say that physical activity education has a great role to play in the social sciences-that is, students are helped to acquire desirable personality traits through participation in various types of physical education activities. There is, certainly, a concern with society as a group of interrelated, interdependent people, but it is doubtful whether it is wise to be affiliated with the humanities in the sense that the field would serve chiefly as a discipline and as an instrument of factual knowledge only.
Those who emphasize the scientific attributes are anxious to gather as much systematized knowledge as possible through all possible avenues and types of research. In this, of course, there must be continual borrowing from mathematics and the physical sciences as well as psychology. The present trend seems to be to make progress through statistics (i.e., proving right

103

through a coefficient of correlation). Certainly there must be borrowing from everywhere possible in order to get all the facts.

Immediate concern about a high place for physical activity education in the curriculum hierarchy may help, but the aim should be to raise the physical fitness standards of *all* students–and ultimately of all citizens. Education "through the physical" is the correct slogan so long as rugged, healthy bodies for boys, girls, men, and women are the end result. The development of physical attributes belongs uniquely to the field of physical activity education. This should never be forgotten!

For Consideration and Discussion

As an exercise, it is recommended that two students each make a 10-minute presentation, one telling to what extent his high school lived up to the characterization here of what might be considered a fine program of physical activity education and athletics, while the other explains the inadequacies of the program he/she experienced. Then a third student should conduct a class discussion on the topic.

CHAPTER 5

A COMPETENCY-BASED APPROACH
TO MANAGEMENT DEVELOPMENT
IN
PHYSICAL ACTIVITY EDUCATION
(INCLUDING ATHLETICS)

The inauguration of the North American Society for Sport Management (NASSM) in 1986 with its solid *Journal of Sport Management* available through Human Kinetics Publishers has proved to be a boon to the development of the field of sport and physical activity management. (The subsequent addition of the Sport Management Education Journal in 2007 is another "solid plus" for the field.) In addition, the blossoming emphasis within the National Association for Sport and Physical Education (NASPE) of the American Alliance for Health, Physical Education, Recreation, and Dance (AAHPERD) looking toward solid sport management curriculum development has also provided a further, much-needed stimulus. Further, the fact that NASSM and NASPE have several ongoing joint projects bodes well for the future of this area of development within the field.

Nevertheless, the movement toward the almost 100% "scientification" of the *overall* field of physical activity education, characterized by the adoption of names like "kinesiology," "human kinetics," and "sport sciences" at the university level, has mitigated efforts to improve the burgeoning development of what seems destined to be called sport management. Obviously, no one should be denigrating any effort to provide a substantive scholarly base for the profession's development. It should be clear to all, however, that how and to what effect people of all ages move their bodies should be the paramount emphases within this scholarly foundation.

Yet, unless men, women, and children understand the background development of the overall field and the need for lifelong involvement in developmental physical activity, we will have an inadequate body of knowledge upon which to build our drive toward professional status. This means that a social science and humanities under–girding is required along with the natural science emphasis. It also means that the professional aspects of the field's development should be studied concurrently. This is where investigation regarding the theory and practice of programs of developmental physical activity must be included, as well as emphasis on the study of management theory and practice applied to sport, physical activity, and expressive movement.

For these reasons, therefore, we state once again that we are absolutely convinced that a scholarly social-science approach to management science as it relates to this field is more urgently needed than *ever* before. This is even more necessary because managers are being challenged as *never* before. In what appears to be an era of budgetary cutback or "management decline" as termed by some, our programs are in many instances being reduced drastically, with some even eliminated. Managers are finding that they can no longer make unilateral decisions, despite the return of the past 25 years to a more conservative and traditional attitude toward politics, religion, education, and other pivotal social forces. In addition, and this takes some explanation, despite the fact that the growth of programs in exercise science has been matched by programs in sport management, there has only been nominal movement toward improving the theoretical aspect of management training.

Brief Historical Background

To look back before we look ahead: Approximately 60 years ago the inadequacy in our theoretical and practical training for management was recognized by this author who was then a veteran of 10 years of teaching and coaching in the field. In an effort to improve the situation, the case-method approach of teaching human relations and administration in physical education and athletics was subsequently introduced (Prentice-Hall, 1959). This beginning effort was transferred from The University Western Ontario to The University of Michigan (Ann Arbor) in 1956. Then in 1963 a research orientation to administrative theory and practice was introduced at the University of Illinois (Champaign-Urbana) with direct assistance from King McCristal, Laura Huelster, and David Matthews. As a result a substantive group of doctoral and master's theses by outstanding young professionals were completed in this specialized area, a number of which were included in another innovative publication (Zeigler & Spaeth, Prentice-Hall, 1975).

Unfortunately, the field of physical activity education and athletics has moved relatively slowly to meet the demand for well-qualified sport and physical activity managers. Colleges and universities traditionally offered one course only in physical education and athletics administration. (This basic-course approach was usually only strengthened slightly when repeated at the graduate level.) Such a lecture course was usually characterized by a dull, "nuts and bolts" approach, often taught by the current (or the former) administrator. Thus, it was just this type of course experience at both the undergraduate and graduate levels that was maligned so devastatingly by Professor Conant in 1962 that we are still feeling the effects. (In fact, it was Dr. Conant's ridiculing of the physical education administration course of that era that can be labeled as the critical incident that occasioned much of the rapid action in the direction of a disciplinary, body-of-knowledge approach for the field in the 1960s.)

In the mid-1960s, it became increasing evident that the offering of only one, more or less traditional, professional course for undergraduate students was inadequate for both job placement and the demands that were being made of our graduates. This situation began to change in the 1970s when a variety of areas of specialization were introduced into the basic major program in most colleges and universities on the continent. Interestingly, we then also witnessed a great demand for a specialization that is now almost universally called sport management. Even though many of our natural-science oriented colleagues find it "somewhat deplorable" to waste time on such an option, it can be stated unequivocally that the sport management specialization rapidly became the "success story" of the 1980s and 1990s. Further, the outlook for the immediate future at least is still bright, although the gains made must be consolidated carefully due to the ongoing financial stringencies in higher education.

During the last quarter of the 20th century, a steady advancement was made also in management science in both business and educational administration. This built–in the business world especially–on the already strong foundation developed in the decades before and after World War II. However, it was still apparent that little had been done similarly to develop management *competencies and skills* in physical activity education and athletics management programs. Nevertheless, our field was still not ready to take a progressive step forward. Therefore, our volumes promoting the case method approach to the teaching of human relations and management, as well as management competency development in sport and physical education, were seemingly premature. Undaunted, we now are reasonably secure in the knowledge that progress in understanding the complexity of professional management training has been made during this intervening decade since this approach was first offered to the field in the early years of the 1980s. Of course, we don't argue here that a "supermanager" who has mastered most management competencies and skills can manage any organization, any place, any time. Nevertheless, everything being equal–including desirable personality traits for the task at hand--we put our confidence in a manager who has taken the time to acquire an irreducible minimum of knowledge, competencies and skills in the various categories presented in our management competency development laboratory manual (2007).

Justification for this Approach

Despite the above, another text about management thought, theory and practice in physical activity education (including athletics) still requires justification. It has been argued that the 20th century was a transitional one in human history–that the period from 1900-2000 has taken us from one historical era to another. Maybe this is true, but only history–in due time–will provide the answer. At any rate, changing times are occasioned by the impact of a variety of social forces on society.

Such change has its accompanying influence on the professional training of leaders in the many fields that make up the society in which the change is taking place. In this instance we are concerned with this development within North American culture primarily, although sport and physical activity management training is taking roots in Europe and Japan notably. More specifically we addressed the professional preparation of those men and women who will presumably administer and manage developmental physical activity programs delimited to sport, exercise, play, and expressive movement.

And so, looking ahead in the 21st century, we will not present a detailed historical analysis of what transpired in the final quarter of the 1900s, both good and bad. However we *can* state again that more attention should undoubtedly be devoted to both management theory and practice--not to mention training through laboratory experiences in the skills required to be an effective and efficient manager. Below in Figures #1 and #2, I have repeated diagrams included in Chapter 2 that offer (1) an analysis of the component of what *any* profession needs for full development (Fig. 1), and (2) an analysis of how this may be carried out in the development of a profession of sport and physical activity management in society at large (Fig. 2).

> **Note:** If this format were followed within the profession of education, it would be identified as management competency development for the field of physical activity education and athletics.

We believe that close to a majority of our colleagues are now aware of this deficiency in respective "environments" at present. We can only trust that those involved with management training will steadily take steps to implement these positive changes fully in the near future. We believe further that social trends and the job market are forcing professionals in the field to develop sufficiently strong attitudes (psychologically speaking) to bring about this much-needed change.

A Comprehensive Listing of Desirable Management Competencies

What then, specifically, are these "desirable management competencies or skills" that are needed by the aspiring sport and physical education manager? Through a careful analysis of the literature and responses from knowledgeable colleagues, we are prepared to offer a lengthy, but probably incomplete listing of competencies and skills subdivided into the five areas or category of skills that we have determined. (The competencies or skills are categorized below in relation to understandings developed, skills acquired, assessments carried out, plans devised, experiments undertaken, evaluations made, instruments employed, etc.. whereby the development of such competency or skill may be effected to

Figure 1

A Model for Optimum Development of a Field Called "X"

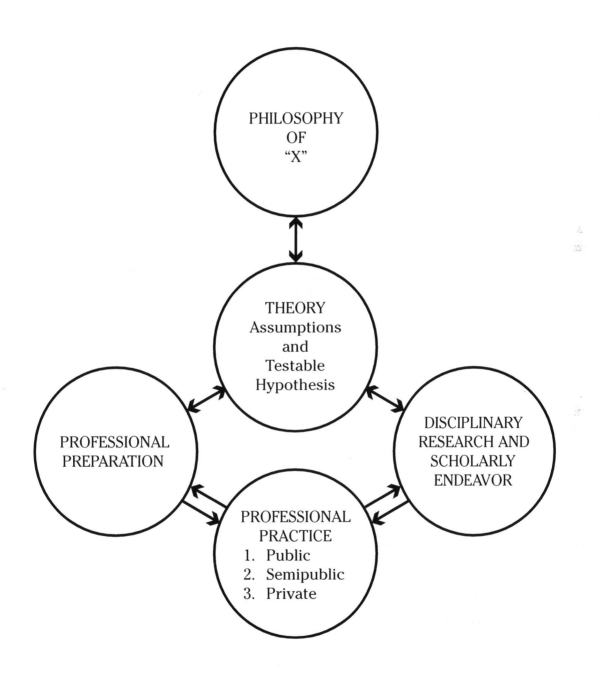

PHILOSOPHY
OF
"X"

THEORY
Assumptions
and
Testable
Hypothesis

PROFESSIONAL
PREPARATION

DISCIPLINARY
RESEARCH AND
SCHOLARLY
ENDEAVOR

PROFESSIONAL
PRACTICE
1. Public
2. Semipublic
3. Private

Earle Zeigler, Ph.D.

Figure 2

A MODEL FOR MANAGEMENT DEVELOPMENT: A COMPETENCY-BASED APPROACH

Earle F. Zeigler, Ph.D.

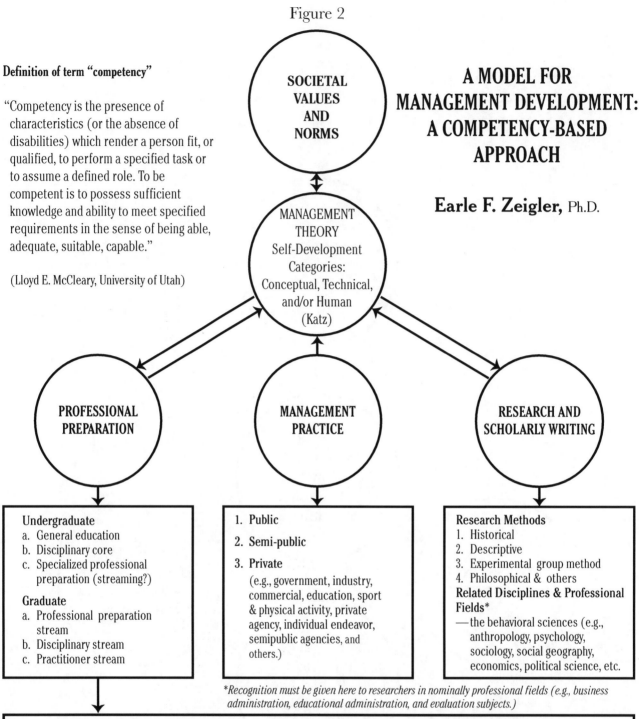

Definition of term "competency"

"Competency is the presence of characteristics (or the absence of disabilities) which render a person fit, or qualified, to perform a specified task or to assume a defined role. To be competent is to possess sufficient knowledge and ability to meet specified requirements in the sense of being able, adequate, suitable, capable."

(Lloyd E. McCleary, University of Utah)

SOCIETAL VALUES AND NORMS

MANAGEMENT THEORY Self-Development Categories: Conceptual, Technical, and/or Human (Katz)

PROFESSIONAL PREPARATION

MANAGEMENT PRACTICE

RESEARCH AND SCHOLARLY WRITING

Undergraduate
a. General education
b. Disciplinary core
c. Specialized professional preparation (streaming?)

Graduate
a. Professional preparation stream
b. Disciplinary stream
c. Practitioner stream

1. Public
2. Semi-public
3. Private
   (e.g., government, industry, commercial, education, sport & physical activity, private agency, individual endeavor, semipublic agencies, and others.)

Research Methods
1. Historical
2. Descriptive
3. Experimental group method
4. Philosophical & others
Related Disciplines & Professional Fields*
—the behavioral sciences (e.g., anthropology, psychology, sociology, social geography, economics, political science, etc.

Recognition must be given here to researchers in nominally professional fields (e.g., business administration, educational administration, and evaluation subjects.)

A Plan for Competency-Based Management Education (Including the Teaching/Learning Process)

1. Ascertain professional functions & needs.
2. Specify competencies (including self-development and those under conceptual, technical, human, and "conjoined" categories).
3. Determine performance levels.
4. Specify program content & instructional, methodology (involving a problem-solving approach in achievement of performance levels: what needs to be known; where obtained; organization of the learning experience; probable results, and others.
5. Identify and evaluate competency attainment.
6. Validate process periodically.

Teaching/Learning Techniques
(e.g., lecture, discussion, case, role-playing, action research, pure and applied research, independent study, debate, computer-assisted or programmed instruction, internship, game theory, panels, forums, and others—depending upon technique's applicability to learning of a competency)

(Adapted from McCleary & McIntyre 1973)

some degree.) The five general areas of competency or skill are (1) personal skills, (2) interpersonal skills, (3) conceptual skills, (4) technical skills, and (5) conjoined skills.

1. The Manager's *Personal* Competencies/Skills

    a. determine one's personal philosophy of life and/or religion

    b. establish priorities in personal values clarification

    c. develop a personal mission statement

    d. devise a plan that tentatively maps out one's future (i.e., goal-setting in relation to stages of maturity)

    e. conduct a personal analysis to assist in the development of an individual time-management plan (i.e., planning a work schedule for the day, week, month, year. etc.)

Additional *Personal* Competencies/Skills:

- learning self-management
- practicing positive thinking
- learning a second language
- employing the requisite amount of assertiveness
- improving one's perception
- strengthening one's motivation
- acquiring ability at self-analysis
- avoiding stress through biofeedback
- improving one's reading skills
- evaluating personal communication skills (e.g., writing and speaking)
- determining one's overall physical fitness and a "recreational quotient" based on self-assessment
- learning to think critically (based on informal logic)
- evaluating one's position on a socio-political spectrum (i.e., assessment of opinions about controversial social issues)
- employing a cognitive style instrument to determine how one thinks about information received
- learning about useful techniques for the

111

elimination of encounters and situational
stressors
- self-assessing one's daily work habits
by completion of a checklist
- learning a systems analysis approach to
optimal health achievement through human
ecological interaction
- completing a personal fitness inventory
(including initial assessment of strength,
flexibility, and endurance)
- passing a basic computer "literacy" test
- completing a scale designed to assess one's
creativity and innovation abilities
- testing one's understanding of the meaning of
statistical terms used in everyday life
- determining one's "attitude adjustment
quotient"

II. The Manager's *Interpersonal* Competencies/Skills

f. develop an understanding of self
(i.e., self-concept) as required for
successful interpersonal competency
g. assess interpersonal communication
skills (e.g., empathetic listening and
responding)
h. execute an interpersonal style inventory
i. evaluate interpersonal management skills
(e.g., selling ideas)
j. learn about one's leadership attributes and
effectiveness; assessing present leadership style

Additional *Interpersonal* Competencies/Skills:

- assessing one's basic management skills
- carrying out a simulated job interview
(e.g., a "structured " interview)
- completing a debating experience on a
controversial issue
- completing a team development scale
- learning how to negotiate
- developing a leadership style based on a
sound management theory
- role-playing a situation involving the
counseling of staff members (including working
with a disturbed colleague)

112

- discharging a staff member
- disciplining a staff member
- learning to combat staff mobility
- detecting the managerial or employee "hustler"
- understanding how to relate to minority personnel
- handling conflicts (i.e., conflict resolution)
- assessing the organizational climate of an organization
- taking part in a leaderless group discussion (including performance assessment)
- chairing a case method discussion as an example of an approach to managerial decision-making
- serving as chairperson of a discussion group to consider qualities that should be required for admission to a sport management training program
- knowing about successful strategies employed to gain organizational power and then being able to convert it to influence
- developing a supporting rationale for a proposal to implement an affirmative action program for the hiring of either women, ethnic minorities, or handicapped persons

III. The Manager's *Conceptual* Competencies/Skills

k. understand the development of twentieth century management thought and theory
l. analyze the general (external) and immediate (internal) environments
m. plan in the management process (levels and tools)
n. organize in the management process (guidelines and types of organizational structures)
o. staff in the management process (human resources management)
p. direct in the management process (leadership theory and techniques)
q. control in the management process (including setting standards, developing an annual budget, and performance evaluation)
r. relate Mackenzie's Management Process Model to a systems approach for sport and physical education management

Additional *Conceptual* Competency Skills

- executing an assignment designed to improve conceptual blockbusting
- understanding of a mathematical model that explains management process in sport and physical education
- demonstrating an awareness of the historical development of management thought, theory, and practice in sport management
- understanding the variety of organizational concepts
- creating a statement of aims and objectives for a sport organization
- determining one's own management philosophy (presumably derived from one's personal life philosophy determined in Category I above)
- understanding of selected current management theories and their implications for practice
- explaining (including diagramming of) a systems approach to theory & research in sport management
- based on data presented about a sport management problem presented, executing a simulated exercise designed to produce a solution to the situation
- writing a case for subsequent consideration of those concerned with a sport management problem
- based on careful observation, preparing a model delineating an organization's structure
- developing a mission statement delineating long range aims and specific objectives of an organization with which one has had experience
- formulating one's approach to professional ethics
- explaining the steps one must follow to implement a management by objectives approach (MBO) in an organization
- understanding how to establish work priorities
- distinguishing between managing and doing
- analyzing information that comes to one's attention

IV. Developing the Manager's *Technical*
Competencies/Skills

    s. learn how to use the meeting as an effective
       tool for the work group
    t. learn about team-building (i.e., developing
       an understanding of how work groups are formed
       and maintained)
    u. execute an "in-basket analysis" as the manager
       approaches a day on the job (including a request
       for an assessment of how computer information
       technologies & networking might be employed)
    v. understand legal liability in relation to
       sport management

Additional *Technical* Competencies/Skills

    - acquiring minimum computer skills (i.e.,
      word processing, spread sheet, data storage)
    - learning everyday office techniques (e.g.,
      telephone usage, dictation, interviewing)
    - using a computer as an aid to decision-
      making
    - developing a plan for facility and equipment
      maintenance
    - learning how to apply for various types of
      grants
    - acquiring an elementary understanding of
      accounting
    - learning how to order supplies and equipment
      competitively
    - knowing what is involved in the preparation of,
      and "checking out" of, a personal resume
    - discussing the topic of computer technology
      and networking knowledgeably
    - determining cost-benefit analysis
      that compares present condition to two
      competing alternatives (using a spreadsheet)
    - developing a year-end balance sheet for an
      organization
    - developing an outline for a manual on
      facilities management
    - understanding of the concept of "the automated
      office" (including networking)
    - explaining research methodology available to
      sport managers (including so-called action

115

research) and the research techniques available to each type of research
- developing an understanding of public relations and learning how to prepare media releases
- preparing an instrument designed to assess an organization's marketing status
- executing a fact-finding investigation to assist with the solving of a specific problem or issue
- carrying out of an action research project (e.g., in-house survey)
- developing a format for the implementation of the following categories of operations research models: (1) comparison and/or classification (e.g., statistical sampling), (2) operational process (e.g., linear programming), (c) future prediction (e.g., break-even & profitability)
- employing an administrator evaluation instrument in a specific organizational situation
- analyzing an applicant's resume, including ways to determine its accuracy and the applicant's true abilities
- using an evaluative grid, completing a structured interview to employ a sport manager
- demonstrating competency in chairing a meeting
- after observing a meeting, appraising its effectiveness and efficiency
- mapping a program for fund-raising within the internal environment of an organization
- writing the following documents effectively: an inter-office memorandum, a letter, and an agenda for a meeting
- learning how to develop a successful sport sponsorship
- developing a plan to obtain a sport sponsorship
- keeping the necessary criteria in mind, developing a plan for the organization and management of a sport tournament
- organizing and developing one's own resume for possible use in obtaining a position in sport management

- learning how to implement a management
  information system (MIS)

V. The Manager's *Conjoined* Competencies/Skills

v. develop an outline of a policies and
   procedures manual for a special event (e.g.,
   a sports tournament)
x. develop an approach to decision-making
   in relation to one's personal and professional
   philosophy (including ethical decision-making
   where applicable)
y. carry out a strategic market-planning
   assessment for a sport- and/or physical
   activity-based program
z. understand how to manage for change

Additional *Conjoined* Competencies/Skills

- creating an organizational climate within
  which people can accept advice from others
- planning for the implementation of an on-
  the-job training program
- learning how to use the informal organization
  in the achievement of organizational goals
- using a problem-solving approach with a small
  group, development of a change process model
- using a quantitative technique based on an
  applied mathematical model, determining the
  solution to a sport and physical education
  problem (operations research)
- developing an organization's "future
  orientation" (e,g, by developing a format
  for a standing committee on the topic)
- developing an organizational approach to
  ethical decision-making
- assessing the ecological implications of a
  physical recreation program
- constructing a mechanism to assess the
  cost-effectiveness of competitive sports at
  an educational institution
- after selecting a sport management problem for
  consideration, roleplaying by a management team
  (selected from the group) of a human relations
  situation while working toward a solution of
  the issue

117

- understanding how to manage a complex project
  (e.g., Critical Path Method <CPM>)
- allocating designated resources through
  case analysis of a specific administrative
  situation employing such factors as human
  capital, scarcity, effectiveness, efficiency,
  optimization, competition, and monopoly
- based on actual case situation, determining
  what actions to take (and what not to take)
  in regard to a situation where the question of
  legal liability arises
- developing a crisis management plan and
  adapting it to a specific situation (e.g.,
  budgetary shortfall in the middle of a fiscal
  year)

Advice to the Instructor

Obviously there is insufficient time in one undergraduate course to offer all of experiences listed above that can lead to the development of all of the management competencies and skills listed above. (In fact, it may not even be possible to complete the 26 fundamental experiences that have been delineated for special attention under the five categories (i.e., personal, interpersonal, etc.) within the span of one course experience.) In addition, there may be some needed experiences (as the instructor sees it) that are not listed here. Whatever the situation may be (e.g., using the related laboratory manual as the only course text or using it in conjunction with this text–or another!), and also depending on the length and extent of the course experience (i.e., quarter, term, or semester), the successful student should demonstrate achievement and/or completion of at least a representative sampling of the experiences provided in this text/workbook under the five categories as delineated. Due to space limitations, it has obviously not been possible to include the multitude of different exercises that would be needed to fulfill every possible expectation.

Those planning the broad physical activity education and athletics management training program in a particular college or university should offer an entire course devoted to the development of management competencies and skills. In such a case, the instructor could easily build on what we have called a "representative sampling" of laboratory exercises under each of the five aspects of "total management competency." In this way more complex, advanced experiences could be provided.

The best advice here would seem to be that a minimum number of "laboratory" exercises and tasks for a one-semester course (app. 15 weeks) should be included. Obviously, depending on the extent to which the

118

instructor and his/her class wish to follow this approach, more or less use can be made of these laboratory exercises or assignments in the laboratory manual (see Zeigler and Bowie, 2007). Further, the instructor may have his or her own tasks and exercises that could supplement, or substitute for, some of those that are included here.

In regard to course organization, the instructor, based on previous experience and student evaluation, has to decide how much he or she will lecture and how much laboratory experience to offer in the course. Certainly this is an individual matter and depends on a number of factors. We believe that this lecture/laboratory experience approach to competency development is urgently needed in our field and wish you success with its use.

> **Note:** In addition to the occasional quiz, the instructor and/or a teaching assistant will have a set of exercises to correct with each of the five categories of skills (e.g., personal, technical). In addition, there will normally be some sort of a "knowledge final" based on this course text. Hence, it would probably best for the instructor to have the student hand in each set of laboratory experiences by specified dates throughout the semester. When returned, the student could then insert them in a loose-leaf binder for a (possible) final review by the instructor and student at the end of the semester (or quarter or term). The suggested laboratory manual is titled *Management Competency Development for Physical Activity Development and Sport: A Laboratory Manual*. It was written by Earle F. Zeigler and Gary W. Bowie. The publisher is Trafford and the bookstore can be reached by e-mail at www.trafford.com. Information about the text and the workbook can be had at the author's website www.earlezeigler.com by clicking on the book's cover there. Anyone interested can get further information–and can also go directly to the publisher through the Web.

For Consideration or Discussion

As an exercise at the end of this chapter, it is recommended that two students each make a 10-minute presentation, one discussing the make-up of Figures 1 and 2, while showing how one relates to the other, while the other explains the five types of competencies and skills needed by the manager along with several examples of each he/she may have already encountered.. Then a third student should conduct a class discussion on the topic.

CHAPTER 6

MANAGERIAL DECISION-MAKING THROUGH THE EMPLOYMENT OF COMPUTER TECHNOLOGY

(Terry Haggerty, Ph.D., Univ. of New Brunswick, is co-author.)

Change takes place typically through the impact of a variety of social forces. In this instance we are concerned with change primarily within North American culture. Such change has its accompanying influence on the professional training of leaders in the many fields that make up the society. Our concern here is with the professional preparation of those men and women who will manage developmental physical activity education programs related to sport, exercise, dance, and play. We are even more specifically concerned here with one aspect of a subject that has become known as sport and physical activity management. The focus will be on the strengthening and improvement of managerial decision-making by the employment of specific techniques that have become available through steadily improving computer technology.

During the final quarter of the twentieth century, it became evident that the offering of only one, more or less traditional, professional program for undergraduate students was inadequate for both job placement and the demands that were being made of our graduates. Hence, a variety of areas of specialization within the basic major program has gradually been added to departmental offerings in most colleges and universities on the continent. Interestingly, we have witnessed a great demand for a specialization that is now almost universally called sport management. Even though many of our natural science oriented colleagues find this area "something less than academic," it can be stated unequivocally that the sport and physical activity education management specialization became the "success story" of the final quarter of the twentieth century.

For a number of reasons the field of physical activity education had moved relatively slowly to meet this demand. Traditionally the professional curriculum has offered *one course only* in physical education and athletics administration. (For some unexplained reason, this basic course had typically been only slightly strengthened when repeated at the graduate level.) This classroom (lecture) course was characterized by a dull, "nuts and bolts" approach, often taught by the current (or the former) administrator. It was just this type of course "experience" at both undergraduate and graduate levels that was maligned so devastatingly by Professor Conant in 1962 that we are still feeling the effects. (In fact, it was Dr. Conant's ridiculing of the physical education administration course of that era which can be labeled as <u>the</u> critical incident that occasioned much of the rapid action in the direction

120

of a disciplinary, body-of-knowledge approach for the entire field in the 1960s.)

Interestingly, no diligent search for "something different" was necessary to improve the situation.. It had become increasingly obvious to us that the "typical administrator" needed "upgrading" at the first possible moment. This is why efforts have been made to introduce present and future sport and physical activity managers to improved decision-making through the knowledge, competencies, and skills that can be made available through burgeoning computer technology. Such understanding, however, should be more than that represented by a "crash course" in computer literacy. We believe that the need now is for a well-trained administrator who understands the management tools that have become available to him or her through the various computer technologies.

Decisions Must Be Made Every Day!

Managers in sport, physical education, and recreation settings are continually faced with decisions. The importance of a correct decision is obvious; managers who make bad decisions usually suffer the consequences of their actions. Yet many managers make decisions daily on the basis of hunches, intuition, and guesses. That situation can be improved greatly by the application of a variety of quantitative decision-making tools. Until recently, it was not possible to call upon computers to help with decisions because of their size and scope and the complexity and cost of such operations. With the advent of smaller scale computers and accompanying specialized software programs, however, a much more personalized approach has now become possible.

The fact that a variety of highly useful models and tools is now readily available–but are not being utilized!–leads to the suggestion that there is lack of understanding as to their possible effectiveness. It probably also indicates an inability to cope with them. To be fair to those for whom this paper is directed, it should be pointed out that many managers in other fields generally are not using these tools and models either. In fact, even among those who are well versed in their use, computers are often neglected because of a presumed lack of time, a presumed lack of applicability to real-life situations, and the ever-present difficulty of quantifying all of the variables involved.

Research indicated that management courses in physical activity education, sport, and recreation do not provide adequate theoretical instruction and practical laboratory experiences at both the undergraduate and graduate levels (Zeigler and Bowie, 1983, pp. vii-xi, 67-77). Of course, job analyses were necessary in order to determine the extent to which decision-making tools and models are needed. In addition, ongoing research should provide information to categorize the types of problems in this field that could be best solved with the aid of computer-aided analysis.

Recent experience contributes to the view that experimentation with computerization within the workplace will continue because computers do indeed provide improved technological assistance. The computer industry, however, has been slow to recognize the need to make the various systems compatible (although even Apple Computers has announced that it is changing its longstanding policy of independence). "User-friendliness" is absolutely essential if the goal of improved communication is to become a reality; thus, the move in the direction of a common operating system (MS-DOS) was timely.

Within this context, modern managers should learn about computers so that they can improve their managerial decision-making skills. This increased knowledge could be correlated with the ever-developing concept of the :office of the future" as perceived by the computer industry as it struggles to make available more coherent systems that will meet the present and future *actual* needs of users.

Historical Background

An extensive body of literature on management has developed since 1900. However, it has been characterized by steadily increasing complexity, and there now exists what has often been called a "management theory jungle." Interestingly, from the standpoint of the topic of the present paper, one of the schools identified historically views management's primary function as decision-making. In this context, the manager's task is to gather as much information as possible about a subject, and then make decisions based on an analysis carried out with the best quantitative techniques available. In essence, this is what has been referred to as operations research but is now commonly known as "management science."

Although it is recognized that decision-making is an important competency for an executive, this ability has not been well developed. As mentioned above, research has revealed that the large majority of managers in sport and physical education do not use the techniques involved in common decision-making methods when elementary tools are readily available. This situation should be rectified in at least two ways. First, course experiences should be provided in undergraduate and graduate training programs to help in the development of the necessary competencies. Second, professional associations should work cooperatively with computer companies to provide improved, reasonably inexpensive, in-service training programs.

Decision-Making Fundamentals

All creatures on earth have been making decisions since the evolutionary process set in. A problem arose and a decision had to be made--fight, run, or hide, for example. A choice was made according to alternatives present in the situation. As social life has become increasingly complex, the decision-making process has increased in complexity as well. What are some recommended steps that might be taken as an individual strives to make a rational decision? Where do emotions enter into the decision-making process? What relationship do decisions have to the manager's value system? Can a classification system for the various types of decisions (e.g., routine decisions) be established? Under what conditions are decisions made (i.e., degree of uncertainty or risk)? Finally, what techniques have proven to be useful and valuable in the decision-making process (e.g., marginal analysis)?

Small Computer Systems: A Brief Overview

Through gradual, but steady improvement in computer technology and experimentation on the part of the users, the purposes for which the early computers were used are gradually being modified and expanded. Many early operations envisioned the users as interested but passive users of machines that turned out results according to highly precise instructions. With the improved technology available, however, it may be possible for managers and related personnel to be more creative and insightful. In the final analysis, therefore, the level of productivity should gradually increase from the standpoint of both effectiveness and efficiency. To accomplish this goal, managers need to understand how the key components of computer systems work (e.g., system configuration, information processing). Managers in sport, physical education, and recreation settings need to understand (at least) the theory of operating systems, telecommunications programs, general–purpose languages, and graphics equipment and software. Those who are willing to take this a step further and develop the required competencies to maximize their managerial potential will find that there are handsome rewards and dividends for their efforts.

Computer Technology and the Manager

Managers in physical activity education, including sport, now need a reasonable competence in the many aspects of microcomputers. The level of competence needed for the future is uncertain. Familiarity with a microcomputer seems absolutely essential. This is vital since the line of distinction between what a manager does and what a secretary does has now become blurred. However, the complex technical problems that arise in the training of a high level of computer literacy may not be necessary for the manager in most situations. The ability to employ computer systems as management tools, while not having extensive programming knowledge or hardware operations insight, is what today's manager needs. What is basic, therefore, is to establish a set of standards for managers in this field. These standards should include computer applications and techniques that are available to support managers employing decision-making techniques in the performance of the basic management functions. This was called the process school of management when Mackenzie (1969, pp. 80-87) delineated planning, organizing, staffing, directing, and controlling as the steps involved.

Introduction to Computerized Management Applications in Physical Activity Education and Athletics

In many instances now, except when cost and time commitments discourage their use, qualified people in other departments or divisions (or outside consultants) are employed to help in decision-making. It can be argued, therefore, that the manager should now appreciate how the computer can be employed to cut down costs, to save time, and possibly even to improve the quality of the everyday decisions. A qualified manager or associate can write a software program to solve a specific problem, or--perhaps better yet--can purchase a particular software program designed for that purpose and adapt it at reasonable expense to the physical activity education situation.

More specifically, if the quality of the information available to describe the situation is excellent, and if the problem to be resolved is *quantitative* and not primarily *qualitative* in nature, it may be both possible and practical to use one of the fine, general-purpose, spreadsheet programs available. Consider it this way: a quantifiable problem *plus* accurate data *plus* a need for a precise answer means that the manager would be advised to use a modified computer program to solve the problem. The actual techniques to be employed here could be (1) spreadsheet computation programs, (2) statistical analysis packages, and (3) specialized programs and models.

Specific Management Applications for Physical Activity Education and Athletics Settings

In light of the fact that numerous programs or models are available, a study was carried out to determine that could be most useful to sport, physical education, and/or recreation managers, Chung (1982) included six popular, well-established decision-making tools in his study:

> (a) *break-even and profitability analyses*--methods for studying the relationships among revenue, fixed costs, and variable expenses to determine the break-even point where revenue equals (=) expenditure (costs) (Heyel, 1973, p. 70).

124

(b) *cost benefit/cost effectiveness analyses*--mathematics-oriented methods for choosing the preferred alternative by evaluating the potential trade-offs with regards to the benefits or effectiveness to be gained in relation to the costs to be incurred for the alternatives available (Heyel, 1973, p. 130).

(c) *decision-tree analysis*--a graphical method for expressing the alternative actions that are available to the decision-maker and the choices as determined by statistical probability (Hillier and Lieberman, 1974, p. 610).

(d) *linear programming*--an algebraic method for optimizing or maximizing an objective function that is subjected to several constraints or conditions (Hillier and Lieberman, 1974, pp. 15-16).

(e) *PERT/CPM* (program evaluation and review technique/critical path method)--mathematically ordered systems of planning for the best possible use of resources to achieve a given goal within overall time and cost limitations (Heyel, 1973, p. 723).

(f) *queueing theory*--an analytical method for balancing the cost of a service against the cost of time-wasting queues (Hillier and Lieberman, 1974, p. 397).

Analytical tools such as these can be classified in a number of different ways (e.g., methods of analysis, types of information used). Thus, it was decided to approach the problem from the standpoint of the end result desired. Accordingly, in order to meet the needs of the average manager, it was necessary to double the size of the original listing to include examples of tools or models that (a) compare and/or contrast aspects of the present situation, (b) help in the selection of the operational process to be followed, and (c) look to the future by some type of prediction. On this basis, therefore, the following specific models and techniques designed to serve as decision-making tools are recommended for consideration:

1. *Comparison and/or Classification*

a. Decision Table Model

     b. Statistical Sampling Model
     c. Market Share/Growth Model
     d. Comparison Model

2. *Operational Process*

     a. Network Analysis (PERT/CPM)
     b. Linear Programming Model
     c. Inventory Model

3. *Future Prediction Models*

     a. Break-Even & Profitability Model
     b. Decision-Tree Model
     c. Queuing Simulation Model
     d. Econometric Model
     e. Multiple Regression Model

Models Included in the Present Study

For the purposes of the present discussion, three models were selected for inclusion--one from each of the categories outlined. The market share/growth model was selected from the category of *comparison or classification models*, a network analysis model was chosen from the second category of *operational process models*, and, finally, the queueing simulation model was taken from the category of <u>future prediction models</u>. (The remaining nine applications will be developed in the near future for use in sport, physical education, and recreation settings.)

Market Share/Growth Model. One type of decision table model, the Boston Consulting Group market share-growth model, has been used to classify a business into one of four groups (i.e., star, cash cow, problem child, and dog). (See Table 1 below.) It can be adapted for use in the classification of various program entities with an intramural-recreation sports program. Admittedly, program offerings within an intramurals program are not determined only by the amount of money they make. Nevertheless, all programs have been forced increasingly to take the profit-loss issue into consideration. Also, many programs often "cost more than they are worth"-- that is, the cost is too great for the number of people served. Thus, "unprofitable" programs require annual review to determine whether they should be justified and continued on the prevailing or a lesser basis.

The business model could therefore be adapted to an educational institution where worthwhile programs are often subsidized despite their overall cost. This model envisions that "cash cow" businesses will be managed in order to develop profit (cash) for use in the development of new

Table 1
Market Share/Growth Model–
Intramurals-Recreational Sports Program

Competing Program Offering	Estimated Market Growth (1-10 scale)	Market Share	Classification
Sport Clubs	Ten % or less	High (7)	Cash cow
Tennis Lessons	More than 10%	Low (3)	Problem child
Recreational Swim	More than 10%	High (9)	Star
Hockey League	Ten % or less	High (8)	Cash cow
Figure Skating	More than 10%	Low (5)	Problem child
Water Polo	Ten % or less	Low (3)	Dog
Flag Football	More than 10%	High (8)	Star

The value of modeling the Market Share/Growth Model in a spreadsheet is that logically managers are in a position to base the validity of their assessment on the phrase "if..., and..., then" in the sense that the computer can be programmed to scan a table that will indicate which classification should be awarded to a particular program offering. For example, in the case of sport clubs (the top item in Table 1), if market growth is 10% or less, and market share is rated as 7 or more, then classification = cash cow. Also, the benefits of using a spreadsheet for this type of classification becomes more obvious as the size and complexity of the Market Growth/Market Share Model increase.

Network Analysis. A network is a graphical representation of all activities to be completed in a project. There are two basic approaches that can be followed here: PERT (program evaluation and review technique) and CPM (critical path method). Both answer questions such as (1) How long will a project take?, (2) When and where are resources needed?, (3) How can a delay be accepted in each activity?, (4) What are the effects of delays on the total time?, and (5) Which activities are *critical* to the completion of the project on time?

The basic steps to be followed in this type of analysis are as follows:

1. List all activities in a logical order of progression.
2. Determine the immediate predecessor(s).
3. Estimate the time duration of each activity.
4. Determine the earliest start time for each activity.
5. Determine the latest start time for each activity.
6. Subtract the earliest start time from the latest start time to determine the slack for each activity. (Activities with zero slack are on the critical path. They are "critical" in that a delay will result in a requisite delay in the total project.)

The main difference between PERT and CPM is in the determination of the estimated duration of an activity. CPM uses an estimate for each activity, while PERT employs three ratings for each activity; i.e., optimistic (To), most likely (Tm), and pessimistic (Tp). For example, if the *optimistic* time for an activity were 4, the *most likely* 6, and the *pessimistic* time 8, the time estimate used by PERT is 6 and is determined by the following formula:

$$\text{Duration} = \frac{\text{To} + 4(\text{Tm}) + \text{Tp}}{6}$$

A simple example is presented in Tables 2 and 3 and Figure 1. It uses only one time estimate for each activity:

Table 2
PERT Network Analysis I

Activity		Immediate Predecessor	Estimated Time (in weeks)
A	Reserve facility	-	3
B	Advertise event	A	1
C	Hire staff	B	1
D	Promote event	B	5
E	Pick up equipment	C	1
F	Set up equipment	E	1
G	Operate event	D,F	2

+++

Figure 1   Project Network

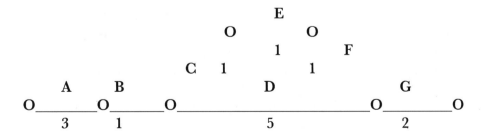

Key: letters A-G = progression of activities; numbers designate weeks needed to complete an activity.

Table 3
PERT Network Analysis II

Activity	Duration	Earliest Start (ES)	Latest Start (LS)	Total Slack (LS-ES)	Critical Path (Yes/No)
A	3	0	0	0	Yes
B	1	3	3	0	Yes
C	1	4	6	2	No
D	5	4	4	0	Yes
E	1	5	7	2	No
F	1	6	8	2	No
G	2	9	9	0	Yes

The Queuing Simulation Model. Queuing theory (or waiting line theory) involves the mathematical study of "queues" or waiting lines that can help sport and physical activity managers make decisions such as: (1) How many attendants/service facilitators (e.g., in ticket booths, locker rooms) are required to restrict average waiting time to "X" minutes?, (2) What are the monetary or time costs (to both organizers and patrons) associated with various arrangements of the queueing system?

Such decisions are important since if clients are forced to wait inordinately long for service, the organization will face complaints and subsequent ill will resulting in loss of business. On the other hand, if there is no waiting line for service, the service component may be excessive. The goal of queuing theory is to achieve an economic balance between the costs of providing adequate service and the costs associated with waiting for service.

To conduct a queuing study, the manager must have the following data: (a) the chronological arrival time of each client, and (b) the actual service time involved for each client. To determine the waiting time for a client (n), the following formula is used:

$$W_n = S_{n-1} + W_{n-1} - t_{n-(n-1)}$$

where Wn = waiting time for client n
   Sn-1 = service time of previous client
   Wn-1 = waiting time for previous client
   tn-(n-1) = between time arrival (i.e., the
         time of arrival of client n - time
         of arrival of client n-1)

In the example of queuing theory application, the manager enters the data required in Columns B and D. The spreadsheet can be programmed, using the above formula, to automatically insert the data in columns C and E, as well as to calculate the average waiting time and service time.

Table 4
Queuing Theory Application

A	B		C		D		E
Client #	Service Time for Previous Client		Waiting Time		Between Time of Arrival		Waiting Time
	(S_{n-1})	+	(W_{n-1})	-	$(t_n-(n-1))$		(W_n)
1	0		0		0	=	0 min.
2	2 min.		0		1 min.	=	1 min.
3	4 min.		1 min.		2 min.	=	3 min.
4	3 min.		3 min.		.5 min.	=	5.5 min.

Results: Average service time = 2.25 min.
     Average waiting time = 2.4 min.

A continuation of the above example will assist the manager to answer the waiting line questions posed earlier more definitively.

Looking to the Future

The need for more and better knowledge to provide guidance for sound decision-making in the increasingly complex internal and external environments of physical activity education and athletics is gradually being recognized by administrators. Thus, a sampling of fundamental decision-making tools based on models that readily adaptable to sport, physical education, and recreation settings have been offered. It is recognized that there are identifiable links between what has been called the quantitative (managerial) school of thought and the management process school (i.e., planning, organizing, staffing, etc.). Also, it can be argued that a further link can and/or should occur between the quantitative approach and what has been identified as a behavioral management school of thought.

There is no doubt that the use of models and techniques such as these (i.e., comparison and/or classification, operational process, and future prediction) can be most helpful. In a specific situation where sufficient knowledge is not available to make the best possible decision, the results obtained from the application of one or more of these models can be used to help the decision process.

The use of the techniques outlined in the present paper does not rule out the continuing need for experience, wisdom, and inspiration in decision-making. Nevertheless, using these decision-making tools should help to reduce daily reliance on what might be called "intuitive wisdom."

References

Benton, F. W. (1983). *Execucomp.* New York: John Wiley.

Chung, S. (1982). *The use of operations research techniques in sport and \ physical education administration in higher education in Ontario.* M.A. thesis, The University of Western Ontario.

Heyel, C. (ed.). (1973). *The encyclopedia of management.* New York: Van Nostrand Reinhold.

Hillier, F. S. & Lieberman, G. J. (1974). *Operations research.* San Francisco: Holden-Day.

Mackenzie, R. A.. (1969) The management process in 3-D, *Harvard Business Review,* 47: 80-87.

Zeigler, E. F. & Bowie, G. W. (1983). *Developing management competency in sport and physical education.* Philadelphia: Lea & Febiger.

For Consideration and Discussion

As an exercise at the end of this chapter, it is recommended that two students each make a 10-minute presentation, one discussing computerized management applications *generally*, while the other explains two different applications specifically, Then a third student should conduct a class discussion on the topic.

CHAPTER 7

DECISION-SUPPORT SYSTEMS FOR MANAGERS
IN PHYSICAL ACTIVITY EDUCATION AND ATHLETICS

(Terry Haggerty, Ph.D., Univ. of New Brunswick, is co-author.)

Introduction

Many lists of management problems and functions have been delineated within the business world. For example, there are those that were detailed most carefully by Mackenzie in 1969 (pp. 80-87) as planning, organizing, staffing, directing, and controlling. This approach belongs to what has been called the process school of management. If research were carried out to delineate, categorize, and evaluate the totality of such problems and functions within the field, a set of standards for managerial education in physical activity education (including sport) would soon emerge. Such standards, when developed, would presumably include a categorization and listing of the best and most appropriate computer applications and techniques available to support managers using decision-making techniques in the performance of the basic management functions.

Management decision and information systems are becoming ever more useful and popular in the various aspects of management within our increasingly complex culture. However, management–training courses in sport and recreation do not typically provide theoretical instruction and practical laboratory experiences in management decision and information systems at either the undergraduate or graduate levels (Zeigler and Bowie, 1995 and 2007, pp. ii-iv, 3-10). Three useful categories of such computer applications within information systems that should probably be incorporated into programs include electronic data processing systems (e.g., a payroll), management information systems (e.g., a sales analysis), and decision support systems (e.g., spreadsheet modeling for comparison, prediction, or process analysis). Of course, job analyses are necessary in order to determine the extent to which specific decision-making tools and models are needed in our professional education programs.

Classification of Decision-Making Tools:

In light of the fact that numerous decision-making programs or models are available, a study was carried out to determine which of these could be most useful to sport, physical education, and/or recreation managers (Chung, 1982). For the purposes of this investigation, six popular, well-established, decision-making tools were included:

(1) <u>break-even and profitability analyses</u>--methods for studying the relationships among revenue, fixed costs, and variable expenses to determine the break-even point where revenue equals (=) expenditure (costs) (Heyel, 1973, p. 70).

(2) <u>cost benefit/cost effectiveness analyses</u>-- mathematics-oriented methods for choosing the <u>preferred</u> alternative by evaluating the potential trade-offs with regards to the benefits or effectiveness to be gained in relation to the costs to be incurred for the alternatives available (Heyel, 1973, p. 130).

(3) <u>decision-tree analysis</u>--a graphical method for expressing the alternative actions that are available to the decision-maker and the choices as determined by statistical probability (Hillier and Lieberman, 1974, p. 610).

(4) <u>linear programming</u>--an algebraic method for optimizing or maximizing an objective function that is subjected to several constraints or conditions (Hillier and Lieberman, 1974, pp. 15-16).

(5) <u>PERT/CPM (program evaluation and review technique/critical path method)</u>--mathematically ordered systems of planning for the best possible use of resources to achieve a given goal within overall time and cost limitations (Heyel, 1973, p. 723).

(6)) <u>queuing theory</u>--an analytical method for balancing the cost of a service against the cost of time-wasting queues (Hillier and Lieberman, 1974, p. 397).

Analytical tools such as these can themselves be classified in a number of different ways (e.g., methods of analysis, types of information used). Here it was decided to approach the problem from the standpoint of the end result desired. Accordingly, in order to meet the needs of the average manager, it was necessary to double the size of the original listing to include examples of tools or models that (a) compare and/or contrast aspects of the present situation, (b) help in the selection of the operational process to be followed, and (c) look to the future by some type of prediction (Benton, 1983, pp. 65-90). On this basis, therefore, the following specific models and techniques designed to serve as decision-making tools were recommended for consideration:

Classification of Related Analytical Tools

1. Comparison and/or Classiciation
   a. Decision Table Model
   b. Statistical Sampling Model
   c. Market Share/Growth Model
   d. Comparison Model

2. <u>Operational Process</u>

   a. Network Analysis (PERT/CPM)
   b. Linear Programming Model
   c. Inventory Model

3. <u>Future Prediction Models</u>

   a. Break-Even & Profitability Model
   b. Decision-Tree Model
   c. Queuing Simulation Model
   d. Econometric Model
   e. Multiple Regression Model

Proceeding from Chung's (1982) findings that managers in physical activity education and athletic settings are not typically using models and tools readily available to assist them, the investigators carried out a study (1) to show what selected, computerized management applications were available to help the manager improve the quality of everyday decisions where the problem to be resolved is largely quantitative in nature, and (2) to demonstrate how to carry out selected applications effectively and efficiently (Zeigler and Haggerty, in Slack & Hinings, 1987).

It is generally agreed that using spreadsheet computation programs is the simplest and best way for managers to get small-scale assistance for decision-making. All integrated software packages offer the spreadsheet technique as a powerful yet simple approach to data collection and analysis. In this way an electronic two-dimensional table is created and stored in a computer's memory. Usually the horizontal rows correspond to persons, products, or cases, while the vertical columns relate to characteristics of each person, product, or case (i.e., in the latter instance, cost, availability, or size). In creating the electronic table, specific numbers or labels are entered in the columns and rows and typically are defined in terms of one or more other columns and rows. The idea is to start with what is known, and then additional rows and columns are added in some sort of a logical and/or computational relationship to what already exists.

135

To be somewhat more precise, but not absolutely definitive, an equipment manager might have a (project) budget for various types of balls used in an intramurals and recreational sports program. To create a spreadsheet table, the columns would be labeled with letters and the rows with numbers. The four columns are designated as (A) Item, (B) Unit Cost, (C) Number Purchased, and (D) Total Cost. The six rows (and this figure is arbitrary here, of course) are (1) Basketballs, (2) Footballs, (3) Soccer Balls, (4) Volleyballs, (5) Softballs, and (6) Project Budget. To construct a spreadsheet table, the program would require the following instructions:

> LABEL the columns: A=Item, B=Unit Cost, C=Number Purchased, and D=Total Cost
> LABEL the rows: 1=Basketballs, 2=Footballs, 3=Soccer Balls, 4=Volleyballs, 5=Softballs, and 6=Project Budget.
> ASSIGN the following values to positions in the table you are creating: B1=50, B2=42, B3=36, B4=29, B5=8; C1=60, C2=40, C3=30, C4=30, C5=36 (Note: "B2" refers to "Column B, Row 2"; "C1" refers to "Column C, Row 1", etc.)
> MULTIPLY the numbers in column B by the numbers in column C for rows 1, 2, 3, 4, and 5, and ASSIGN the resulting values to column D.
> ADD the values in positions D1, D2, D3, D4, and D5, and
> ASSIGN the sum to D4 (adapted from Benton, 1983, p. 62).

Execution of the steps indicated above would result in an elementary spreadsheet table explaining the "project budget" for balls in a program. Keep in mind, of course, that each software program including spreadsheet modeling has its own specific (exact!) language that must be followed. Also, the computational capabilities vary from program to program. A strong point for the use of this technique is that tables can be created, used, stored, called up again with another program, and required to perform a different function or purpose. And, vice versa, stored information and data can be called up and analyzed through the introduction of a desired spreadsheet program.

In the 1987 study, three spreadsheet models to aid in the decision-making process were selected from the twelve applicable spreadsheet models (described above) for development and presentation. The market/share/growth model was selected from the category of *comparison or classification models*; the network analysis was chosen from the second category of *operational process models*. Finally, the queuing simulation model was taken from the set of *future-prediction models*.

In the present investigation, three additional models were developed, one from each of three categories listed above: (a) from the classification model category, a *statistical model* was developed to show how involvement of students in the various years in a physical recreation and intramurals

136

program may be determined in a type of ongoing market research project; (b) from the operational process model category, an *inventory model* was created to help determine whether it would be desirable to purchase and store athletic equipment in quantity; and (c) from the future-prediction models, an elementary *decision-tree or flow model* was implemented to describe the marketing process involved in estimating future potential for the sale of season tickets in one or more sports.

What is needed is a plan designed to facilitate the implementation of these applications into an ongoing situation by the eventual development of templates available on software for use within the fields of sport, physical education, and recreation. The result would be an improved means of assistance for managers who desire to make sound decisions based on the best information available.

Statistical (Sampling) Model Related to an Intramurals & Recreational Sports Program

The plan with this first model is to estimate the extent of expressed interest and subsequent involvement of categories of students attending an educational institution in the various programs offered by an intramurals and recreational sports program. For example, samplings of such sub-groups as male, female, student level (i.e., first year, second year, etc.), those in residence, those living off campus, those participating in voluntary physical recreation and fitness, those participating in instructional programs, those participating in competitive sport, and those participating in sport clubs would be taken. Elementary statistical tools of measurement and evaluation (i.e., descriptive statistics) would be applied to the data collected. The procedures used to estimate from samples would be based on probability. The computer would first help in the summarization and analysis of the findings of the survey, but the concern here is to help in the <u>interpretation</u> of the findings. Thus, the idea is to convert the information obtained into a spreadsheet model that could be employed by the manager each year as an ongoing market research project.

The table developed uses a basic statistic called a standard deviation (described in any elementary statistics text). (See Table 1 below). What this statistic defines basically is the extent to which scores in a random sample or group vary from the average score of the sample or group.

Table 1. Basic Statistics re Participation Rates

Participation Rates

	Year	Year	Year	Year			Projections 68% chance that #s will be between Col H&I	
	2006	**2007**	**2008**	**2009**				
A	B	C	D	E	F	G	H	I
					Avg.	SD	Mean -1 SD	Mean +1 SD
Male	2,000	2,200	2,300	2,100	2,150	129	2,021	2,279
Female	1,600	1,800	2,000	1,900	1,825	171	1,654	1,996
Total	3,600	4,000	4,300	4,000	3,975		3,675	4,275

Table 1. Basic Statistics re Participation Rates

Participation Rates

	Year 2006	Year 2007	Year 2008	Year 2009	Avg.	SD	Mean -1SD	Mean+1 SD
	A	B	C	D	E	F	G	H
Male	2000	2200	2300	2100	=AVERAGE(B7:E7)	=STDEV(B7:E7)	=F7-G7	=F7+G7
Female	1600	1800	2000	1900	=AVERAGE(B8:E8)	=STDEV(B8:E8)	=F8-G8	=F8+G8
Total	=SUM(B7:B8)	=SUM(C7:C8)	=SUM(D7:D8)	=SUM(E7:E8)	=SUM(F7:F8)		=SUM(H7:H8)	=SUM(I7:I8)

Developing the spreadsheet program might involve the following steps:

1. Define the row and column labels.
2. Enter the number for the size, mean, and standard deviation columns for each category (or characteristic of that category).
3. Define the A column as the mean minus .675 of the standard deviation.
4. Define the range of the B column as the A column figure and the mean.
5. Define the range of the C column as the mean plus 1 and the mean plus .675 of the standard deviation.
6. Define the D column as the mean plus 1 plus .675 of the standard deviation.

The findings from a mini-survey employing statistical sampling could be recorded and then compared on a year-by-year basis. Such information could be most helpful to the intramurals and recreational sports manager in regard to future planning and budget development.

Inventory Model Related to Purchase of Sports Equipment

The plan for the inventory model is to provide a method for the planning and evaluation of the operational process employed in the purchasing of sports equipment. This model can help the manager to determine the most efficient combinations relative to stock inventory and transportation deliveries.

Typically, a manager concerned with expending funds wisely needs to know when he/she should restock the many items of sports equipment required for the successful operation of a program. Since both purchasing and carrying costs are involved, as well as possible rental or sales losses, the most profitable point at which to re-order is very important. For example, it may offer potential gain to increase storage facilities and then to order in larger lots for volume discounts and to save on transportation costs.

A spreadsheet model can provide a flexible calculation program in which through enumeration the costs of the possible solutions to the problem can be calculated. For example, the manager could do an analysis to determine which of the various items purchased (e.g., a squash racquet) in the past few years have been re-ordered more than once during a given budgetary year (e.g., 1, 2, 5, 10 times). An ongoing inventory model can then be created to indicate how much could be saved on discounts, transportation, and possible warehousing costs in connection with each item if larger numbers were purchased.

139

Table 2. Inventory Model Related to Purchase of Sports Equipment

Equip. Item	Nbr. Ordered	Cost/ Set	Total Cost	Interest	Storage	Gross Cost	Sale Price	Est. Sales	Profit per Item
Squash Racquet	12	$35.00	$420.00	$42.00	$144.00	$50.50	$86.00	6	$120.00
	10	$38.00	$380.00	$38.00	$120.00	$53.80	$86.00	6	$130.00
	7	$40.00	$280.00	$28.00	$84.00	$56.00	$86.00	6	$164.00
	6	$43.00	$258.00	$25.80	$72.00	$59.30	$86.00	6	$160.20
	3	$46.00	$138.00	$13.80	$36.00	$62.60	$86.00	3	$70.20
	1	$46.00	$46.00	$4.60	$12.00	$62.60	$86.00	1	$23.40

Equip. Item	Nbr. Ordered	Cost/ Set	Total Cost	Interest	Storage	Gross Cost	Sale Price	Est. Sales	Profit per Item
Squash Racquet	12	35	=C4*B4	=D4*0.2*0.5	=0.5*B4*24	=(D4+E4+F4)/B4	86	6	=((H4-C4)*I4)-(E4+F4)
	10	38	=C5*B5	=D5*0.2*0.5	=0.5*B5*24	=(D5+E5+F5)/B5	86	6	=((H5-C5)*I5)-(E5+F5)
	7	40	=C6*B6	=D6*0.2*0.5	=0.5*B6*24	=(D6+E6+F6)/B6	86	6	=((H6-C6)*I6)-(E6+F6)
	6	43	=C7*B7	=D7*0.2*0.5	=0.5*B7*24	=(D7+E7+F7)/B7	86	6	=((H7-C7)*I7)-(E7+F7)
	3	46	=C8*B8	=D8*0.2*0.5	=0.5*B8*24	=(D8+E8+F8)/B8	86	3	=((H8-C8)*I8)-(E8+F8)
	1	46	=C9*B9	=D9*0.2*0.5	=0.5*B9*24	=(D9+E9+F9)/B9	86	1	=((H9-C9)*I9)-(E9+F9)

Such a spreadsheet model to determine saving through volume purchasing, for example, could be created in a table with the following steps:

1. Define the rows and columns.
2. Enter the alternative numbers of orders, numbers of items or sets per order, and total cost per order.
3. Define the "cost per set" column as the total cost divided by the number of sets.
4. Define the total interest (at 20% per year) as 20% of one-half of the total cost. (Use of one-half assumes that half of the items will be sold, thereby reducing the interest costs. Also, it costs 2 dollars a month to store specific quantities (a gross?) of items elsewhere.)
5. Define the interest per gross of items as the total interest divided by how many gross are purchased and stored.
6. Define warehouse rental for storage as one-half of the number

After developing this model for one piece of sports equipment (e.g., a squash racquet), the IRS manager knows money can be saved by purchasing X gross of squash racquets and paying storage and carrying costs. Also, through the process of enumeration with the spreadsheet, alternative solutions may be calculated if interest and/or storage rates go up or down.

Decision-Tree/Flow Model Related to Purchase of Season Tickets

Intercollegiate athletics face the problem of the number of season tickets sold. At one extreme, there is the happy situation for the Denver Broncos of the NFL that thousand and thousands of people are on a waiting list. Typically, however, a business manager is faced with the need to increase the number of season ticket holders in football or basketball (or any other revenue-producing sport).

In such a situation, an approach to prediction about this important item that can be employed is the basic decision-tree or flow model. Such a model describes simply the breakdown of a group of people (or units) as they move through a process. Such a model maintained on an annual basis can be employed comparatively as well as for a particular season. It can demonstrate the subsequent effects of actions or decision taken previously.

Although a spreadsheet approach is not suited to complex decision-tree modeling where specialized software must be employed, it can be used to describe *a specific path* in a complex model. For example, a business manager of athletics could describe marketing process from the first advertising contact to the eventual sale of season tickets to X number of people.

1. Define the rows and columns.
2. Enter the initial number (i.e., the size of the total market).
3. Enter the possible percentage (%) of persons who would be interested (e.g., 5%, 8%)
4. Calculate potential customers (market size x interested)
5. Using the "rule of 45" to estimate number of season tickets (i.e., 45% of interested would purchased if followed up for 1 year, 26% after 6 months, and 12% after 3 months)

Table 3. Season Ticket Scenario.

James Obermayer, Managing Sales Leads: Turning Cold Prospects Into Hot Customers, Thomson/South-Western and Racom Books

Market Size	If: Interest Level	Potential Customers	3 Months of Follow-up	6 Months of Follow-up	12 Months of Follow-up
			12%	26%	45%
200,000	5%	10,000	1,200	2,600	4,500
"	8%	16,000	1,920	4,160	7,200
"	10%	20,000	2,400	5,200	9,000
"	15%	30,000	3,600	7,800	13,500

Market Size	If: Interest Level	Potential Customers	3 Months of Follow-up	6 Months of Follow-up	12 Months of Follow-up
			0.12	0.26	0.45
200000	0.05	=$A$6*B6	=$D$5*C6	=$E$5*C6	=$F$5*C6
"	0.08	=$A$6*B7	=$D$5*C7	=$E$5*C7	=$F$5*C7
"	0.1	=$A$6*B8	=$D$5*C8	=$E$5*C8	=$F$5*C8
"	0.15	=$A$6*B9	=$D$5*C9	=$E$5*C9	=$F$5*C9

The description of this pathway on an annual basis (and then comparatively over a period of years) permits the business manager to assess the effect of implementing various marketing strategies (e.g., spending more on radio advertising, implementing a telephone campaign to alumni by alumni). (This example is a simple spreadsheet approach that can be implemented with ease. Sophisticated software is now available commercially for the development of a more complex model if and when needed.)

Concluding Statement

In conclusion, we repeat that the need for more and better knowledge to provide guidance for sound decision-making in the increasingly complex internal and external environments of sport, physical education, and recreation settings is apparent to us. We can only hope that it will gradually be recognized by managers in the field as well. For this reason, we have offered an additional sampling of three more fundamental decision-making tools based on models that are readily adaptable to sport, physical education, and recreation settings.

We recognize that there are identifiable links between what has been called the quantitative (managerial) school of thought and the management process school (i.e., planning, organizing, staffing, etc.). Also, it can be argued that a further link can and/or should occur between the quantitative approach and what has been identified as a behavioral management school of thought. Accordingly, we will continue our effort to support our belief that the use of models and techniques such as these (i.e., comparison and/or classification, operational process, and future prediction) can be most helpful. In a specific situation where sufficient knowledge is not available to make the best possible decision, the results obtained from the application of one or more of these models can be used to help the decision process.

It is true, of course, that the use of the three additional techniques outlined here (i.e., three originally in 1986 and now three more in 1996) does not rule out the continuing need for experience, wisdom, and inspiration in decision-making. We can only hope that "new-generation" sport managers will experiment with models such as these. We also believe that "old dogs can be taught new tricks"; thus, we hope further that managers of all ages will experiment with management techniques or decision-support models of this nature that have the potential to improve managerial effectiveness and efficiency significantly.Here we would create a spreadsheet that describes a particular pathway leading to the sale of the season ticket. The following steps could be taken to create the spreadsheet:

References

Benton, F. W. (1983). *Execucomp.* New York: John Wiley.

Chung, S. (1982). The use of operations research techniques in sport and physical education administration in higher education in Ontario. M.A. thesis, The University of Western Ontario.

Heyel, C. (ed.). (1973). *The encyclopedia of management.* New York: Van Nostrand Reinhold.

Hillier, F. S. & Lieberman, G. J. (1974). *Operations research.* San Francisco: Holden-Day.

Mackenzie, R. A.. (1969) The management process in 3-D, *Harvard Business Review*, 47: 80-87.

Zeigler, E. F. & Bowie, G. W. (1995). *Developing management competency in sport and physical education.* Champaign, IL: Stipes.

Zeigler, E.F. & Haggerty, T. (1987). Improving managerial decision-making through spreadsheet modeling. In *The Organization and Administration of Sport* (T. Slack & C.R. Hinings, Eds.), Note: This is the *Proceedings of the First Canadian Symposium on Sport Management. London, Canada: Sport Dynamics.*

For Consideration and Discussion

As an exercise at the end of this chapter, it is recommended that two students each make a 10-minute presentation, one discussing the break-down of the classification of selected decision-making tools along with how the classification of related analytical tools meshes with it. The other student should then explain the essence of the three examples offered in this chapter. Then a third student should conduct a class discussion on the topic in a "concerted search" for other instances where tools like this could be helpful

CHAPTER 8

SPORT MANAGEMENT MUST SHOW SOCIAL CONCERN AS IT DEVELOPS TENABLE THEORY

Introduction

An epoch in civilization approaches closure if the basic convictions of the majority of the populace are challenged by a substantive minority. It can be argued that indeed the world is moving into a new epoch as the proponents of postmodernism have been affirming over recent decades. Within such a milieu there are indications that the sport management profession is going to have great difficulty crossing this chasm, this so-called, postmodern divide (Zeigler, 2003, p. 93).

Nevertheless, there is no question but that sport has become recognized as one of humankind's fundamental social institutions. However, I believe that there are now strong indications that sport's presumed, overall recreational, educational, and entertainment role in the "adventure of civilization" is not being fulfilled adequately. Municipal recreation programs, private sport clubs, and school sport programs are "doing the best that they can" often with limited funding. At the same time the commercialized sport establishment gets almost all of the media attention and is prospering as never before. Hence, an intelligent, concerned citizen can reasonably ask, "What evidence do we have that sport as a social institution is really making a positive contribution to society?" Therefoe, I find myself forced to ask whether commercially organized sport is actually "talking a better game than it plays." Where or what is sport management's tenable theory? Recalling the well-known fairy tale. I find that I must declare--not that "the king doesn't have any clothes on"--but that "The king should prove (to society) that he is sufficiently clothed to justify our continuing support!"

The sport industry is obviously "charging ahead" driven by capitalistic economic theory that overemphasizes ever-increasing gate receipts with an accompanying corollary of winning fueled somehow by related violence. One of the "principal principles" of physical education espoused in the early 1950s by Dr. Arthur Steinhaus (George Williams College) was that "sport was made for man, not man for sport"(1952). *It is being countermanded day by day, week by week at all levels around the world.* Interestingly, but disturbingly, a societal majority seems to lend support to this surge in the popularity of professionalized competitive sport. The athletes--those relatively few happy people of the total on the way to the bank who do not mind being used as commodities--typically don't understand what is happening. They don't even recognize this as a problem. Neither do many (most?) aspiring sport management students in professional programs.

Everything considered, I am therefore forced to ask, "What are we helping to promote--we who have associated ourselves with sport management--and exactly why are we doing it?" I fear that we are simply going along with the seemingly inevitable tide. In the process we have become pawns to the prevailing sport establishment by "riding the wrong horse." Our present responsibility--to the extent that we are educators and scholars--should be to devote our efforts to provide sport management with tenable theory. This tenable theory should relate to sport and physical activity involvement for all people of all ages in society whether they are normal, accelerated, or special in status.

Governmental agencies sponsoring "amateur" sport competition should be able to state in their relationship to sport that: if "such-and-such" is done with reasonable efficiency and effectiveness through the sponsorship of sporting activities, then "such-and-such" will (in all probability) result. Personnel in these same agencies are striving to do just this, but not necessarily in an acceptable way consonant with overall societal values. Instead of working assiduously for a "from-the-ground-up" development of young athletes in the hope that they would achieve relatively superior status eventually, they are proceeding in what might be called a fast-track approach. By that I mean that governments are focusing primarily on the recruitment and development of potentially elite athletes who somehow come to their attention, athletes whom they hope will bring fame and glory to their country. (Canada has been calling it the "own-the-podium approach...") So, again, I ask, where is the evidence that organized sport's goal is based on tenable theory consonant with societal values that claim to promote the welfare of all?

I am heartened, however, by selected publications in the *Journal of Sport Management* that discuss future directions in research. Frisby's EFZ Lecture (2005) , in referring to "The Good, The Bad, and The Ugly" strikes just the right note in her conclusion by urging a broadened outlook for sport management. Next Costa's study (2005) using Delphi technique provided excellent discussion based on the opinions of leaders in the field as to future directions. Concern was expressed about the ability to achieve the goals outlined (e.g., additional cross-discipline research) within our own discipline. Then, the entire "Expanding Horizons" issue offered interesting insights and approaches about research for consideration (2005). Finally, Chalip's analysis in his 2005 EFZ Lecture titled "Toward a distinctive sport management discipline," points us toward the achievement of "distinctive relevance" for our field. (This idea of a distinctive approach for a sport-management model strikes a resounding chord with me. Below I will seek to add a bit to the profession's consideration of this problem.)

Fortunately, also, there is a growing minority within the populace that supports a more humanistic position that accepts the steadily mounting evidence that all people--not just elite athletes striving for personal fulfillment and fame--need to be active in physical recreational activities throughout their entire lives. This leads me to inquire as to what role the professional sport management societies worldwide should play in the guidance of its members toward this end. Hopefully these men and women, serving as qualified professionals seeking the achievement of their society's most desirable values, will increasingly be in a position to assist sport and related physical activity to serve all people in our world society in the best possible way.

Before such a dream can become a reality, however, we need to dig deeply in our respective "cultural psyches" to begin to understand how society got itself in the presently questionable situation. Until at least the majority of people in our world's culture understand what has happened, what should be done, and what can be done, there is little hope for improvement in what I believe to be an increasingly untenable situation.

In retrospect, the 18th century in the Western world witnessed revolutionary thought that had caused it now to be known as the Age of Reason (or "enlightenment"). This outlook was based on ideals of truth, freedom, and reason for all humans. In the United States, however, the Enlightenment vision of Thomas Jefferson that promised political and social liberation was somehow "turned upside down." What happened in American life in the 19th century was that "progress" came to mean "technocratic progress." This was not the anticipated social progress for all people that was planned by the inculcation of such values as justice, freedom, and self-fulfillment. These vital goals of a democratic political system were simply subjugated to the more immediate instrumental values. As Leo Marx explains, this technological advancement "became the fulcrum of the dominant American world view" (p. 5).

In the realm of physical (activity) education there was a "battle of the systems" of exercise and gymnastics that took place in the final quarter of the 20th century. However, it was the burgeoning interest in sport that permitted sport to infiltrate in the program of school physical education as sport skills. This type of experience was expanded further in (what was termed) extracurricular activity with team sports for the more highly skilled boys and girls. Earlier physical education programs, where available, as well as programs in wartime eras, undoubtedly stressed the concept of education "of the physical" more than the "roll-out-the-ball" approach so evident in physical education in subsequent decades. There was also the concept of "education through the physical" was also promoted to a degree by the educational "progressivists" influenced by Deweyan pragmatism. Typically this broader emphasis waned during periods of war and international unrest.

Careful historical analysis of this situation has led me to believe that the steady development of the social institution of competitive sport in the United States over the past 150 years has reached a crossroads (Zeigler, 2005, Chaps. XI & XII). If a claim can reasonably be made that organized sports may be doing as much harm as it does good can be made, I am forced to ask, "Where is the sport management theory needed to refute such a proposition?" In the United States especially, and in much of the remainder of the world, there is seemingly little awareness that such a negative contention about organized sport can be made. The developing world permits without question the commercialization that has brought about sport's expansion and current gargantuan status. The conventional wisdom seems to be that "highly organized sport is good for people and our country. The more involvement an individual can have with sport, either actively or passively, the better he or she will be."

In the meantime, however, the vast majority of the population is getting inadequate involvement in regular, physical activity designed to help them live healthy, active, fulfilling lives. Many of these same people now possess--what Herbert Spencer in the mid-nineteenth century--called "seared physical consciences" He argued that in increasingly urbanized society there is inadequate physical activity education in the schools (1949). These same people simply don't know or appreciate what vigorous physical health "feels like." At the same time throughout their lives they are constantly being encouraged to pay increasing amounts of money to watch "skilled others" play games. (The resultant inactivity has created a crisis situation that will be discussed in some detail below.)

Hard Questions About Present Social Institutions

Social institutions are created and nurtured within a society ostensibly to further the positive development of the people living within that culture. Take democracy, for example, as a type of political institution that is currently being promoted vigorously by the United States throughout the entire world. (Such worldwide change will take time!) Within this form of social development, democracy has "struck up a deep relationship with economics and has found an eager bedfellow with whom to associate"--i.e., the institution of capitalism. Economics, of course, is another vital social institution upon which a society depends fundamentally. As world civilization developed, a great many of the world's countries have enacted with almost messianic zeal the promotion of such social institutions as democracy, capitalism, and --now!--an increasing involvement with competitive sport. The "theory" is that the addition of highly competitive sport to this mix will bring about more "good" than "bad" for the countries involved. But has it? Disturbing questions have now begun to arise in various quarters.

What does this all mean as we move along in the 21st century? Think of the example being set in North America, for example. Is there reasonable hope that the present brand of "combined" democratic capitalism that uses up the world's environmental resources inordinately will somehow improve the world situation in the long run? Can we truly claim with any degree of certainty that this "mix" of democracy and capitalism (with its subsequent inclusion of big-time sport) is producing more "good" than "bad"? (Admittedly, we do need to delineate between "what's 'good'" and "what's 'bad'" more carefully) There is no escaping the fact that the gap economically between the rich and the poor is steadily increasing. This means that "the American dream for all" is beginning to look like a desert mirage. Will the historical "Enlightenment Ideal" remain as an unfulfilled dream forever?

One of the results of the increasing development of the social institution of competitive sport is the creation of sport management societies in the respective regions and countries where such expansion has occurred. At the same time the question may be asked whether this development has reached a point where a claim can be made that highly competitive sport as a social phenomenon may be doing more harm than good in society. It is not that competitive sport does not have the potential for good that is being questioned here. (The world seems to have accepted this as fact!) It's the way that it is being carried out that is the problem. The world community does not really know whether this contention is true or not. However, sport's expansion is permitted and encouraged almost without question in all quarters. "Sport is good for people, and more involvement with sport of almost any type--extreme sport, professional wrestling--is better" seems to be the conventional wisdom. Witness, also, the millions of dollars that are being parceled out of tax revenues for the several Olympic enterprises perennially. So long as there's "a buck's to be made," also, permit even aging Evander Holyfield to box professionally in what's called a sport until he won't be able to remember his own name!

In the meantime, the large majority of the population in the developed world is getting inadequate involvement in physical activity, with obesity increasing unduly at all ages and levels. This is a highly significant problem that is increasing daily. Conversely there is rampant starvation in the underdeveloped world where most people, including children, must labor inordinately just to survive. At the same time the public in the technologically developed world is being expected to pay increasing amounts of money to watch "skilled others," either on television or "in the flesh," play types of games and sports increasing in complexity and danger almost exponentially. At the same time, "The National Institutes of Health estimates that Americans will take five years off the average life span," reports Randolph in "The Big, Fat American Kid Crisis" (*The New York Times*, 2006). The eventual outcome of what is happening today can be encapsulated in the grim predictions that the bulk of children and youth in the coming generation of

149

the developed world may be the first to die before their parents because of obesity, less physical activity, and related health problems.

Resultantly, I am forced to ask "What really are we promoting, and do we know why are we doing it?" I do not have a complete answer to these questions, of course. But I do believe this strongly: we need to develop a theory of sport that will permit us to assess whether what we call "competitive sport" is fulfilling its presumed function of promoting good in a society. To achieve this. we will need to establish connections and relationships with a variety of disciplines in the academic world. Some that come to mind immediately are sport sociology, sport history, sport psychology, sport philosophy, sport economics, as well as selected other fields where research findings could well have application to sport and related physical activity. Some of these fields are anthropology, social geography, and political science--all academic fields that could well help in any assessment of the findings of sport management.

I want to emphasize, also, that the field of sport management must keep a healthy balance between the theoretical and the practical in its ongoing scholarship and research. To do otherwise would be courting the same fate that befell the former Philosophic Society for the Study of Sport (now the IAPS). I'm sad to report that sport philosophy "went disciplinary" in the late 1960s and has never descended from that lofty perch. As the third president, my warning on this point in 1975 was to no avail (Zeigler, 1976). Today the International Association for Sport Philosophy has very few members and "they speak to no one," relatively speaking, except each other. This is an outcome that the field sport management will need to guard against assiduously. (Nevertheless, the disciplinary aspects of sport management should be pursued diligently, but there must be an accompanying pragmatic emphasis on applied research that is regularly and consistently downloaded to the "real world" where sport in its many forms takes place daily.)
.

Sport should be conducted in its various settings now and in the future, both generally and specifically, in a manner that will encourage its proper professional, educational and recreational uses, as well as its semiprofessional and professional concerns To guarantee such a state of affairs, sport must be challenged on an ongoing basis by people at all levels in a variety of ways. If this were to be the case, sport might possibly regain and retain those aspects that can contribute significant value to individual and social living.

In making these assertions, I must first define my terms accurately so that you are fully aware of what I am seeking to explain and also critique here. This is necessary because the term "sport," based on both everyday usage and dictionary definition, still exhibits radical ambiguity. Such indecision undoubtedly adds to the present confusion. So, when the word "sport" is used here, it will refer--unless indicated otherwise--to "competitive physical activity, an individual or group competitive activity involving physical exertion or skill, governed by rules, and sometimes engaged in professionally" (*Encarta World English Dictionary*, 1999, p. 1730).

Analyzing Sport's Role in Society

In this process of critiquing competitive sport, I believe further that society should strive to keep sport's drawbacks and/or excesses in check to the greatest possible extent. In recent decades we have witnessed the rise of sport throughout the land to the status of a fundamentalist religion. For example, we find sport being called upon to serve as a redeemer of wayward youth, but--as it is occurring elsewhere--it is also becoming a destroyer of certain fundamental values of individual and social life.

Wilcox (1991), for example, in his empirical analysis, challenged "the widely held notion that sport can fulfill an important role in the development of national character." He stated that "the assumption that sport is conducive to the development of positive human values, or the 'building of character,' should be viewed more as a belief rather than as a fact." He concluded that his study did "provide some evidence to support a relationship between participation in sport and the ranking of human values" (pp. 3, 17, 18, respectively).

Assuming Wilcox's view has reasonable validity, those involved in any way in the institution of sport--if they all together may be considered a collectivity--should contribute a quantity of redeeming social value to our North American culture, not to mention the overall world culture (i.e., a quantity of good leading to improved societal well-being). On the basis of this argument, the following questions are postulated initially for possible subsequent response by concerned agencies and individuals (e.g., federal governments, state and provincial officials, philosophers in the discipline and related professions):

(1) Can, does, or should a great (i.e., leading) nation produce great sport?

(2) With the world being threatened environmentally in a variety of ways, should we now be considering an "ecology" of sport in which the beneficial and disadvantageous aspects of a particular sporting activity are studied through the endeavors of scholars in other disciplines as well?

(3) If it is indeed the case that the guardian of the "functional satisfaction" resulting from sport is (a) the sports person, (b) the spectator, (c) the businessperson who gains monetarily, (d) the sport manager, and, in some instances, (e) educational administrators and their respective governing boards, then who in society should be in a position to be the most knowledgeable about the immediate objectives and long range aims of sport and related physical activity?

(4) If the answer to question No.3 immediately above is that this person should be the trained sport and physical activity management professor, is it too much of a leap to also expect that person's professional association (!) to work to achieve consensus about what sport and closely related physical activity should accomplish? Further, should the professional association have some responsibility as the guardian (or at least the assessor) of whether the aforementioned aims and objectives are being approximated to a greater or lesser degree?

Answering these questions is a truly complex matter. First, as I have stated above, sport and related physical activity have become an extremely powerful social force in society. Secondly, if we grant that sport now has significant power in all world cultures--a power indeed that appears to be growing--we should also recognize that any such social force affecting society can be dangerous if perverted (e.g., through an excess of nationalism or commercialism). With this in mind, I am arguing further that sport has somehow achieved such status as a powerful societal institution without an adequately defined underlying theory. Somehow, most of countries seem to be proceeding generally on a typically unstated assumption that "sport is a good thing for society to encourage, and more sport is even better!" And yet, as explained above, the term "sport" still exhibits radical ambiguity based on both everyday usage and dictionary definition. This obviously adds even more to the present problem and accompanying confusion.)

As we consider this matter more seriously, we may be surprised. We may well learn that sport is contributing significantly in the development of what are regarded as the *social* values--that is, the values of teamwork, loyalty, self-sacrifice, and perseverance consonant with prevailing corporate capitalism in democracy and in other political systems as well. Conversely, however, we may also discover that there is now a great deal of evidence that sport may be developing an ideal that opposes the fundamental moral virtues of honesty, fairness, and responsibility in the innumerable competitive experiences provided (Lumpkin, Stoll, and Beller, 1999).

Significant to this discussion are the results of investigations carried out by Hahm, Stoll, Beller, Rudd, and others in recent years. The Hahm-Beller Choice Inventory (HBVCI) has now been administered to athletes at different levels in a variety of venues. It demonstrates conclusively that athletes will not support what is considered "the moral ideal" in competition. As Stoll and Beller (1998) see it, for example, an athlete with moral character demonstrates the moral character traits of honesty, fair play, respect, and responsibility whether an official is present to enforce the rules or not. Priest, Krause, and Beach (1999) reported, also, that--over a four-year period in a college athlete's career--ethical value choices showed decreases in "sportsmanship orientation" and an increase in "professional" attitudes associated with sport.

On the other hand, even though dictionaries define social character similarly, sport practitioners, including participants, coaches, parents, and officials, have come to believe that character is defined properly by such values as self-sacrifice, teamwork, loyalty, and perseverance. The common expression in competitive sport is: "He/she showed character"--meaning "He/she 'hung in there' to the bitter end!" [or whatever]. Rudd (1999) confirmed that coaches explained character as "work ethic and commitment." This coincides with what sport sociologists have found. Sage (1998. p. 614) stated that "Mottoes and slogans such as 'sports builds character' must be seen in the light of their ideological issues" In other words, competitive sport is structured by the nature of the society in which it occurs. This would appear to mean that over-commercialization, drug-taking, cheating, bribe-taking by officials, violence, etc. at all levels of sport are simply reflections of the culture in which we live. Where does that leave us today as we consider sport's presumed relationship with moral character development?

This discussion about whether sport's presumed educational and recreational roles have justification in fact could go on indefinitely. So many negative incidents have occurred that one hardly knows where to turn to avoid further negative examples. On the one hand we read the almost unbelievably high standards stated in the Code of Conduct developed by the Coaches Council of the National Association for Sport and Physical Education (2001). Conversely we learn that today athletes' concern for the presence of moral values in sport declines over the course of a university career (Priest, Krause, and Beach, 1999).

With this as a backdrop, we learn further that Americans, for example, are increasingly facing the cost and consequences of sedentary living (Booth & Chakravarthy, 2002). Additionally, Malina (2001) tells us that there is a need to track people's involvement in physical activity and sport across their life spans. Finally, Corbin and Pangrazi (2001) explain that we haven't yet been able to devise and accept a uniform definition of wellness for all people. The one thought that emerges from these various assessments is as follows: We give every evidence that we desire "sport spectaculars" for the few much more than we want people of all ages and all conditions to have meaningful sport and exercise involvement throughout their lives.

Sport Management Theory and Practice

Defined traditionally, we might say that the sport manager is one who plans, organizes, staffs, leads (or directs), and controls (i.e., monitors and evaluates) progress toward predetermined goals within programs of sport for people of all ages, be they in normal, accelerated, or special populations. To place the current topic in historical perspective (i.e., the beginning of investigation about the management [or administration] of sport and physical activity in educational institutions largely), master's and doctoral degrees about the subject within departments and schools of education in the United States were completed initially at Columbia Teachers College and New York University starting in the mid-1920s. Individually, there were many well-intended, seemingly worthwhile studies completed. However, it was impossible to say what these--literally--thousands of investigations "added up to" 35 years later at the beginning of the 1960s decade was really not known.

In the 1960s, however, research and scholarship in administrative theory and practice related to physical education and athletic administration began to receive attention in several quarters. Through the efforts of King McCristal (and the author (University of Illinois, U-C), we were able to get this area included as one of six subject-matter areas in the Big Ten Body-of-Knowledge Project. In the fall of 1972, a symposium was held on the subject at The University of Michigan, Ann Arbor. In a volume published in 1975, the results of 20 doctoral dissertations related to sport and physical education management carried out at Illinois were published (Zeigler and Spaeth, 1975). However, financial and other constraints in higher education of the 1970s slowed this development down considerably.

Then the rise of a so-called disciplinary approach to the field of physical education, plus the perennial claim of the "educational essentialist" that it is only the hard sciences that provide the basic knowledge, resulted in the introduction of the term kinesiology to supplement (or even supplant!) that of physical education at the university level. This tended to severely downgrade the importance of administrative theory and practice programs within the field, while job opportunities for professors related to biomechanics, exercise physiology, and motor learning increased. Concurrently, however, burgeoning interest in commercialized, highly

154

competitive sport within higher education and in the public sector created a need for the establishment and development of college and university curricula in sport management. So the essence of what was often being eliminated in one program appeared to be springing up in a new curriculum stream--sport management. It was at this point on February 24, 1986 that a small group of us witnessed the successful creation of the now-successful North American Society for Sport Management.

Most of those behind the establishment of NASSM actually envisioned an association with a broad emphasis leading to the promotion of sport and physical activity for all people of all ages. However, interest in highly organized, elite sport seems to have "engulfed" conference presentations in the various aspects of competitive sport management. Sport management has rapidly become a mushrooming field in its own right that increasingly has its own curriculum independent of former physical education and athletics administration courses in educational institutions. Concurrently, the "eager scientists" in kinesiology, who conceptually relegated administrative theory and practice for physical education and athletics to the dustbin insofar as its place in their disciplinary curriculum is concerned, are presumably now quite happy and relieved in those sites where such separation has actually occurred.

Intramural and recreational sport is actually doing quite well at the college and university level, but is almost nonexistent at the high-school level and lower. Finally, the near demise of physical activity programs "for the many"--required within education at all levels within education prior to 1950– does not even appear on the radar screen of the large majority of professional preparation personnel in universities. Yet, because of the decline of required physical education, it has become starkly apparent that the health and physical fitness of the populace needs a strong shot in the arm to again establish a firm foothold in public consciousness. (It doesn't seem that the "War on Terrorism" will bring this change. Do we need another world war to accomplish this?) This is true even though--almost daily--reports of scientific studies tell us of the beneficial effects of regular physical activity on the human organism in so many different ways.

In such a developing world environment, then, what is the mission of a field called sport management, still a fledgling profession but one that ha rapidly caught on all over the world? Frankly, I believe strongly that our profession needs to understand (define?) its mission much better than appears to be the case at present. Exactly what is its fundamental purpose in society? Further, how does the mission of sport management globally relate to the mission of the various professional associations composed primarily of men and women involved in the professional education of future sport managers? (Keep in mind that the typical professional sport promoter worldwide presently lives in "another world"!)

Unfortunately, as I see it, the outlooks or aims of those people who today promote sport competition professionally, and that of those who believe they are promoting such competition educationally, appear to be getting closer all the time. I am referring here to the people involved, for example, in the National Basketball Association or the National Collegiate Athletic Association in the United States, respectively. Granted that the people in both of these associations are operating on the assumption that the provision of highly competitive sport opportunities in society is a good thing. Also, they appear to believe that promoting ever more opportunity for the masses to observe such activity is worthwhile. The fact that the cultivation of a "fan club" for professional sport also provides exorbitant income for the "accelerated few" athletes and a dubious future for the vast majority of athletes who don't "make it" appears to be of little concern. This is unfortunate for that "vast majority" because their educational background has typically been stunted by excessive involvement in competitive sport while enrolled at universities.

Frankly, I believe this assumption of "goodness " for society has become a dubious premise or principle upon which most of these promoters and/or educational administrators are operating. I maintain that this is so unless they can provide accompanying evidence to substantiate to society that the continuation and enlargement of the present trend to increasing commercialization in sport is contributing positively to society as a social institution. To repeat, all social institutions must have an underlying theory to justify their continuing existence. The basic question, I submit, is simply this: In this evolving situation, what kind of "good"--philosophically speaking--can we claim is currently being made by competitive sport?

To one who has followed and written extensively about this development down through the 20th century from both a historical and a philosophical standpoint, I can only report (sadly!) that the excesses and corruption of competitive sport have increased steadily decade by decade. And, even more sadly, the seemingly jaded public (as fans) does not seem to realize--or seems to accept--that sport's status as a desirable social institution is being lowered steadily with each passing year. (I won't even get into the question of the taking of one or more of 400-500 drugs to enhance performance that the sport establishment is facing today.) Competitive sport is forced to stay within the law, but its typically laudable creed espoused so freely requires an enforceable code of ethics in the present--not as a dream for the future.

Concurrently, the low status perennially accorded to physical education-- except in times of war when referred to as "physical fitness"--continues. This is true even though ongoing research in kinesiology and physical education--and the field's related disciplines--is steadily making the

156

case for regular, developmental physical activity as an essential, if not a vital, social institution to be employed for the benefit of all. Nevertheless the term "sport," and what it connotes to the average mind, largely overrides the need for the provision of necessary funding of developmental physical activity as a social institution. I firmly believe that provision for the managing and promoting developmental physical activity in sport, exercise, and physical recreation for people of all ages, be they part of accelerated, normal, or special populations, should at least be an auxiliary part of our mission in sport management. Yet we find that our professional associations and disciplinary societies relayed to "physical activity" are steadily and increasingly becoming more disjointed as they grow farther apart. Other professions and disciplines are "filling in" where we should be "producing" (e.g., recreation, medicine).

You can see where I am heading with this analysis. I believe it is now incumbent upon the field of sport management (i.e., these professional organizations worldwide) to investigate and subsequently understand precisely what effect sport, however defined and with all of its ramifications, is having on society. Is it more good than bad? Who knows? The professional and semiprofessional sport managers can't answer this basic question. (Many probably wouldn't want to know anyhow if it meant a possible shifting of emphasis in their offerings.) Therefore I urge the world's various professional sport management associations to take a hard look at what appears to be a steadily growing problem. They need to determine (1) what effect sport is having on society; (2) if there is a problem with the present development, and to what extent the professional associations (e.g., in North America) may unwittingly be part of the problem; and (3) in what ways professional sport management associations can ensure that sport as a whole, and more specifically its many programs at all levels, are moving in the right direction? These questions can't be answered satisfactorily without an underlying theory of sport management that meets the needs of all people.

Need for a Theory of Sport Management

Returning to the assertion made earlier, a theory underlying sport management could contribute greatly to the answering of the questions raised immediately above. It would need to be related basically to the social sciences and to certain professions that carry out their own independent research as well (e.g., business administration). It should contain "propositions of fact" that can, at least in principle, be verified empirically. "Propositions of value" are subjective and therefore typically conform to societal values and norms. Therefore, it would not be a philosophy of sport management, although a concerned individual or group might well philosophize about such human activity.

Table 1

SPORT MANAGEMENT:
SCHOLARLY AND PROFESSIONAL DIMENSIONS

Areas of Scholarly Study & Research	Related Disciplinary Aspects	Professional Aspects
I. BACKGROUND, MEANING, & INTERCULTURAL SIGNIFICANCE	-History -Philosophy -International & Comparative Study	-International Relations -Professional Ethics
II. SOCIO-CULTURAL & BEHAVIORAL ASPECTS	-Sociology -Economics -Psychology (individ.& social) -Anthropology -Political Science -Geography -Law	-Application of Theory to Practice
III. SPORT MANAGEMENT THEORY	-Management Science -Business Administration (e.g., sport marketing sport finance, facility management, sales)	-Application of Theory to Practice
IV. CURRICULUM THEORY & PROGRAM DEVELOPMENT	-Curriculum Studies	-Application of Theory to Practice

1. *General* Education: universities and colleges typically have a distribution requirement for all students in the humanities, social-science, and natural sciences.

2. *Professional* Core Subjects: an irreducible minimum requirement in the following subjects is required: communication & media relations, economic theory & sport finance, sport marketing, sponsorship & sales, legal aspects, sport governance, sport ethics, the international sport industry, and sport & physical activity interneships.

3. *Specialized* Undergraduate Professional Preparation; streaming possibilities may be added in the degree program.

4. *Graduate* Education; three types of specialization are desirable: (1) professional preparation stream; (2) disciplinary stream, (3) practitioner stream)

V. MEASUREMENT & EVALUATION	-Theory about the Measurement Function	-Application of Measurement Theory to Practice

(Note: Reactions and/or recommendations for
change or additions to Table 1 would be
appreciated at <zeigrog@axion.net>)

A theory is not a taxonomy, however, although a taxonomy of sport management will necessarily evolve as scientific and scholarly investigation about it is carried out. "A taxonomy may be defined as a classification of data according to their natural relationships, or the principles governing such classifications…In fact, one could probably make a good case to support the contention that any science begins with a taxonomy…" (Griffiths, 1959. p. 17)

A Taxonomy for Sport Management. Above as Table 1, I have included a sample of what a taxonomy of sport *management* might look like. It includes both scholarly and professional dimensions with three headings defined as (1) areas of scholarly study and research, (2) related disciplinary aspects, and (3) professional aspects. The possibility of "streaming" is mentioned at the undergraduate level. Also, there are three categories of graduate education postulated.

A Model for Sport Management. The development of a model could also be important for evolving theory, because it would enable a researcher not only to ask questions, but also to speculate as to how they might be answered. (See Figure 1 below.) The term "model" has a number of meanings. The one that concerns a developing theory of sport management would be: "a description of a set of data in terms of a system of symbols, and the manipulation of the symbols according to the rules of the system. The resulting transformations are translated back into the language of the data, and the relationship discovered by the manipulations are compared with the empirical data." (Griffiths, p. 44)

The idea of competency and skill-acquisition into the model based on the recommendation by Lloyd McCleary, formerly of the University of Illinois, C-U. I subsequently realized that this entire model configuration fits very well into a description of the ongoing status of the sport-management profession.

Note here, however, the difficulty of "manipulating symbols" unless , for example, one is trying to explain anything other than present social developments. To seek to determine those that occurred in history, one would be well advised initially to attempt to estimate the strength of each conceivable influence that might have caused a past social occurrence or historical phenomenon.

By now governmental, educational, and commercial agencies and organizations should be able to argue convincingly that sport is a "relatively homogeneous substance" that can serve at least reasonably well as an

159

Figure 1

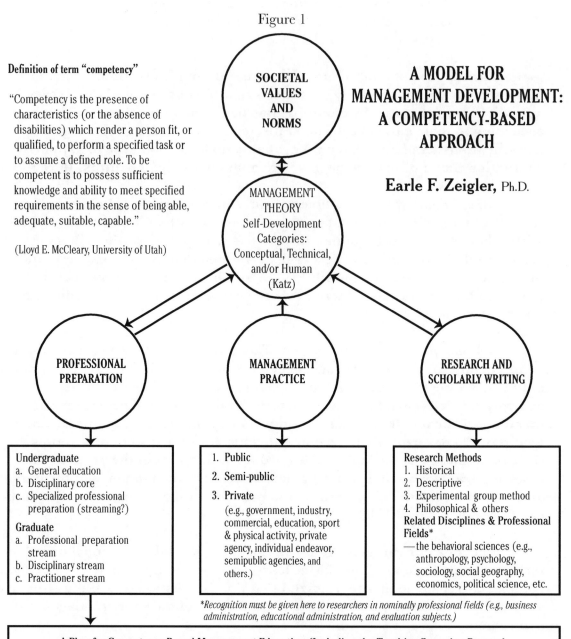

Definition of term "competency"

"Competency is the presence of characteristics (or the absence of disabilities) which render a person fit, or qualified, to perform a specified task or to assume a defined role. To be competent is to possess sufficient knowledge and ability to meet specified requirements in the sense of being able, adequate, suitable, capable."

(Lloyd E. McCleary, University of Utah)

SOCIETAL VALUES AND NORMS

A MODEL FOR MANAGEMENT DEVELOPMENT: A COMPETENCY-BASED APPROACH

Earle F. Zeigler, Ph.D.

MANAGEMENT THEORY Self-Development Categories: Conceptual, Technical, and/or Human (Katz)

PROFESSIONAL PREPARATION

MANAGEMENT PRACTICE

RESEARCH AND SCHOLARLY WRITING

Undergraduate
a. General education
b. Disciplinary core
c. Specialized professional preparation (streaming?)

Graduate
a. Professional preparation stream
b. Disciplinary stream
c. Practitioner stream

1. Public
2. Semi-public
3. Private
   (e.g., government, industry, commercial, education, sport & physical activity, private agency, individual endeavor, semipublic agencies, and others.)

Research Methods
1. Historical
2. Descriptive
3. Experimental group method
4. Philosophical & others
Related Disciplines & Professional Fields*
—the behavioral sciences (e.g., anthropology, psychology, sociology, social geography, economics, political science, etc.

*Recognition must be given here to researchers in nominally professional fields (e.g., business administration, educational administration, and evaluation subjects.)

A Plan for Competency-Based Management Education (Including the Teaching/Learning Process)

1. Ascertain professional functions & needs.
2. Specify competencies (including self-development and those under conceptual, technical, human, and "conjoined" categories).
3. Determine performance levels.
4. Specify program content & instructional, methodology (involving a problem-solving approach in achievement of performance levels: what needs to be known; where obtained; organization of the learning experience; probable results, and others.
5. Identify and evaluate competency attainment.
6. Validate process periodically.

Teaching/Learning Techniques
(e.g., lecture, discussion, case, role-playing, action research, pure and applied research, independent study, debate, computer-assisted or programmed instruction, internship, game theory, panels, forums, and others—depending upon technique's applicability to learning of a competency)

(Adapted from McCleary & McIntyre 1973)

(**Note**: As it happens, these elements also describe
the basic elements of *any* profession earlier; see
Zeigler, 1972.)

indispensable balm or aid to human fulfillment within an individual life
(adapted from Barzun [speaking about art], 1974, p. 12). However, the idea of
"sport and developmental physical activity for all" on a lifelong basis
continues to receive more "lip support" than actual investment based on the
monetary input of government toward overall fitness and physical
recreational involvement for the general population. Yet the logical argument
that--through the process of total psycho-physical involvement--sport
provides highly desirable "flow experience" may well be true. The question is
"for whom does the bell toll?" (Csikszentmihalyi, 1993, p. 183).

The inclusion of "Societal Values & Norms" as an overarching entity in
the model is based on the sociologic theory that the value system (i.e., the
values and the norms) of a culture will be realized eventually within the
society--if all goes well! Values represent the highest echelon of the social
system level of the entire general action system. These values may be
categorized into such "entities" as artistic values, educational values, social
values, sport values, etc. Of course, all types or categories of values must be
values held by personalities. The social values of a particular social system
are those values that are conceived of as representative of the ideal general
character that is desired by those who ultimately hold the power in the
system being described. The most important social values in North America,
for example, have been (1) the rule of law, (2) the socio-structural facilitation
of individual achievement, and (3) the equality of opportunity (Johnson, 1994).

Norms--not to be confused with values--are the shared, sanctioned
rules that govern the second level of the social structure. The average person
finds it difficult to separate in his or her mind the concepts of values and
norms. Keeping in mind the examples of values offered immediately above,
some examples of norms are (1) the institution of private property, (2) private
enterprise, (3) the monogamous, conjugal family, and (4) the separation of
church and state.

Put simply, this means that decisions regarding the development of a
profession are based on the prevailing values and norms over and above any
scientific and/or scholarly evidence that may become available to strengthen
existing theory. Fundamentally, there is a hierarchy of control and
conditioning that operates within the culture that exerts pressure downward
affecting all aspects of the society. (Keep in mind that this pressure may be
exerted upward as well.)

Moving downward from the top of Figure 1, the second phase of the
model is called "Sport Management Theory." This is the systematic

arrangement of proven facts or knowledge about a professional field (or discipline in the case of a subject-matter). From such theory we can also derive assumptions and testable hypotheses that should soon amplify as a result on ongoing scholarship, research, and experience. In the process scholars and researchers will also clarify a developing (and presumably) coherent group of general and specific propositions arranged as ordered generalizations) that can be used as principles of explanation for the phenomena that have been observed. Obviously, any profession must have a sound under girding body of knowledge if it hopes to survive with its professional status fully recognized in society. Unfortunately. at present there is no such inventory of scholarly and research findings about sport management theory readily available for those involved in sport management practice, professional preparation, and research and scholarly writing contributing to disciplinary development.

Moving downward once again, the model now expands both downward and to the right and left so that there is a total of three circles. In a sense these three circles would typically "feed" or "draw" knowledge and information from the middle circle above designated as "Sport Management Theory." Note that there are arrows going backward and forward in all directions to explain necessary "reciprocity" among these entities. These arrows show the complexity of the evolving subject.

The circle on the left is designated as "Professional Preparation." It includes the planned program designed to educate the professional practitioner, the teacher of practitioners, and--arguably--the scholar and/or researcher about the subject of professional preparation. The undergraduate program would presumably include (1) general education, (2) a disciplinary core, and (3) specialized professional preparation (conceivably with streaming possibilities). The graduate program could conceivably contain three distinct streams: (1) a professional-preparation stream; (2) a disciplinary stream. and (3) a practitioner stream.

The second of the three circles alongside each other in the upper half of the model is titled "Sport Management Practice." This would include those professional practitioners with degree programs involving general education, a sport management disciplinary-base, and specialized knowledge about the theory and practice of sport management in the range of public, semipublic, and private agencies and programs involved with varying types of sport and physical activity programs.

The third of the three circles (on the right) has been given the title of "Research and Scholarly Writing." Such research knowledge and scholarly writing is developed on an ongoing basis employing existing research methods and techniques to gather knowledge (i.e. propositions of fact) about the subject of sport management at all levels and under all conditions). Such

162

research and scholarly writing is typically carried out by university professors and qualified professionals wherever employed. Obviously, there has been great--continuing!--help in the past provided by scholars and researchers in related disciplines and professional fields (e.g., the behavioral sciences and business administration).

The Next Step for the Sport Management Profession

Now that we have had a look at where sport management has been, and where it is currently, where should it go from here? The obvious answer would appear to be to build on--i.e., add scholarly sport management literature--to the available inventory of completed research on physical education and athletics management that has been made ready for entry into both departmental and personal data banks and/or retrieval systems by the efforts of scholarly people in the field since the mid-1920s. This historical literature has been delineated and recorded for sport and physical education management.

As it exists, it can be stored in such a way that an ongoing data base can be originated, maintained, and developed. To this should be added as soon as possible the results of investigations reported in the Journal of Sport Management and similar publications worldwide (e.g., the International Journal of Sport Management). This is the bare minimum that should be carried out by someone or some group on behalf of . If completed, when professors or graduate students contemplate further research, they could at least determine what research has already been carried out on the particular topic at hand being considered for further research.

Despite the fact that this embryonic inventory of completed research is now available for easy storage and retrieval in a database, what we have been able to accomplish with this data represents merely a "scratching of the surface." So much more needs to be done by our scholars in sport and related physical activity. Presently, practitioners have been "overwhelmed" by periodical literature, monographs, and books from our field, from the allied professions, and from the related disciplines. Much of this information is interesting and valuable. However, it is so often not geared to the interests of professionals who are fulfilling many duties and responsibilities in the various positions they hold. Also, there is undoubtedly much overlapping material emanating also from the allied professions (notably recreation and park administration). Further, much of the available material--when a person by intent or chance happens to discover it--may be unintelligible, partially understandable, or not available in its essence and in a condensed form to the professional in sport management. Thus, one can only conjecture in what form such information will (or unfortunately won't) be conveyed to the many legislative or advisory boards on whose behalf we are carrying out our endeavor.

To make matters worse, because of provinciality and assorted communication barriers, our field is missing out on important findings now becoming available in Dutch, German, Japanese, Chinese, Italian, and the Scandinavian languages. Further, in addition to the above reason, because of a plethora of rules, regulations, and stipulations, people may not be receiving information about substantive reports of various government agencies at all levels. Such reports should become part of personal and departmental retrieval systems of those carrying out scholarly work in sub-disciplinary and sub-professional areas of investigation.

Interestingly, Joo and Jackson (2002) analyzed scholarly literature that had appeared in the *Journal of Sport Management* since its inception in 1987. Their analysis of 242 articles published showed that, although Trevor Slack's study in 1996 revealed that 65% of the published articles involved the delivery of either physical education or athletics programs, the emphases in research had shifted in the 1990s to marketing studies. More recently, however, there was a move to the area of organizational behavior. The results of research published in the *Journal of Sport Management,* as well as in the more recent *International Journal of Sport Management* should be entered into our bibliography and inventory as soon as possible. These findings should be correlated with studies reported as part of Zeigler's (1995) and Baker's (1983 and 1995) ongoing thesis and dissertation project with Collins and Zarriello, respectively. (Note: Contact author at <zeigrog@axion.net> to have bibliographic data from 1925-1972 downloaded.)

It is true that bibliographies of scholarly publications are occasionally made available. Further, printouts of bibliographies on specific concepts or uniterms can sometimes be purchased commercially. However, a bibliography is just that--a bibliography. Such a listing is typically not annotated to any degree, and one can hardly recall the last time a thorough bibliographical *commentary* on a topic related to sport management has been published.

The Most Important Point: The Need for an Ongoing Inventory. Still further--and this is really the most important point--it can be argued that the profession simply does not know where it stands in regard to the steadily developing body of knowledge in the many sub-disciplinary and sub-professional aspects of sport management (e.g., sport ethics, sport law, sport economics, sport marketing). Our profession--any profession for that matter!--needs such information as an inventory to form the basis--the theory, intellectual "underpinning," evidence, body of knowledge--for an evolving professional (practitioner's) handbook. In our case it would immediately become an essential component of every person's professional practice in the field of sport management. Nowhere does our professionals (and scholars, also) have such a steadily evolving "Inventory of Scholarly,

Scientific Findings Arranged as Ordered Principles or Generalizations" in their hands (and also online) as an ever-evolving professional handbook to help them in their work daily--be they general manager, ticket manager, marketer, athletic director, head coach, management scholar or researcher, or whatever. Such information is obviously vitally important to the professional practitioner who could make use daily of the essence of this proposed "action-theory marriage." If such an inventory were to be made available, the profession should then carry such an inventory forward on a yearly, 2-, 3-, or 5-year basis of renewal for all practitioners in the profession. This deficiency can--and indeed must--be rectified as we move on into the 21st century.

Formulation of an Inventory of Scientific Findings. This recommendation to develop an inventory of scientific findings about sport management would not be unique to this field. Bernard Berelson and Gary Steiner (1964) postulated such an inventory 42 years ago in what they called the behavioral sciences. In their publication, *Human behavior: An inventory of scientific findings*, the editors and associates reported, integrated, assessed, and classified "the results of several decades of the scientific study of human behavior (p. 3). The basic plan of this formidable undertaking is fundamentally sound; thus, many of their ideas concerning format could be employed in the development of a scientific inventory of findings about sport management. Actually, it could well be carried out in all of the world's existing disciplines and then updated at regular intervals on a worldwide basis in one or more agreed-upon languages. Of course, varying emphases and certain significant differences might be introduced, but the basic approach is still valid. Berelson and Steiner summarized their task as the development of "important statements of proper generality for which there is some good amount of scientific evidence" (p. 5).

How the Inventory Would Be Constructed. The type of inventory recommended would develop through the combined effort of people in the various aspects of sport management and related disciplines and professions. The goal would be to present an inventory of knowledge on the subject of sport management--that is, to assess the present state of knowledge and scholarly thought. Thus, those who prepare this information would be writing as reporters and knowledge-integrators, presenting what they know, and what they think they know, based on the available evidence. Every effort would have to be made to avoid presenting what they hope will be known. Down through the years there appear to have been frequent occasions in many professions where this latter approach has been followed, intentionally or otherwise, where people make declarative statements arguing that such thoughts are indeed based on documented evidence.

In such an inventory, the reader would find series of verified findings, principles and/or generalizations in an ordered 1-2-3-4 arrangement, typically with the citation of sources that generated the information. For example, several general theoretical propositions relative to "organizational behavior" could be considered according to several categories from Berelson and Steiner. The following findings about "The Organization," arranged as ordered generalizations, have been extracted from Berelson & Steiner (1964, pp. 365-373):

A1 The larger, the more complex, and the more heterogeneous the society, the greater the number of organizations and associations that exist in it.

    A1,1 Organizations tend to call forth organizations: If people organize on one side of an issue, their opponents will organize on the other side.

    A1.2 There is a tendency for voluntary associations to become more formal.

A2 There is always a tendency for organizations (of a nonprofit character) to turn away, at least partially, from their original goals.

    A2.1 Day-to-day decisions of an organization tend to be taken as commitments and precedents, often beyond the scope for which they were initially intended, and thus they come to affect the character of the organization.

In reporting the available material, the language used should be as free as possible from scientific jargon. It should be understandable to the intelligent layperson and, of course, to professional practitioners in the area of physical activity education management. This would be difficult, because the findings would range from sport marketing to sport ethics to management competencies in a field that includes many areas of specialization. In any case, what would be presented is currently not available elsewhere in this form. This involves more than delineating by descriptive research technique what might be called "sport management literacy" (see, for example, Zeigler [1994] that presents "physical education and sport foundations" from which certain generalizations as explained above might be drawn). This type of inventory would represent a truly significant contribution to the profession of sport management, as well as the public for whose benefit sport is presumed to serve as a social institution.

To clarify this process further, the reader should understand that it may be necessary to select a particular study for inclusion in the inventory from among similar items available in the sport management literature--and also from among studies carried out in closely related fields (e.g., management science) that have a direct bearing on the major topic at hand The knowledge integrator or synthesizer (i.e. a *qualified* analyst) would be looking primarily for theory, findings, principles, generalizations, and propositions that apply to this field (i.e., the management of sport in its various forms worldwide). After accepting a finding for inclusion, it would be necessary to condense it and similar findings to one distinct principle or generalization. Next, the investigator would organize the material into subheadings that could subsequently be arranged in a logical, coherent, descending manner (e.g., Proposition A1, then A1.1, A1,1a, A1.1b, A1,1c, etc., depending upon the complexity of the proposition at hand). Finally, the resultant material would be reviewed and analyzed in order to eliminate certain technical language that might only confuse the majority of professionals for whom the inventory is primarily intended.

The goal of this project would be an inventory representing a distillation of the literature relating to the management of sport in all its forms, one that would communicate what scholars believe is known about the field to those professionals who are not specialists in the specific sub-disciplinary or sub-professional area described. This is not to say, of course, that such an inventory could not be helpful to the specialist in his or her own specialty. Further, to some extent there would at first be reliance on secondary summaries of the available literature, but this should be kept to a minimum. However, such reliance would be necessary because of the great bulk and variety of material. Also, the investigators could obtain the benefit of the evaluative judgment of the specialist who may have originally developed a summary or evaluation. Such material would be temporarily helpful in those instances where gaps in the field's own literature still exist (of which there are undoubtedly many).

Then, too, as more evidence is forthcoming, it would provide a base for improved professional operation as the fundamental and specialized management theory grows broader and deeper. Even then, the scholar, as well as the professional user of the generalized theory, would appreciate the necessity of using some qualifying statements in the development of ordered principles or generalizations (e.g., "under certain circumstances"). This inventory could be made available as an evolving professional handbook on the assumption that a steadily growing body of scientific findings about the management of developmental physical activity in sport and exercise is needed *now* by the many professionals in the field--be they managers, supervisors, teachers, coaches, or researchers in public, semipublic, or private agencies.

How This Inventory Would Be Constructed. The type of inventory recommended would develop through the combined effort of people in sport management, its allied professions, and its related disciplines (those that have any direct or tangential interest in the management of sport). The goal would be to present an inventory of knowledge on the subject of the management of sport and related physical activity--that is, to assess the present state of knowledge and scholarly thought. Thus, those who prepare this information would be writing as Reporters and Integrators presenting (1) what they know and (2) what they think they know based on the available evidence. (As mentioned above, every effort would have to be made to avoid presenting what they hope will be known.)

In such an inventory, the reader would find series of verified findings, principles and/or generalizations in an ordered 1-2-3-4 arrangement, typically with the Citation of Sources that generated the information. For example, the following general theoretical propositions relative to human behavior in managerial situations could be considered according to several categories (as adapted from Berelson and Steiner in the area of small-group research). The following theory relating to the athletic director in a university--that is, assumptions or testable hypotheses--might be included in an inventory:

1. That the manner in which the director of athletics leads his/her program is determined more by existing regulations of the educational institution itself, and the expectations of coaches and staff, than the manager's own personality and character traits.
2. That a director of athletics will find it most difficult to shift the department away from established norms.
3. That a director of athletics will receive gradually increasing support from coaches and staff members to the extent that he/she makes it possible for them to realize their personal goals.
4. That a director of athletics who attempts to employ democratic leadership will experience difficulty in reaching his/her own personal goals for the program if there are a significant number of authoritarian personalities in it (adapted from Berelson & Steiner, pp. 341-346).

Concluding Statement

In offering this perspective to the field of sport management, Daniel Wren's cautionary thought was in my mind. In the epilogue of his outstanding *History of Management Theory and Practice* (2005), he stated: "Management is more than an economic activity, however; it is a conceptual task that must mold resources into a proper alignment with the economic, technological, social, and political facets of its environment. We neglect the 'social facets' at our peril!"

It is these very "social facets" of the enterprise that the field of sport management needs to consider more carefully in the twenty-first century. Sport, as all other social institutions, is inevitably being confronted by the need to become truly responsible. Many troubling and difficult decisions, often ethical in nature, will have to be made as the professor of sport management continues the development of this profession/discipline as it seeks to prepare those who will guide sport in the years ahead. The fundamental question facing the profession is: "What *kind* of sport should the profession promote to help shape what sort of world in the 21st century? Professional sport management societies need to decide to what extent they wish to be involved with all types of sport for all types of people of all ages as they take part in healthful sport and physical activity promoted by public, semipublic, or private agencies.

There is no doubt but that the field of sport management made great strides in the closing years of the twentieth century. Nevertheless I believe that the field--both the profession and its related disciplinary effort--must develop underlying management thought, theory, and practice in an ongoing manner to support its professional practitioners. I stress again that practitioners "on the fire line" daily in sport management should be provided with an evolving inventory of ordered generalizations as to the best ways of carrying out their endeavor.

Finally, whatever decisions are made in regard to the future, we must continue to make all possible efforts to place professional preparation for administrative or managerial leadership within our field on a gradually improving, sound academic basis. The question of leadership confronts us from a number of different directions. Our field, and undoubtedly many others, desperately needs a continuing supply of first-class leaders. Any organization or enterprise soon begins to falter and even to stumble if it doesn't have good leadership. We should maintain our efforts to find more fine people who will take charge in the behaviorally oriented, sport management environment of today's world.

References

Baker, J. A. W., & Collins, M. S. (1983). *Research on administration of physical education and athletics 1971-1982*: A retrieval system. Reseda, CA: Mojave.

Baker, J. A. W. & Zarriello, J. (1995). *A bibliography of completed research and scholarly endeavor relating to management in the allied professions (1980 1990 inclusive)*. Champaign, IL: Stipes.

Barzun, Jacques. *The use and abuse of art*. Princeton: Princeton University Press, 1974, pp. 123-150.

Berelson, B., & Steiner, G. A. (1964). *Human behavior; An inventory of scientific findings*. New York: Harcourt, Brace & World.

Booth, F. W., & Chakravarthy, M. V. (2002). Cost and consequences of sedentary living: New battleground for an old enemy. *Research Digest (PCPFS)*, 3(16), 1-8.

Chalip, L. (2006). Toward a distinctive sport management discipline. *Journal of Sport Management*, 20(1), 1-22.

Corbin, C. B. & Pangrazi, R. P. (2001). Toward a uniform definition of wellness: A commentary. *President's Council on Physical Fitness and Sports Research Digest*, 3, 15, 1-8.

Costa, C. A. (2005). The status and future of sport management: A Delphi study. *Journal of Sport Management*, 19(2), 117-143.

Csikszentmihalyi, M. (1993), *The evolving self: A psychology for the third millennium*. NY: HarperCollins.

Encarta World English Dictionary, The. (1999). NY: St. Martin's Press.

Frisby, W. (2005). The good, the bad, and the ugly. *Journal of Sport Management*, 19(1), 1-12.

Griffiths, D. E. (1959) *Administrative Theory*. NY: Appleton-Century-Crofts.

Hahm, C.H., Beller, J. M., & Stoll, S. K. (1989). *The Hahm-Beller Values Choice Inventory*. Moscow, Idaho: Center for Ethics, The University of Idaho.

Johnson, H. M. (1994). Modern organizations in the Parsonsian theory of action. In A. Farazmand (Ed.), *Modern organizations: Administrative theory in contemporary society* (p. 59). Westport, CT: Praeger.

Joo, J. & Jackson, E. N. (2002). A content analysis of the *Journal of Sport Management*: An analysis of sport management's premier body of knowledge. *Research Quarterly for Exercise and Sport*, 73(1, Suppl.), A111.

Journal of Sport Management. (A special issue of the journal was devoted to the question of sport management research. Dated October, 2005, Vol. 19, No. 4. It was titled "Expanding Horizons: Promoting Critical and Innovative Approaches to the Study of Sport Management".)

Kavussanu, M. & Roberts, G. C. (2001). Moral functioning in sport: An achievement goal perspective. *Journal of Sport and Exercise Psychology*, 23, 37-54.

Lumpkin, A., Stoll, S., & Beller, J. M. (1999). *Sport ethics: Applications for fair play* (2nd ed.). St. Louis, MO: McGraw-Hill.

Malina, R. M.. (2001). Tracking of physical activity across the life span. *Research Digest (PCPFS)*, 3-14, 1-8.

Marx, L. (1990). Does improved technology mean progress? In Teich, A. H. (Ed.), *Technology and the future*. NY: St. Martin's Press.

National Association for Sport and Physical Education. (2001). The coaches code of conduct. *Strategies*, 15(2), 11.

Priest, R. F., Krause, J. V., & Beach, J. (1999). Four-year changes in college athletes' ethical value choices in sports situations. *Research Quarterly for Exercise and Sport*, 70(1), 170-178.

Randolph, E. (2006). The big, fat American kid crisis...And 20 things we should do about it. *The New York Times*. (see:http://select.nytimes.com/2006/05/10/opinion/10talkingpoints.html?pagewanted=all).

Rudd, A., Stoll, S. K., & Beller, J. M. (1999). Measuring moral and social character among a group of Division 1A college athletes, non-athletes, and ROTC military students. *Research Quarterly for Exercise and Sport*, 70 (Suppl. 1), 127.

Sage, G. H. (1998). Sports participation as a builder of character? *The World and I*, 3, 629-641.

Spencer, H. (1949). *Education: intellectual, moral, and physical.* London: Watts.

Steinhaus, A. H. (1952). Principal principles of physical education. In *Proceedings of the College Physical Education Association.* Washington, DC: AAHPER, pp. 5-11.

Stoll, S. K. & Beller, J. M. (1998). *Sport as education: On the edge.* NY: Columbia University Teachers College.

Wilcox, R. C. (1991). Sport and national character: An empirical analysis. *Journal of Comparative Physical Education and Sport.,* XIII(1), 3-27.

Wren, D. A. (2005). *The history of management thought.* NJ: John Wiley & Sons.

Zeigler, E. F. (1972). A model for optimum professional development in a field called "X." In *Proceedings of the First Canadian Symposium on the Philosophy of Sport and Physical Activity.* Ottawa, Canada: Sport Canada Directorate, pp. 16-28.

Zeigler, E. F. & Spaeth, M. J. (1975). *Administrative theory and practice in physical education and athletics.* Englewood Cliffs, NJ: Prentice-Hall.

Zeigler, E. F. (1976). In sport, as in all of life, man should be comprehensible to man. *Journal of the Philosophy of Sport,* III, 121-126

Zeigler, E. F. (ed. & au.). (1994). *Physical education and kinesiology in North America: Professional and scholarly foundations.* Champaign, IL: Stipes.

Zeigler, E. F. (1995). *A selected, annotated bibliography of completed research on management theory and practice in physical education and athletics to 1972 (including a background essay).* Champaign, IL: Stipes.

Zeigler, E. F. (2003). Sport's plight in the postmodern world: Implications for the sport management profession," *International Journal of Sport Management,* 4(2), 93- 109.

Zeigler. E. F. (2005). *History and status of American physical education and educational sport.* Victoria, BC: Trafford.

For Consideration and Discussion

As an exercise at the end of this chapter, it is recommended that two students each make a 10-minute presentation, the first one critiquing the various aspects of the body-of-knowledge taxonomy presented what has been termed sport *management*. The other student should then explain the essence and ramifications of the proposed inventory of social-scientific findings to be developed. Then a third student should conduct a class discussion on the topic in a search for the way and means to bring the project to fruition.

CHAPTER 9

PROFESSIONAL ESSENTIALS:
FROM BITS TO WISDOM
ABOUT
DEVELOPMENTAL PHYSICAL ACTIVITY

Introduction

Present developments in the field of physical activity education have convinced me that the leaders of our professional associations in the United States and Canada should forthrightly ask themselves what the future holds for our field within education. Of course, the answer to this question has great implications for the organizations themselves as well. In this chapter I have put together the results of about 25 years of thought on this topic, a subject on which a number of others have contributed. As I see it currently, if we achieve the specific objectives and the long range aims outlined in this chapter (i.e., how we can best upgrade our profession and the service it is prepared to offer its members), we will have begun to live up to the potential that seems inherent in developmental physical activity in exercise, sport, dance, and play to become a "socially useful servant" designed to improve the quality of people's lives.

The answer seems obvious as to what will happen to the field if it doesn't meet this objective: "Splintering in all directions"! Thus, I believe that the choice is before us right now: either we move ahead steadily and consistently to become a full-fledged, recognized field within education–and elsewhere too, or we will most certainly maintain the present "uneasy role" as a lesser field within the education profession with some of the characteristics of a *trade* with ongoing lesser status within the teaching ranks! In my opinion there is no middle ground.

(There is another issue here that we somehow have never come to grips with: What obligation [opportunity?] do we have in society at large? The people "out there" selling their services as some sort of a "physical activity educator" with a crazy amalgam of titles have never been tallied. Whether we will ever try to incorporate them within our ranks in the 21st century remains to be seen...)

If we choose the "professional enhancement route"--the "from bits to wisdom" approach outlined in this chapter that merges scientific findings with computer technology--as opposed to the present inadequate approach semi-professional and semi-"trade route"–we will most definitely have to re-double our efforts as we "stumble along striving to "put it all together by getting our act together as best possible." There are examples out there for us to follow in regard to what a full-fledged profession should accomplish in society at large. The medical profession comes to mind. Further, we know that fine professional practice can only be built on a sound body of knowledge that is readily available to practitioners.

Emerging fields such as physical activity education (including athletics)--or whatever name we in this field finally decide upon--must continually be aware of the extent to which they have achieved what society demands of a respected field with the profession of education. The now legendary Abraham Flexner (1915) recommended six criteria as being characteristic of a profession, but Bayles (1981) subsequently maintained that there is still no definition of the term that is generally accepted. This latter position appears to be the situation in 2010.

However, Bayles did suggest an approach whereby *necessary* features are indicated along with a number of other common features that would serve to elevate an occupation to professional status. The three necessary aspects or components of a profession that are generally recognized are (1) the need for an extensive period of training. (2) a field where there is a significant intellectual component that must be mastered before the profession is practiced, and (3) a recognition by society that the trained person can provide a basic, important service to its citizens. Right now I believe the "significant intellectual component" (#2 above) needs to be upgraded theoretically *and* practically before "general acceptance" is accorded by society (#3).

I have stressed again the importance of the field of physical activity education's developing a "significant intellectual component that must be mastered before our field is practiced within education." Specifically, then, I am concerned about the body of knowledge that the field does (or does not) have available at the present. I am further concerned about (1) who is developing it; (2) how it is being developed; (3) in what form it is being made available; and (4) how we should be going about providing such knowledge to our professional practitioners. Therefore, proceeding from the general to the specific, I will seek to answer the following questions:

1. What are some of the terms we need to define so as to understand the topic at hand?

2. How has knowledge been communicated historically?

3. How do individual humans gain knowledge?

4. In what form is knowledge available?

5. Where is *our* knowledge (i.e., what we think we know about developmental physical activity in sport, dance, play, and exercise")?

6. What might a knowledge taxonomy for our field look like?

7. How would this taxonomy fit into a proposed model for optimum development in our field?

8. What should this taxonomy of our body of knowledge look like by the year 2025?

9. What other techniques and services do we need to achieve this objective and others demanding attention?

10. Exactly what are ordered principles or generalizations that can be developed from our profession's expanding body of knowledge?

11. Could we implement the plan that is proposed here so that an ever-expanding body of knowledge in our field will result after the establishment of a systems approach?

12. How might we as a profession obtain what appears to be needed to make this plan a reality?

13. Keeping present status in mind, how should we proceed initially as we move toward our eventual goal?

14. What might the future hold for us if we carry out this task successfully?

Definition of Terms

There are a number terms that should be defined for an understanding of the ideas to be included in the following discussion. (Note: They have been gleaned from various sources (e.g., *Dictionary of computing*, 1983) Some terms used here have been employed in earlier chapters, but they are repeated at this point again so that they will be clear to all readers. In addition, since they may typically be used ambiguously at present, certain terms have been given a specific meaning that may needs further clarification. Therefore the following are brief definitions of terms that can be used.

Allied Profession. A profession that is closely related to the field of physical activity education (e.g., health education, recreation).

Bits = acronym (plural) for binary digit (i.e., the binary digit used in the number system most commonly employed in computers; a bit is either 0 or 1).

Data = facts, that which is given.

Developmental Physical Activity in Sport, Exercise, and Related Expressive Movement. A term recommended for what might be called the disciplinary aspect of the profession of sport and physical education by th National Association for Sport and Physical Education of the American Alliance for Health Physical Education, Recreation, and Dance.

Expert Systems = computer programs built for commercial application using the programming techniques of AI (i.e., the product-directed approach to Artificial Intelligence) for problem-solving (e.g., a hypothetical medical expert system for diagnosing liver cancer) (Schank, 1984).

Hypothesis = a theoretical assumption used as a basis for investigation.

Information = information is data (raw facts) placed in context so that it (the information) changes the receiver's perceptions, beliefs, or knowledge base (T. Haggerty).

> Note: Information may be created, transmitted, stored, retrieved, received, copied, processed, or destroyed.

Inventory = a listing, accounting, or catalogue of ideas, facts, things, principles, or generalizations.

Knowledge = facts, truths, or principles resulting from study or scientific investigation.

> Note: Knowledge engineering is the subdiscipline of AI (Artificial Intelligence) concerned with the building of expert systems.

Physical activity education. A term recommended as a replacement for the term "physical education" to describe a subject-matter taught with public and/or private education.

Physical activity and recreation. The term currently used by the American Association for Physical Activity and Recreation within the AAHPERD.

Physical and Health Education. The term used to name the field of study with the system of public education in Canada.

175

Principles or Generalizations (Ordered) = a series of ordered statements or findings in a 1-2-3-4 arrangement (Berelson and Steiner, 1964).

Related Discipline. A field of scholarly endeavor or branch of learning, the findings from which should be employed by professional educators in "physical activity education" as they perform their duties and responsibilities (e.g., physiology, psychology, history).

Sport and physical Education. The term adopted to describe the profession by the National Association for Sport and Physical Education.

Sub–disciplinary Aspects. Those aspects of developmental physical activity (as defined above) that make up a substantive segment of the essential components of the body of knowledge upon which professional practice in physical activity education (including athletics) is based (e.g., the functional effects of physical activity, which some call exercise physiology).

Sub–professional Aspects. Those aspects of developmental physical activity (as defined above) that make up the remaining segment of the essential components of the body of knowledge upon which professional practice in physical activity education (and athletics) is based (e.g., program development, measurement and evaluation).

Systems Approach. For example: A plan designed for the management of an operation or organization that involves the determination of exactly what is to be accomplished and how such an achievement of objectives may be executed successfully. Another definition might be the following: An analysis that stresses the necessity for maintaining the basic elements of input-process-output and for adapting to the larger environment that sustains the organization (Rosenberg, 1978, p. 430).

Taxonomy = a classification into categories based on natural relationships (e.g., chemical elements).

Theory = a systematic arrangement of facts with respect to some real or hypothetical laws (e.g., Einstein's Theory).

Ways That Knowledge Has Been Communicated Historically

In 1970 Asimov warned that a "fourth revolution" in the realm of communications was rapidly occurring within the social development of people on earth. These revolutions in chronological order have been as follows: (1) the invention of speech, (2) the invention of writing, (3) the mechanical reproduction of the printed word, and (4) the development of relay stations in space.

To most of us the idea of relay stations in space seems most beneficent. The eventual result of this advancement means that all people will be confronted with a blanketing communications network that is steadily and increasingly making possible interpersonal relationships hitherto undreamed of by humans. However, Asimov (1970) predicts that this fourth revolution means that a great danger lies before us as well. His point is that we are being well informed about the world's tragic happenings before we have created a "fully cooperative world situation," or at least a situation where some sort of responsible world government has been brought into play. Obviously, this is a factor that must be reckoned with in our quest for the greater dissemination of knowledge.

How Humans Gain Knowledge

More specifically, how do people gain knowledge of any type? For example, how do we "know what we know" about society in general, about the process of education, or specifically about developmental physical activity in sport, exercise, or dance?

Royce (1964) offers considerable insight into this question when he offered a model explaining that throughout history knowledge has been gained in four different ways as follows: (1) thinking (known more formally as rationalism); (2) feeling (or intuitionism), perhaps "intuiting" would be a better term here; (3) sensing (or empiricism); and (4) believing (or authoritarianism.

The Form in Which Knowledge Is Available

Keeping the above four ways in which humans gain knowledge in mind, we should review briefly the actual form in which knowledge is available to us. Keep in mind that knowledge has been defined above as "facts, truths, or principles resulting from study or scientific investigations." Further, a theory is "a systematic arrangement of facts with respect to some real or hypothetical laws," and a hypothesis is a "theoretical assumption used as a basis for investigation."

On this basis, one category might be the "depth," "quality," "intensity," or "power" of the facts or truths provided. Moving from the elementary to the most complex, then, this categorization of the form in which knowledge is available might progress from (1) common sense, (2) informational articles, (3) descriptive studies based on specific concepts, (4) ad hoc theories or hypotheses with a fairly low level of abstraction, (5) "middle range" (Merton) incomplete "segmental" theories, and (6) explicit, complex, grand theories based on a model and a perspective (e.g., Parsonian theory in the discipline of sociology, Marxian theory).

A second category, on a more practical basis for the seeker of knowledge in the form of specific facts or truths (possibly through the use of the computer and an on-line service), would be that made of the actual informational material. Thus the searcher for available knowledge might turn (through the use of a specific on-line service) to (1) a bibliographic listing, (2) an abstract of the item in question, (3) a specific page from the article, or (4) the entire article or publication. Of course, if the listing is not available through an on-line service, then the professional person or investigator will have to go to a library to track down the actual article in a magazine or journal, or possibly in the book or monograph in which it appears.

Where Our Knowledge Is Located

Julius Caesar is purported to have said, "A funny thing happened as I entered the Forum!" Our profession might say today, "A funny thing happened as we left the sheltering umbrella of starting down the path toward our becoming a fully recognized profession!" That "funny thing" is that we simply do not know where we stand in regard to the steadily increasing body of knowledge about "developmental physical activity in sport, exercise, and dance." Like Julius. we too could be 'eliminated!"

Although other established and embryonic professions, may be facing an identical or similar problem, that's their particular worry at this stage of society's development. Our own problem is that our professional practitioners are gradually and increasingly being overwhelmed by information, opinions, and facts available in newspapers, periodicals, monographs, proceedings, and books.

However, although this quantity of material is often interesting, valuable, and occasionally vitally important, it is typically not presented in such a way as to be readily useful to the physical educator/coach as a practitioner. Interestingly, this information and knowledge is also available to us under a great variety of headings through such on-line services as SIRC, SIRLS, ERIC, *The Physical Education Index*, *Sport Dokumentation* (FRG), and now *Sport Search* through Human Kinetics Publishers. Nevertheless, the great questions to be answered are, "What is it? "Where is it? and "Who is using it?" Thus if very few people are availing themselves of this widely dispersed, documented material, we must discover why this is so, and then try to improve the situation.

A Proposed Taxonomy of Knowledge
for Developmental Physical Activity
in Exercise, Sport, and Related Expressive Movement

First, I would like to suggest that we simply must reach some agreement on a proposed taxonomy of knowledge for our field. Reaching consensus will undoubtedly be most difficult; however, it is absolutely essential that we strive for such an objective. A number of years ago, Dr. Laura J. Huelster, late Professor at the University of Illinois, C-U) and I, appreciating fully while yet deploring the rift that was developing in the field between the so-called scholars and the so-called practicing professionals, decided that we would "conjure up" a taxonomy that would included both the "professional" and the scholarly dimensions of our work.

With this thought uppermost in our minds, we decided upon a balanced approach between the sub–disciplinary areas of our field and what might be identified as the sub–professional or concurrent professional components. By this we mean that what many have called scholarly professional writing (e.g., curriculum investigation) will be regarded as scholarly endeavor, just as what many have considered to be scholarly, scientific endeavor (e.g., exercise science) should indeed be regarded as professional writing too (i.e., writing that should ultimately serve the profession).

As part of an effort to close what we regarded as a disturbing and widening rift with the field, we developed a taxonomical table to explain the proposed areas of scholarly study and research using our nomenclature (sport and physical education terms only) along with the accompanying disciplinary and professional aspects. *We agreed upon eight areas of scholarly study and research that are correlated with their respective sub–disciplinary and sub–professional aspects in Table 1 below.* Most importantly, the reader will note that the names selected for the eight areas do not include terms that are currently part of the names of, or the actual names, of other recognized disciplines that are therefore usually identified with these other (related) disciplines primarily by our colleagues and the public (Zeigler, 1982, p. vii)

Our position is that we must promote and develop *our own* discipline of sport and physical education as described above, while at the same time working cooperatively with the related disciplines (to the extent that interest is shown in our problems). We maintain that by continuing to speak of *sociology* of sport, *physiology* of exercise, etc., it will just be a matter of time before these other disciplines and professions awaken to the importance of what we believe to be *our* professional task (i.e., the gathering and dissemination of knowledge about developmental physical activity through the media of sport, dance, play, and exercise, and the promotion of it to the extent that such promulgation is socially desirable. (Such "awakening" is not

Table 1
DEVELOPMENTAL PHYSICAL ACTIVITY IN SPORT, EXERCISE, AND RELATED EXPRESSIVE MOVEMENT

Areas of Scholarly Study & Research	Subdisciplinary Aspects	Subprofessional Aspects
I. BACKGROUND, MEANING, & SIGNFICANCE	-History -Philosophy -International & Comparative Study	-International Relations -Professional Ethics
II. FUNCTIONAL EFFECTS OF PHYSICAL ACTIVITY	-Exercise Physiology -Anthropometry & Body Composition	-Fitness & Health Appraisal -Exercise Therapy
III. SOCIO-CULTURAL & BEHAVIORAL ASPECTS	-Sociology -Economics -Psychology (individ. & social) -Anthropology -Political Science -Geography	-Application of Theory to Practice
IV. MOTOR LEARNING & CONTROL	-Psycho-motor Learning -Physical Growth & Development	-Application of Theory to Practice
V. MECHANICAL & MUSCULAR ANALYSIS OF MOTOR SKILLS	-Biomechanics -Neuro-skeletal Musculature	-Application of Theory to Practice
VI. MANAGEMENT THEORY & PRACTICE	-Management Science -Business Administration	-Application of Theory to Practice
VII. PROGRAM DEVELOPMENT	-Curriculum Studies	-Application of Theory to Practice

(General education; professional preparation; intramural sports and physical recreation; intercollegiate athletics; programs for special populations--e.g., handicapped--including both curriculum and instructional methodology)

VIII. EVALUATION & MEASUREMENT	-Measurement Theory	-Application of Theory to Practice

How a Taxonomy of a Discipline Taxonomy Might Fit Into A Model for Optimum Development of a Field Called "Sport and Physical Education"

Carrying the above recommendation one step farther, we now need to show how such a taxonomy of our profession's body of knowledge might relate to a model that might be employed for the optimum development of the profession. Actually this model could well be employed for development of *any* profession, but in this case it is applied specifically to our field as it is known in the United States; for example, as "sport and physical education" within the National Association for Sport and Physical Education of the American Alliance for Health, Physical Education, Recreation, and Dance. In Canada the professional association is now called PHE Canada. In the schools there it is typically still called "physical and health education," whereas in the universities the designation ranges from physical education to human kinetics or kinesiology. (See Fig. 1 below)

Societal values and norms could well be placed at the top of the model. This is based on the theory that (1) a society's values and norms have a watershed quality, (2) in the final analysis progress will be made toward their achievement, and (3) they exert control and conditioning over the lower levels in the social system as the culture moves gradually and unevenly toward what might be considered progress. Assuming this designation–that the values of a society overarch what appears below–note that the model includes the following subdivisions: (1) an operational philosophy for the profession, (2) a developing theory embodying assumptions and testable hypotheses, (3) professional, semiprofessional, and amateur involvement as practitioners, (4) professional preparation and general education, and (5) scholarly endeavor and disciplinary research.

On top in the model is the overriding philosophy of sport and physical education in a society, or the values according to which the conducts its practice within education. At this level we appreciate that especially in a democracy pluralistic philosophies are allowed to exist (Zeigler, 1977, pp. 7-9).

The second level involves the assumptions and testable hypotheses of a steadily evolving theory--a knowledge base upon which professional practice is predicated and executed. This theory should comprise a coherent group of general and specific propositions that can be used as principles to explain the phenomena observed in human motor performance in sport, dance, play, and exercise.

Figure 1

A Model for Optimum Development of a Field Called "X"

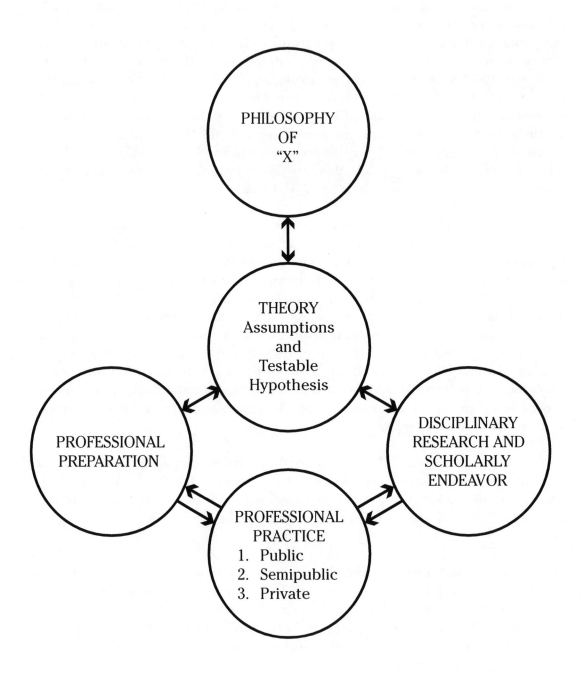

Earle Zeigler, Ph.D.

The third level in the model is depicted as professional, semiprofessional, and "amateur" involvement in the practice of the profession. This is subsumed under the categories of public, semipublic (or semiprivate), and private involvement or practice. To the left of this is the area of professional preparation and general education. Professional preparation should include (1) the performer, (2) teachers/coaches, (3) administrators/supervisors, (4) teachers of teachers/coaches, (5) scholars and researchers, and (6) people in alternative professional careers. So-called general education should now be elevated so that it is regarded as part of a broad liberal arts and science background rather than merely as a "service" course. To achieve this it will be necessary to provide a sound educational experience in the theory and practice of human motor performance in sport, dance, and exercise.

To the right at the fifth level is the area of disciplinary research and scholarly endeavor as explained in Figure 1 above. Once again the reader should note carefully that by the year 2025 we are recommending a complete changeover from the use of the terms belonging to the related fields (e.g., physiology, sociology) to those terms that are solely ours and that will in time help us earn the status that can be rightfully ours (Zeigler, 1982, pp. 39-41).

Other Techniques and Services That Are Needed

"What else is needed other than the development of a sound body of knowledge?" you may ask. Basically, what we need most urgently as well are better ways to actualize our potential first during the periods of professional preparation and thereafter for the rest of our lives. We need improved competency development training in what I have called (1) personal skills, (2) conceptual skills, (3) technical skills, (4) human skills, and (5) conjoined skills (some combination of nos. 2-4 above). I have been particularly concerned that those responsible for management development add a dimension of a laboratory experience in their programs to help university students in this regard (Zeigler and Bowie, 1983b).

Additionally, and most importantly, we need greatly improved and more readily accessible information services. These can be categorized in a fourfold manner, although they are not always discrete or completely distinguishable one from the other as follows:

1. On-Line Services (via a modem and personal computer) for bibliographic data, abstracts, complete articles, etc. (i.e., electronic libraries). Obviously these are already available to us through (for example) SIRC and SIRLS in Canada and ERIC in the United States through Knowledge Index of DIALOG. However, professionals are not yet geared up to use such services because of lack of money, equipment, etc.

2. <u>Electronic Bulletin Boards</u> (via a modem and personal computer, also at all levels--i.e., local, regional, national and--possibly--international). If these were to be developed and become fully operative, professionals could quite easily get the benefit of ongoing dialogue with colleagues at all levels and of varying abilities. Additionally, there should be an opportunity for our professional associations (AAHPERD in the U.S. and CAHPER in Canada to work cooperatively with designated universities insofar as the concept of an 'electronic university' is concerned. Such an arrangement would mean that students could elect credit courses leading to various degrees. Further, in-service courses and clinics could be made available regularly to mature professionals who need assistance and possible upgrading in a variety of degree programs. (At present there is an organization called Electronic University operating out of San Francisco that offers college credit courses through a linkage with some 25 colleges and universities in the United States.)

3. <u>Comprehensive Professional Handbook</u> available to all. Such a handbook would be open-ended and loose-leaf for updating and expansion at 6-month intervals. <u>This handbook would be developed on the basis of ordered principles or generalizations</u> at a nominal cost to members of the leading professional association (e.g., AAHPERD in the USA and CAHPER in Canada), but would also be made available on a sales-for-profit basis to any other interested person.

4. <u>Interactive, Electronic Data Base</u> (from which the Professional Handbook in #3 above is developed). With this service a professional seeking an answer to a problem (urgent or otherwise) could "carry on a conversation with Hal" (remember 2001 and 2010!), and at the present time would be given the best available answer to his/her problem in return at the so-called "making-sense" level.

Here, of course, we are getting into the realm of Artificial Intelligence, or AI, the so-called 5th generation computers. As Schank (1984) tells us, there are three fairly distinct levels of understanding that can be differentiated (i.e., making sense, cognitive understanding, and complete empathy). At the "making sense" level computers can make sense because they are given "rules for how to produce certain outputs on the basis of having processed corresponding inputs" (p. 57). The "cognitive understanding" level is harder because it requires a computer to understand how it comes to a new conclusion about a problem with certain information it has processed. At present some second-level AI programs have been developed, but whether that level can be surpassed (and how we will be certain that progress has been made toward the achievement of "complete empathy")) are problems or questions to which there are no answers currently available (Ibid.). Thus, we need to appreciate that we are probably still years away from AI in the profession of sport and physical education at

184

the second or "cognitive understanding" level. <u>Nevertheless,</u> now is the time to at least begin at the first (making-sense) level.

5. Finally, keeping in mind the potential services available if and when Electronic Bulletin Boards and on-line services become available at <u>all</u> levels, the top-flight practitioner wants and needs <u>wisdom</u> as he or she confronts truly difficult problems in carrying out professional responsibilities and duties. Here we need the opportunity to discuss difficult and intricate problems with specialists in each of the many subdisciplinary and subprofessional aspects of our field. Such specialists would help us to reach the "complete empathy" level that may never be possible with reactive computers functioning at the cognitive understanding level. Of course, each of us must work to develop the required maturity that will afford a modicum of wisdom--the faculty to discern right or truth and to judge or act accordingly based on the advice obtained from specialists.

What Ordered Principles or Generalizations Are

In #3 immediately above where the idea of a professional handbook is discussed, the plan to devise and develop series of ordered generalizations about developmental physical activity in sport, exercise, and related expressive movement available to professionals in the form of a loose-leaf, expandable handbook was recommended. However, we need to answer the question as to exactly what <u>ordered principles or generalizations</u> are.

Ordered principles or generalizations are simply important and verified findings about (1) what we really know, (2) what we nearly know, (3) what we think we know, and (4) what we claim to know. These principles or generalizations are arranged in an ordered, 1-2-3-4 arrangement--<u>and in as plain English as is possible!</u>

As an example, the following findings about "the organization," arranged as <u>ordered</u> principles or generalizations have been extracted from Berelson & Steiner (1964, pp. 365-373):

The Organization.

A1 The larger, the more complex, and the more heterogeneous the society, the greater the number of organizations and associations that exist in it.
A1.1 Organizations tend to call forth organizations: if people organize on one side of an issue, their opponents will organize on the other side.
A1.2 There is a tendency for voluntary organizations to become more formal.
A2 There is always a tendency for an organization (of a non-profit character) to turn away, at least partially, from its original goals.

A2.1 Day-to-day decisions of an organization tend to be taken as commitments and precedents, often beyond the scope for which they were initially intended, and thus come to affect the character of the organization.

A2.1a The very effort to measure organizational efficiency, as well as the nature of the yardstick used, tends to determine organizational procedures.

A3   The larger the organization becomes, the more ranks of personnel there will tend to be within within it.

[Etc.--keeping in mind practical limitations, of course.]

A Plan Leading Toward an Ever-Expanding Body of Knowledge Through the Implementation of a System Approach

To this point an effort has been made to present the "why" and "what" of a proposed inventory of scientific findings covering developmental physical activity as it relates to our field, but now we will discuss the "how" in relation to the way in which this proposed development can be effected. It has been recommended further that such an inventory be based on a revised taxonomy including both the sub–disciplinary and the sub–professional aspects of the profession.

We can appreciate that the first such inventory of ordered principles or generalizations would assuredly have certain gaps or deficiencies caused obviously by our own inadequacy. For example, despite the amazing scope of ERIC (Education Resources Information Center), as one calls its "knowledge" up with almost unbelievable rapidity via a modem through the medium of Knowledge Index of DIALOG, the response seems so meager when one asks for references on sport management. Since we know this is now such a popular subject, we wonder why this is so. The answer is that we used the wrong term; it should have been "administration!" Then when we ask we get a figure like 26,474! The task, then, is to isolate those references that relate to sport and/or physical education, etc. Further, we need to know exactly when the particular on-line service began (i.e., because it reports only studies that were published in sources after a specific date).

The first such inventory that we in our own profession develop primarily for *our own* use would have additional gaps or deficiencies of our own making. There would be no need for apology, however, because such an effort would represent a meager beginning compared to what may be possible in 10, 20, or 50 years. However, this development will not come about unless substantive change occurs in present practice. To this end, a recommendation is being made for the gradual implementation of a systems approach, so that university personnel, professional practitioners in this field, scholars and researchers in other disciplines, and the general public may visualize the scope of the development needed to make available a sound, complete body of knowledge about developmental physical activity. (See Fig. 2 below.) We need this service available in such a way that it can be called up instantaneously--whether it be a bibliographic listing, an abstract, the complete article, or a series of ordered generalizations indicating where this new knowledge coincides or clashes with our present understanding.

Figure 2

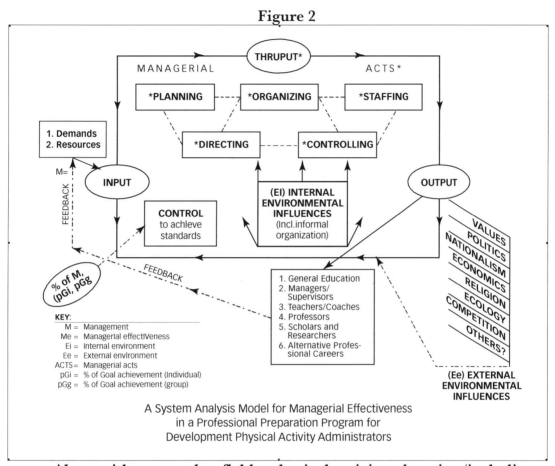

A System Analysis Model for Managerial Effectiveness
in a Professional Preparation Program for
Development Physical Activity Administrators

Along with many other fields, physical activity education (including athletics) does not yet appreciate the need to promote and subsequently implement a "total system" concept. There are many urgent reasons why this field must take a holistic view if the profession hopes to merit increased support in the future. The promotion of this "evolving entity" of developmental physical activity, characterized as it is with so many dynamic, interacting, highly complex components, would require the cooperation of innumerable local, provincial (state), national, and international professional associations so that full support for the <u>total</u> professional effort could be provided.

The model presented here explains how to achieve a common purpose in the development and use of theory and research to achieve managerial effectiveness (Figure 2 above). It explains a system with interrelated components that could be functioning as a unit--admittedly with constraints--

187

execution of such an approach would be complex, the several components of the model being recommended are basically simple. As can be observed from Figure 2, the cycle progresses from *input to thruput to output* and then, after sound consumer reaction is obtained and possible corrective action is taken, moves back to input again (possibly with altered demand or resources) as the cycle is renewed (Zeigler, 1983a, p. 62).

How to Obtain What Appears to Be Needed

Moving to obtain what appears to be needed for our profession is "much easier said than done!" However, I would recommend that AAHPERD in the USA or PHE Canada (or perhaps working cooperatively) should take the lead in promoting this development that could be *coordinated* on a North American scale at first.

A first step that may be difficult, of course, will be the most careful definition of exactly what it is that we do--or have responsibility for--as professional persons. Can we agree, for example, that our task is to employ professionally the application of developmental physical activity in exercise, sport, and related expressive movement with normal, accelerated, and special populations of all ages so as to enhance their quality of life?

Next I believe that we will need advice and financial assistance from governmental or private funding agencies (such as Fitness Canada and Sport Canada at the federal level in Canada and probably private foundations in the USA)--and, of course, also from the appropriate offices offering these services in the various provinces and territories in Canada and educational departments at the various levels in the USA.

It seems self evident further that we will need to work cooperatively with both the Sport Information Resource Centre (SIRC of Fitness and Amateur Sport) and the Sport Information of Recreation and Leisure Studies (SIRLS of the University of Waterloo) in Canada and the Education Resources Information Center (ERIC) in the United States in the development of a complete, on-line data base.

Finally, and this listing is not all inclusive, we could well need cooperation and assistance from selected people in our profession and others in allied and related professions and disciplines in regard to the development of an electronic bulletin board consulting service.

How to Proceed From This Point

How shall we begin right now to implement this plan to help our developing profession obtain sound theory and knowledge to achieve its lofty goals? Some wise person is purported once to have said, "If you want to accomplish something big in this life, do not expect people to roll stones out of your path; in fact, do not be surprised if they heap boulders in your way."

Frankly, at this point I am not looking for stones of any size to be heaped on our path in the years immediately ahead. However, based on past experience, I just know that they are going to be there. The powers that be are simply not going to say "Eureka, you've got it! Here's a million dollars to organize, develop and begin the administration of a plan to make sport and physical education a full-fledged, respected profession. I don't propose to repeat here and now what might be their arguments and rebuttals to any proposals. Further, I would not be the least surprised if we as professionals were to prove to be our own worst enemies as we traverse this rocky path.

Nevertheless, without attempting to enumerate specifically where any stumbling blocks might confront us, I would like to propose four major processes (March and Simon, 1958, pp. 129-131) that could be employed chronologically, as we seek to realize the desired objective as follows:

1. *Problem-solving*: Basically, what is being proposed here is a problem for our profession to solve or resolve. We must move as soon as possible to convince others of the wisdom of moving ahead with this proposal. Part of our approach includes assurance that the objectives are indeed operational (i.e., that their presence or absence can be tested empirically as we progress). In this way, even if sufficient funding were not available--and it well might not be--the various parties who are vital or necessary to the success of the venture would at least have agreed-upon objectives. However, with a professional task of this magnitude, it is quite possible, even probable that such consensus will not be achieved initially.

2. *Persuasion*: For the sake of argument, then, let us assume that our objectives on the way toward the achievement of long range aims are not shared by the others whom we need to convince, people who are either inside our own profession or are in allied professions or related disciplines. On the assumption that the stance of the others is not absolutely fixed or intractable, then this second step of persuasion can (should) be employed on the assumption that *at some level* our objectives will be shared, and that disagreement over sub–goals can be mediated by reference to common goals. (Here we should keep in mind that influencing specific leaders in each of the various "other" associations with which we are seeking to cooperate can be a most effective technique for bringing about attitude change within the larger membership group of each larger association--as recommended by J. J. Jackson.)

Note: If persuasion works, then the parties concerned
can obviously return to the problem-solving level (#1).

189

3. *Bargaining*: We will now move along to the third stage of a theoretical plan on the assumption that the second step (persuasion) didn't fully work either. This means obviously that there is still disagreement over the operational goals proposed at the problem-solving level (the first stage). Now the profession has a difficult decision to make: do we attempt to strike a bargain or do we decide that we simply must "go it alone?"

The problem with the first alternative is that bargaining implies compromise, and compromise means that each group involved will have to surrender a portion of its claim, request, or argument. The second alternative may seem more desirable, but following it may also mean eventual failure in achieving the final, most important objective.

> Note: We can appreciate, of course, that the necessity of proceeding to this stage, and then selecting either of the two alternatives, is obviously much less desirable than settling the matter at either the first or second stages.

4. *Politicking*: The implementation of the fourth stage (or plan of attack) is based on the fact that the proposed action of the first three stages has failed. The participants in the discussion cannot agree in any way about the main issue. It is at this point that the organization (or professional association) involved has to somehow expand the number of parties or groups involved in consideration of the proposed project. The goal, of course, is to attempt to include potential allies so as to improve the chance of achieving the desired final objective. Employing so-called "power politics" is usually tricky, however, and it may indeed backfire upon the group bringing such a maneuver into play. However, this is the way the world (or society) works, and the goal may be well worth the risk or danger involved.

> Note: Obviously, we hope that it will not be necessary to operate at this fourth stage continually in connection with the development of our profession. It would be most divisive in many instances and time consuming as well. Therefore, we would be faced with the decision as to whether this type of operation would do more harm than good (in the immediate future at least).

In this chapter I have argued that the evolving field of physical activity education should develop a revised taxonomy of developmental physical activity in exercise, sport, and related expressive movement as soon as possible. Second, because developments of the past 25 years in our "allied professions and related disciplines" have exceeded our field's capability to assimilate the scientific findings that have accumulated, physical activity educators should plan to develop an inventory of scientific findings arranged as verified, ordered principles or generalizations. Third, to effect the development of an inventory *before others carry out the field's task for it*, it is recommended that the field implement a systems approach on the North American continent at least. Finally, it is recommended that the evolving field of physical activity education mount an all-out effort to reverse the present trend toward dispersion of the "allied professions and the sub–disciplinary areas of scholarly study and research.

At present the field is hampered immeasurably by a lack of focus on its unique mission. This continues the prevailing confusion and vitiates the field's overall effect. In addition, it causes confusion for those in "the allied professions, the related disciplines, and the general public." (They see gaps to be filled, and they are moving steadily to fill those cracks and crevices-- primarily those that will meet the needs and interests of the public at large outside of the educational system.) Our field to fulfill its role best must focus on developmental *physical* activity for the accelerated, the normal, and the exceptional or special populations of all ages. Working in this direction will help the field's focus to become sharpened. Concurrently we will be able to continue efforts to coordinate the efforts of the many splinter groups now often working at cross-purposes with poor or non-existent inter-group communication.

The prevailing system of providing service to people of all ages and abilities can only be realized if the sub–disciplinary and sub–professional inputs are sufficient and timely. Further, the entire field (i.e., professional educators and professional physical activity educators in the public sector) can prosper *only if* a satisfied public rewards it with a continuing demand for services--and accordingly provides the necessary funding for the delivery of such services. In the following chapter, I will explain how the inventory of scientific findings as explained here could fit into a broader scheme whereby the entire field's ability to serve effectively and efficiently could be raised to a new level hitherto undreamed of. If the physical activity education does not make the efforts explained in this chapter, such a golden opportunity many never present itself again.

What the Future Holds for the Profession
If It Achieves Its Desired Objective

In this presentation we have discussed the means whereby the sport and physical education field could move to obtain an ever-expanding body of knowledge based on ordered principles, and how our United States and Canadian professional associations (AAHPERD & CAHPER) could right now take the lead nationally and internationally by moving steadily ahead toward the achievement of this objective. I truly believe that our field could become a leading profession according to all recognized standards.

Penultimately, may I suggest that you think ahead a bit to the year 2050--a year when we will almost all be memories in someone's mind. When we are dead and gone, history will have recorded the answers to the following questions:

1. In the late 20th century were the professional organizations known as the American Alliance for Health, Physical Education, Recreation, and Dance <u>and</u> the Canadian Association for Health, Physical Education, and Recreation (l'ACSEPL) able to achieve a focus about their unique mission?

2. If the answer to Question #1 is "yes," were professionals in the field able to coordinate the efforts of the many splinter groups in both countries often working at cross purposes to achieve the profession's avowed goals?

3. If the answers to Question #1 and #2 are "yes," did the profession, the federal governments, and the various states, provinces ,territories, and commonwealths work cooperatively in this endeavor?

4. If the above questions can be answered affirmatively, did the profession and others concerned employ a systems approach to develop an inventory of ordered scientific findings about the possible role of developmental physical activitry in improving the quality of people's lives?

5. If the answers are still affirmative, did this body of knowledge arranged as ordered principles or generalizations continue to grow? Further, was it gradually made readily available on an "interactive data" basis to practitioners seeking to serve Americans and Canadians of all ages through the medium of developmental physical activity?

6. Assuming affirmative answers above, did a satisfied public truly recognize the importance of the profession and reward it with a continuing demand for high-level services?

Concluding Statement

The large majority of professionals in the field of physical activity education (including athletics) (or whatever we eventually decide to call ourselves) will need to agree that the time is obviously ripe for this vital development described here. The opportunity to achieve such a fine, purposeful goal of solid professional status lies before us right now. If we lay the proper foundation in the years immediately ahead, the answers to the six questions delineated above can indeed all be "Yes"--strongly in the affirmative!

References and Bibliography

Asimov, I. (1970). The fourth revolution. *Saturday Review*, Oct. 24, 17-20.

Bayles, M.B. (1981). *Professional ethics*. Belmont, CA: Wadsworth.

Berelson, B. & Steiner, G. (1964). *Human behavior: An inventory of scientific findings*. NY: Harcourt, Brace and World, pp. 365-373.

Dictionary of computing. (1983). NY: Oxford.

Flexner, A. (1915). Is social work a profession? In *Proceedings of the National Conference on Charities and Correction*. Chicago, IL: Hildmann, pp. 578-581.

Haggerty, T. His interpretations and definitions for selected terms used.

March, J.G. & H.A. Simon. (1958). *Organizations*. New York: Wiley.

Research Council of the American Association for Health, Physical Education, and Recreation. (1960). The contributions of physical activity to human well-being. *Research Quarterly*, 31, 2, 261-375.

Rosenberg, J.M. (1978). *Dictionary of business and management*. New York: Wiley.

Royce, J.R. (1964). Paths to knowledge. In *The Encapsulated Man*. Princeton, NJ: Van Nostrand.

Zeigler, E.F. (Ed.) (1982). *Physical education and sport: An introduction*. Philadelphia: Lea & Febiger.

Zeigler, E.F. (1983a). Relating a proposed taxonomy of sport and developmental physical activity to a planned inventory of scientific findings. *Quest*, 35, 54-65.

Zeigler, E.F. & Bowie, G.W. (1983b). *Developing management competency in sport and physical education*. Philadelphia: Lea & Febiger.

Zeigler, E. F. (1979). The past, present, and recommended future development in physical education and sport in North America. In *Proceedings of The American Academy of Physical Education* (G.M. Scott (Ed.), Washington, DC: The American Alliance for Health, Physical Education, Recreation, and Dance.

Zeigler, E. F. (1980). A systems approach to the development and use of theory and research in sport and physical education. *Sportwissenschaft*, 10, 4, 404-416.

For Consideration and Discussion

As an exercise at the end of this chapter, it is recommended that two students each make a 10-minute presentation, the first one critiquing the various aspects of the taxonomy recommended for developmental physical activity. The other student should then differentiate precisely how this differs from the sport management taxonomy proposed in the previous chapter. Then a third student should conduct a class discussion on the topic in a search for the way and means to bring the project to fruition in a way that can serve the best interests of both groups concerned (i.e., those concerned primarily with sport management and those whose interest is primarily developmental physical activity.

CHAPTER 10

CHANGE PROCESS THEORY AND TECHNIQUE

(Note: This chapter was developed from *Change process in sport and physical education management* by E. F. Zeigler, A. Mikalachki, and G.A. Leyshon. Champaign, IL: Stipes Publishing Company, 1988.)

Introduction

The idea of change is now as firmly entrenched in our North American society as is the presumably unchanging presence of death and taxes. Some people go so far as to say that an organization simply must change or it will gradually wither and die. This may or may not be true, but the very idea of "change for change's sake" makes a person stop and take stock of what is happening. If he or she says, "I agree with change because it will help me and my organization keep up with the times--and also help me to continue to progress!" Then that is the ideal--that is, we change because we believe it will help us progress or "make progress" in some way.

However, what does the concept of "progress" mean? Does it mean that our organization is getting bigger, or better, of faster, or more profitable, or more adaptable, or whatever? We are often aware that some sort of progression has taken place, but is this true "progress?" To answer this question affirmatively, we have to ask ourselves if we have determined a criterion by which progress may be judged. Also, it is a bit presumptuous on our part to assume that we can be both "judge and jury" in this connection. What we are saying is that it may well be an acceptable <u>human</u> criterion of progress that we are using to measure what we hold to be an improvement over a previous state or condition. Change made on the basis of a possibly limited criterion must always be viewed with some skepticism.

In the consideration of social change within a social system, Parsons distinguishes, for example, among three levels of analysis: (1) circular flow that treats the process of interchange processes with a social structure as stable typically; (2) the analysis of growth and/or decline in the various outputs of a system (e.g., the effectiveness of goal attainment); and (3) so-called structural change that can take place at the lower levels of the system without changing the uppermost level, that of values itself. Of course, if the strain at the lower levels is too great, actual social revolution may distort the "normal" control and conditioning process to such an extent that finally a new set of values results.

Admittedly, the management of change is still more of an art than a social science. Nevertheless, we should be developing principles viewed as "currently useful generalizations" that are shared to help us meet the changing conditions with which we are seemingly inevitably confronted. They could be viewed as hypotheses that are tentatively accepted as empirical evidence is being gathered. The literature on change can be divided usefully into two categories--social or societal change and organizational change.

Organizational change that occurred in business history indicates that most firms early in the twentieth century did not manage change themselves. On the contrary, change occurred in the external environment, and this forced most of them to adapt their business strategy to cope with the developing situation. This resulted subsequently in a change of the internal environment of the organization from the standpoint of system <u>input</u> and <u>thruput</u>. In the second half of the 20th century, however, the quickening pace of environmental change any period of grace providing substantive "lag time adaptation" has forced companies to develop the ability to "manage change" themselves--if they hope to survive! Thus, in this recent turbulent environment, planning for changes and/or innovation has become ever so much more urgent because a company often cannot wait for the internal structure to change itself even after it has become obvious that a change in strategy *must* be made.

Keeping the history of management thought, theory, and practice in mind, we should realize that planned changes have taken place in organizations when the hierarchy of social control and conditioning was placed under strain for one or more reasons. Also, the increasing complexity of society has meant that earlier management thought has gradually been supplemented by a social science approach to management theory and practice. Within this environment, the managing of planned, significant organizational change has become more important each decade of this century. Further, there is no reason to assume that the importance of the "change factor" will diminish in the twenty-first century!

What appears to be new in recent decades is the rapidity of change. We have been told that this is a century of transition, but we are only now in sport and physical education beginning to appreciate this advice. It is our position that the speed with which changes must be made now seriously affects the decision-making effectiveness of managers. Further, the increasing stress has undoubtedly left its mark on the health of many managers.

Although in the field of education there has been a strong trend toward "management by committee," we are nevertheless being forced by rapidly changing conditions (including deficits and imposed budget-cutting) to consider what has come to be called "crisis management." Situations are occurring in which administrators soon realize that hasty decisions, often imposed from "on high," will drastically affect both the short- and long-range goals of the organization and its units and thereby also threaten the professional and personal values held by personnel at different levels. Because many of these decisions must be made almost immediately, or in short time periods, the manager is resultantly faced with "indigestible" quantities of information presumably to justify unpopular mandates and decisions legislated either at the political level and/or mandated by the governing board and higher administration.

Decisions accordingly passed on by superiors to middle managers under crisis conditions tend to be arbitrary. There is a tendency to present one-sided information as well as gloss over the unpleasant aspects of the situation. Whether the manager appreciates it or not, the process of decision-making under pressure, and the often questionable quality of such decisions, places the manager under considerable stress. Thus, it is very important for "managerial survival" that a process of decision-making for the management of change be developed, one that will both reduce the attendant stress on the parties concerned and improve the quality of the decisions.

Whatever the case may be, times and conditions are changing continually and continuously. As sport and physical education managers we should be aware of such change, how to recognize the need for it, how to plan for it theoretically, and how to work with our associates so that desirable change (progress?) will occur with a minimum of disruption to prevailing human relations in our organization. (This is assuming that such interpersonal relationships are sound and healthy.)

Thus, we are not concerned here with evolutionary change that may occur over a period of years. Instead we will consider briefly the deliberate, conscious acts of managers of organizations, or any person or combination of people within the unit, seeking to alter organizational practices from the present condition to a desired state--a development that will presumably represent a definite improvement. More specifically, we will be primarily concerned with reasonably significant change--that is, altering practices or goals from Situation A to Situation non-A, rather than from Situation A to Situation A1 or Situation A2 (or the like). Of course, the extent of change that is considered significant is a value judgment in the final analysis.

In this present discussion we are concerned with the analysis of change *within* organizations primarily, and only secondarily from the standpoint of the larger social system. This means that the selection of possible alternatives for action or change is influenced strongly by the leading values held by the controllers of the organization itself--values that may be differentiated from the societal value system in favor of the organization's avowed purpose for itself within that society. Thus, in a business firm, we clearly have an organization with economic primacy. Yet it can well be that further distinctions can be made within this category of organization to allow

196

for certain specialization in the "functional imperatives" or problems of the several action systems. These functional imperatives are (1) pattern maintenance, (2) adaptation, (3) goal-attainment, and (4) integration. Accordingly, even though educational institutions that are tax supported are typically directed to pattern-maintenance goals, there is also the need for a certain amount of specialization in the remaining three functional imperatives.

Keeping the above in mind, then, organizational change in the field of sport and physical education involves the introduction of some sort of a change process into the system that will result eventually in the improvement of the product at the output stage. Such improvement could range from the slight to the momentous in nature, but the goal for the manager is by definition a more desirable state of affairs. Such organizational change is generally planned and implemented by internal personnel who are committed to the organization's survival--to the preservation of viability in a rapidly changing social climate.

Attitudinal Blocks Affecting Change.

Our analysis of the historical development of management theory <u>and</u> practice in North America has shown that progress in this area began originally in business and the related social sciences; started to develop within the field of educational administration (as related to public education) in the late 1940s; and finally began to emerge within professional preparation for physical education and sport in the 1960s. On this basis our tentative hypothesis is that interest in, and knowledge about, managing organizational change will progress in roughly the same sequence.

We have noted further that North American managers, whether in business, educational administration, of sport and physical education management, seem to possess some attitudinal blocks that inhibit managing change effectively. Possibly the major obstacle in this regard has been the managers' high orientation to rapid action based on inadequate analysis of the prevailing situation and its many ramifications. Such premature action is frequently ineffective, and thus requires further analysis resulting in a second type of response. Such a pattern of response usually results in less effectiveness and lowered efficiency.

Conversely, it has been observed that Japanese managers in business organizations make an interesting comparison to their North American counterparts. (We do not have the facts in regard to educational administration or our own field.) The Japanese appear to devote boundless energy and a great deal of time on analysis--and then implement their decisions practically overnight! Typically the analysis time is used to promote the involvement of a large range of people in the decision-making process (i.e., all of those who will be affected in some significant way by the proposed change). Once everyone is aware of the planned innovation and appears to be committed to it to a reasonable extent, then the "overnight" implementation goes into high gear. Conversely, there is some evidence that the opposite occurs often in North America: managers over here have tended to carry out overnight analyses and then spend endless time on implementation. This is an obvious exaggeration, of course, but there is sufficient truth in the statement to have it strike home with most of us.

What does the above information tell us? It says that, even though we understand that the rate of change in society seems to be increasing, we must nevertheless provide a sufficient amount of time to analyze the existing state carefully. Secondly, we believe that such careful examination of proposed changes by all those who would be definitely affected by such innovation develops commitment if it turns out that the proposed venture or change is acted upon. The argument that there may not be sufficient time to get everyone involved is often difficult to refute. However, we can only repeat the assertion that too hasty action will result in ineffectiveness and inefficiency. Also, the remedial efforts required to straighten out the ensuing situation may well be more time-consuming and costly in the final analysis than earlier deliberate, slower action. Keep in mind further that an organization cannot be changed significantly overnight because the underlying psychological readiness for change may develop only slowly after the actual physical changes involved have been implemented. This is true regardless of whether there are myriad problems that require attention or only a few. Such will often be true even though most people involved understand that overall costs can be reduced significantly when the planned organizational change occurs.

Another important obstacle to change is the usually prevailing view that explicit theories may sound good, but that they are often impractical in on-the-job situations. Thus, whether we are talking about business, educational administration, or physical activity education (including athletics) management, there is a strong tendency to distrust and even fear theory. Because of this, there is no reason to believe that we will very soon witness the departure from the scene of managers who want to operate "off the top of their heads" or the "seats of their pants." This will be true even though in mid-20th century Kurt Lewin and many others since that time stated: "there is nothing as practical as a good theory." We agree strongly with this assertion. Actually, there is little that anyone does that is not founded on either implicit or explicit theory; we are simply as humans "constructed" that way! However, we definitely believe that it is important for managers to make their theories of organizational change explicit. They should be placed before concerned colleagues who can examine and discuss them. In that way we should strengthen and improve our theories of change. Also, we will understand better why certain processes and innovations worked, and why others did not achieve success. So now, before we offer a model or framework for the management of change, we will continue by first presenting a brief analysis of those factors that in the past have contributed to high or low success in organizational change.

Factors Contributing to High and Low Success in Organizational Change.

Much of the research that has been conducted on the management of organizational change has taken place in so-called blue-collar settings. Here the change dealt mainly with altering the way actual work was done. However, in the white-collar settings where investigations were carried out, the changes were related more to structural changes in the organization itself and these were concerned primarily with the setting of new goals and strategies.

High Success Factors.

In successful changes, top management and the group involved in analyzing the situation participate together in developing alternatives and implementing the changes. The participation of top management ensures that the change is recognized as important and that those responsible for implementing the change have the required formal authority. The involvement of those who will have to behave differently if the change is to be accomplished, the target group in the change process, facilitates their commitment to the change and to carrying out their new responsibilities. In other words, successful change requires the participation of those who will be managing and operating the changed structure.

Change tends to be more successful when the organization has problems or is facing pressures in its task environment. Where technologic changes or changed consumer demands affect an organization's performance, the personnel is more amenable to organizational change. An organization must be adapted to its task environment if it is to survive. Organizational change is more successfully accomplished when the personnel are able to perceive a lack of such adaptation to the environment.

Understanding the effects of the change promotes success. Changes that address day-to-day problems and hold out the prospect of solving these problems tend to be successful. It is also important to be aware of the indirect effects of the change on other parts of the organization, the ripple effect. When the ripple effect is anticipated and dealt with "up front," change tends to be more successful.

Finally, changes are more successful when those proposing the change are flexible and open to new ideas. The successful manager avoids the trap of feeling obliged to prove that the change, as originally conceived, will be successful. Rather, he follows a general plan but modifies it at various points to take into account useful inputs. In addition, those proposing the change must be prepared to abandon it if--when it is tried out for a reasonable period--it does not prove to have been a wise and useful change in practice.

Low Success Factors.

Managing a change by unilateral action has proved to be unsuccessful. The "now hear this" approach tends to generate resistance among those who will have to enact the change. The attitude that "making a particular change arbitrarily is the prerogative of management" is reversed by withholding of support or other overt resistance by the target group.

Delegated action fares no better than unilateral action. In delegated action, top management's participation and commitment is unclear. The target group, which may be favorably disposed to the change, doubts whether the change is really important and whether it will ultimately receive top management's sanction. A target group, which views the proposed change negatively, simply resists it with no concern about top management's pressures.

Changes in which the managers have no general model guiding the change also prove unsuccessful. The lack of a general model contributes more confusion to an already ambiguous situation. With no anticipation of difficult periods and no general plan as to how these difficulties are to be handled, the anxiety of those involved reaches a level that makes everyone impotent. The lack of a general model also generates a lack of confidence in the change agents on the part of the target group.

A "from-on-high-appointed" task force report has also proved to be unsuccessful. When an isolated task force analyzes the situation and recommends changes, those in the task force are generally not the ones who will be responsible for bringing about or operating in the changed state being recommended. The target group is used as a resource (e.g., for information), but is not significantly involved in the study. This approach generally collapses during implementation when the target group's lack of commitment results in alteration or complete abandonment of the proposed changes.

In summary, when the need for change is not perceived by the target group, it is difficult to change an existing situation. The need for changes has probably arisen either because of external, environmental pressures requiring an organizational re-adaptation or because of internal difficulties in managing the organization. In either situation, if the target group is not fully aware of the external pressures or internal difficulties, or does not believe that the proposed change is appropriate, it will not fully involve itself in and truly commit itself to the change.

Change Plan for Organizational Change.

The change plan should focus heavily on the way in which the new system is introduced. A good plan takes into account the potential contributions the target group can make to the new system, as well as how the new system will benefit or otherwise affect target-group members. The objective should be to introduce the change in a manner that minimizes the costs and maximizes the gains to the target group. It should be recognized, however, that the best of implementations result in a new cost for some people. Seldom do all of the affected people in a major change experience a net gain.

Generally, a major change plan takes into account three phases. The *appraisal phase* examines the target group's readiness to become involved in the change process. In the *transition phase*, members of the target group adopt changes in behavior in connection with the changes. In the *continuation phase*, the new behavior should become a part of the on-going structure and behavioral patterns of the organization. The focus of attention in all three phases is the target group. Without a change in behavior by members of this group, there will be no successful change (see Fig. 1 below).

Appraisal Phase. Implementing a change will have the effect of altering significant behavior. Whenever existing relationships, roles, and rewards are changed, considerable tension, anxiety, and resistance will be generated. There is a degree of comfort and stability in following established patterns. Any significant change disrupts the existing stability and is resisted by virtually all parties. This is particularly so if the need for change is not perceived by the parties affected. Under such circumstances, the question, "What is wrong with the way we are doing things now?" is asked time and again by all affected parties. So what is needed for the introduction of a change is a change plan that minimizes resistance; however, no matter how carefully such a plan is presented, there is seemingly no plan that can eliminate all resistance.

The first step in introducing change is to appraise the organization's readiness for change. A field force analysis (Fordyce & Weil, 1979) takes into account the key factors relevant to the change. It looks at the factors conducive to the change as well as those obstructing the change. For any organization, there are unique or situation-specific factors that cannot be anticipated in a general approach to analyzing the readiness for change; however, some of the key factors that should be general to all organizations are diagrammed below (see Fig. 2 below)

FIGURE 1

CHANGING TO A NEW BEHAVIOUR

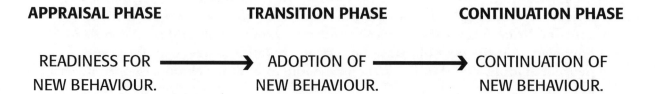

APPRAISAL PHASE	TRANSITION PHASE	CONTINUATION PHASE
READINESS FOR NEW BEHAVIOUR.	→ ADOPTION OF NEW BEHAVIOUR.	→ CONTINUATION OF NEW BEHAVIOUR.

FIGURE 2

APPRAISING THE READINESS FOR CHANGE

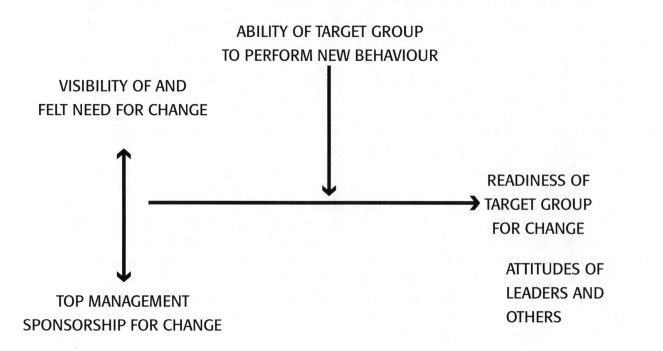

ABILITY OF TARGET GROUP TO PERFORM NEW BEHAVIOUR

VISIBILITY OF AND FELT NEED FOR CHANGE

READINESS OF TARGET GROUP FOR CHANGE

ATTITUDES OF LEADERS AND OTHERS

TOP MANAGEMENT SPONSORSHIP FOR CHANGE

202

Probably the most important stimulus for change is the degree to which the *need for* change is perceived by the target group. If members of the target group do not perceive a problem, it is unlikely they will alter their activities to make a change effective. Therefore, the most critical action step is to establish the need for change (see Fig. 3 below). Until that need is clear to the target group, action is likely to prove ineffectual.

Another key factor is the degree to which top management is prepared to support the change. Does top management recognize the need for a new system? Are they prepared to visibly support such a system? Organization members tend to take their cues of what is important from top management. Conditions in which a number of top managers speak with one voice in support of the change will significantly stimulate acceptance of a new program. Conversely, conditions in which power group members (i.e., top management, governing board, etc.) disagree or are indifferent as to what should be done, usually impede major change programs. Because top management can severely undermine a change, assessing the support or sponsorship of this group is vitally important.

It is also necessary to determine whether the target group members have the knowledge, skills, and aptitudes to deal with the changed state if it were instituted. It is useless to institute a system which the target group is not trained to operate and manage. The proposed change must be such that the target group's attitudes will be favorable; so, this means that the group's members must see some benefit accruing to them. Finally, other appropriate bodies, such as unions, teachers federations, coaches organizations, and other parent groups, must be contacted and fully informed in an effort to enlist their understanding and cooperation.

Transition Phase. As explained above, the adoption of a change depends on the willingness and ability of the members of the target group to behave in a manner that will ensure its success (see Fig. 4 below). There is no question but that a change will alter relationships, roles, and rewards within the organization. For some, after the changeover, the new roles, relationships, and rewards will be more costly than the existing system (i.e., more costs than benefits). The recognition of this fact generates a significant degree of resistance. On the other hand, those who see the new state and accompanying pattern of behavior as leading to valued pay-offs; they like it! For example, if a manager can envision improved productivity because of the change, and consequently improved performance, reduced tension, and increased personal merit reward, such potential pay-offs are almost certain to induce him or her to value the change.

FIGURE 3

ADOPTION OF NEW BEHAVIOUR

LEARNING PROCESS
- COST OF CHANGE
- CREDIBILITY OF CHANGE
  ADVOCATES
  - NUMBER OF ADVOCATES
  - CONGRUENCE OF ADVOCATES
  - IDENTIFICATION OF ADVOCATES

COMMITMENT PROCESS
- PARTICIPATION
- FREEDOM TO SELECT
  NEW BEHAVIOUR
- EXPLICIT STATEMENTS

TRAINING

**NEW BEHAVIOUR MUST
BE VIEWED AS LEADING
TO VALUES PAYOFF**

**ADOPTION OF
NEW BEHAVIOUR**

**ABILITY TO PERFORM
NEW BEHAVIOUR**

The two processes that contribute to the target group viewing the changes as leading to valued pay-offs are (1) the learning process and (2) the commitment process. These two processes should involve members of the target group by educating them about the costs or disadvantages of the current system and by involving them in developing an appropriate action plan. There are two key assumptions regarding efficacy of the learning and commitment processes: (1) any conscientious manager(s) exposed to the present problem will recognize the importance of a change, and (2) one or more managers and close associates, sharing the same information, will develop a useful solution. Given these assumptions, the benefit of target group participation is obvious and will increase commitment to the plan by those who will be implementing it (see Fig. 4 below)

It is self evident that there would be a strong relationship between participation in developing and designing a program and having a strong commitment to it. When individuals have exercised freedom in choosing a new behavior, they are more likely to accept that behavior. Also, *openly declaring* such acceptance results in an even stronger sense of commitment. An open, freely given declaration induces persons to behave in a manner consistent with that behavior.

It is very important, of course, that those responsible for designing and implementing a change are able to do so--that is, that they have the knowledge, competencies, and skills to collect and organize the data, interpret it, and then take remedial where necessary. Making sure that they have these skills may require instituting a training program to facilitate the commitment process. Organizations that do not involve lower-level management in the decision-making process (so-called top-down organizations) will need some training to establish an improved decision-making pattern. This training may require an outside change agent to facilitate group decision-making processes. Outside change agents that are looked upon favorably can help in developing group-consensus, decision-making patterns.

Continuation Phase. Once the behavior patterns are established to the extent that a new system seems to be progressing to a reasonable extent–but not yet to the point where it will be judged successful–it is vital to take steps to ensure that the new system will persist. The continuation phase is aimed, therefore, at institutionalizing the new system so that it will eventually achieve permanency. To do so, the new system must gradually but steadily become an integral or regular part of the existing administrative system that is functioning on an overall basis. (See Figure 4 below.)

FIGURE 4

CONTINUATION OF NEW BEHAVIOUR

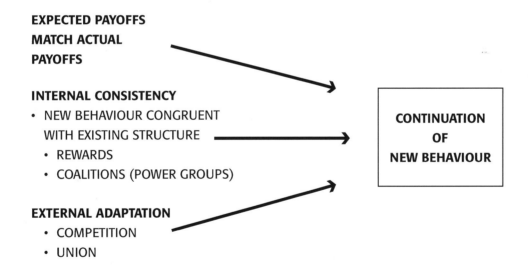

As explained immediately above, the actual pay-offs must match people's expectations. Managers using the new system must be able to deal with problems more effectively. Of course, poor data and insufficient support from higher management could easily nullify the manager's effectiveness and diminish the probability that the change will continue.

205

Concluding Statement

In summary, each organization is unique, and a rigid, detailed change plan may well not work. The change plan must emerge through a process involving many participants. The plan must be general, with flexibility to respond to unexpected resistances, and it must involve the target group heavily. If the change pattern "begins to stumble." the target group should be given the opportunity to recommend modifications. Such modification could well set entire process back on track again.

For Consideration and Discussion

As an exercise at the end of this chapter, it is recommended that two students each make a 10-minute presentation, the first one explaining theoretically the various phases of a plan for change. The other student should then recommend a specific plan to bring about the institution of a comprehensive intramural sports program for boys and girls at a high school where presently there is only a varsity sports program. Then a third student should conduct a class discussion on the topic in a search for the way and means to bring such a project to fruition in a way that can serve the best interests of both groups concerned (i.e., those concerned primarily with varsity sport and those whose interest is primarily intramural sports for all.

CHAPTER 11

A MARKETING ORIENTATION FOR
AN ATHLETIC/RECREATION PROGRAM

(John T. Campbell, M.A., Toronto, ON, Canada is co-author)

Introduction

All North American enterprises faced what has been called a "quality imperative" in the final quarter of the 20th century. The same idea is still paramount today in the face of a recession coupled with increasing global competition. Doing business is simply radically different from the past when customers could be taken for granted. In a global marketplace where quality is the watchword of competition, business needs to rededicate itself to excellence by world standards..

Similarly, all administrators/managers of athletic/physical recreation programs were forced to consider a revised marketing orientation, a whole new set of postulates for them to accept or reject. Competitive athletics and physical recreation and intramurals--all recreation for that matter--have typically been regarded as extra-curricular. A small percentage of people would be willing to accord them co-curricular status. Moreover, an even smaller percentage would accord them curricular status *if* certain conditions prevailed. We fall into this latter category.

Accordingly, our belief does not rest with those who believe that so-called educational athletics and physical recreation should be confined almost completely to club sports, perhaps under the intramurals program, with a separate structure for intercollegiate football and basketball (and any other sport that pays for itself through gate receipts). Nor does it rest with those at the other extreme who argue that the main problem is simply that of "learning to market the product better," thereby creating sufficient profit to meet all demands.

We do believe fully in the "quality imperative," in "striving for excellence" in any activity considered acceptable in the educational environment. This means promoting it to the extent that such striving is compatible with high educational standards (such standards admittedly being difficult to define). Hence, to lay the philosophical groundwork for the first section of this chapter, we are in favor of scholarships for athletes who are striving for excellence, *but only where they have proven financial need*! This is just the same as we are in favor of financial aid for *any bona fide* student with talent in one of a number of recognized "cultural talents"--*where there is proven need*! Our assumption is that worthy, needy students must have sufficient time to devote to the full development of their talents.

Because competitive sport, for example, has only rarely received full educational status at any educational level, full support of athletic programs has been an ever-present budgetary problem. Further, with rare exceptions, gate receipts are *always* of concern, a situation that has often placed great pressure on athletic directors and head coaches of certain revenue sports to produce winning teams. This fact has resulted in a multitude of human and material problems far too numerous to list here. These problems are well known by all, and it would serve no purpose to dwell on any of them at this point.

In the final quarter of the 20th century, at least two factors exacerbated this continuing problem: the financial plight of higher education in general, and the Title IX issue specifically (where increased allotments were mandated for women's competitive sport to achieve a semblance of "equal opportunity"). In addition, a third problem caused concern for all facets of the economy: Those of us related to sport and recreation were victimized by those social forces as well--economic inflation, mini-depressions, and the occasional period of what has become known as "stagflation" (the stagnant economy accompanied by inflation in the 1980s). We began to get the uneasy feeling that college athletics, as we have known it, might eventually be forced to price itself out of the market. As Bole indicated in 1970, alternative methods of financing athletics should be explored before the situation becomes impossible (p. 93). It would indeed be a tragedy if we end up with truncated programs made up of intercollegiate football and basketball only. Under such conditions, all other competitive sports with certain exceptions (e.g., wrestling at Lehigh, hockey at Michigan) would be relegated to minor sport status and would have to follow the extramural or club sport pattern (not to denigrate these activities, of course).

Further, to a greater or lesser extent, the financial outlay for athletic scholarships has hung around the necks of United States athletic directors, especially, like the fabled albatross for many decades. Then, an action that is now history occurred, many state legislatures because of federal Title IX legislation were rightfully required to appropriate funds for athletic scholarships for women as well. Under certain conditions, as mentioned above, we are not questioning this practice for either sex, but the fact cannot be escaped that a tremendous burden has been placed on athletic budgets. This is obviously one more consideration that must evidently be placed into the athletics "planning mix" on a continuing basis.

The question of athletic scholarships has in the 21st century moved-- seemingly almost inevitably--to the forefront in Canada as well. Starting in the 1950s the subject of improvement of national and international sport became a political issue. As governments turned over, there were pressures on the new government to bring competitive sport to parity at least with countries of similar wealth and population. The federal government in Canada did institute so-called, third-party scholarships for "carded athletes" with national standing some years ago. This caused some problems, but by and large this *nondirective* approach (insofar as the universities were concerned) did not cause as many problems as had been anticipated by those who were in opposition to the move. Then some of the provincial government entered the picture similarly (e.g., British Columbia), with both levels of government using lottery receipts to help offset the added financial burden. Some universities in the east and mid–west also began to grant certain financial aid even before the regulations were relaxed. The result in the 1990s was two levels of university competition--one for those who grant athletic scholarships, and one for those who don't (not mentioning the few "under-the-table" institutions. What the future holds is anybody's guess, but we can only hope that academic standards will not be lowered, and that extensive programs of competitive sport for men and women will not have to be curtailed because of continuing inflation and declining income (the latter being derived almost completely from student fees and--more recently--from certain provincial aid programs).

In the United States especially, athletic departments have necessarily felt that they should do all in their power--presumably within the letter and the spirit of the rules within higher education--to produce winning teams. This has been particularly true for those sports that have produced significant amounts of revenue in the past, money that has literally supported teams in other sports where gate receipts were light or nonexistent.

Background of the Marketing Orientation Concept

The time is now long past when a chairperson or director should have given consideration to his or her institution's stance in regard to what is now known as the *marketing concept*. This business phenomenon began in the 1940s and 1950s and has served business and industry and a number of athletic departments so well ever since. The question is whether the many social changes since have created a social climate that requires a whole new set of postulates for the administrator/manager no matter what the size or scope of the sport or physical recreation enterprise. The basic question to be faced, of course, is whether the "Canham marketing philosophy" (the former AD of Michigan at Ann Arbor) can work for all colleges and universities--or whether it is unique for certain universities in specific geographic regions only. To understand this problem more fully, it is necessary first to review briefly the development of the marketing concept since its origination.

Marketing is typically defined as activities that accelerate the movement of goods or services from the manufacturer to the consumer. Thus, it is marketing whether one is talking about advertising, distribution, merchandising, product-planning, promotion, publicity, and even transportation and warehousing. Phrased in a slightly different way, marketing involves the performance of "business activities" that influence the flow of goods and services from the producer to the consumer or user. Certain activities take place before the marketing process sets in (i.e., the identification of marketing needs, desires, and preferences). In other words, the market needs develop, and then typically a business organization is developed to meet those demands.

The development of the marketing concept can be characterized as a response from business to a society that was steadily acquiring more buying power. The personal income of the average family rose steadily so that life's basic essentials used up a smaller proportion of a person's salary. The nature of the consumer's demands changed along with the rising production levels. Then, as the average person's discretionary income increased further, there was a dramatic rise in the demand for services in the final quarter of the 20th century. Concurrently, we witnessed a multitude of technologic innovations with many new variations of distribution patterns.

As the social environment gradually altered, and a different lifestyle emerged for many families, the business community was affected as well. Unions demanded shorter workweeks, but in time the pressure of continuing inflation gradually forced both parents in a family to seek work. This pressure, coupled with increasing freedom enabling women to escape (to a degree) from being homebound almost completely, has resulted in a situation at the beginning of the 21st century where two-thirds of married women are gainfully employed. All of this caused increased demands for commercial recreation, labor-saving devices in the home, opportunities for travel, and opportunities for in-service education.

The result of this societal "upheaval" was a variety of demands for what might be called heterogeneity of goods and services that soon brought about the introduction of the concept of "market segmentation." Each segment had its own discrete desires, needs, and preferences. Thus, businesses found it mandatory to develop and maintain a market-strategy plan. When a company determined which its preferred segment of the market was, decisions could then be made sensibly about which directions should be taken with product development, pricing, distribution, and communication.

Here it is important to distinguish between the concepts of "market segmentation" and "product differentiation." The latter term relates to the different brands of a product *as viewed by* the prospective consumer. Here we are, for example, seeking a better understanding of the marketing orientation for competitive athletics. In this connection, this idea of product differentiation may be one way for athletics to appeal to its presumed market segment. By that we mean that competitive athletics in *educational* institutions can, and probably should be, offered to that segment of the population interested in it on the basis of the *unique* qualities that only it possesses. It may take market research of a social–psychology nature to figure this out scientifically, but it would be worth the time and effort to discover the answers to this important question.

Competitive Athletics During the 1960s

To continue with the example of competitive athletics, it is useful to understand what did happen to athletic budgets as a result of the evolving economy. This is a matter worth considering because of the implications for the future. We know, for example, that the typical budget soon increased more than 100% in the 1960s, but that only approximately one third of that increase could be attributed to the rise in the cost of living. Approximately two-thirds of the college and university athletic programs were losing money with the result that a number of institutions dropped their football programs and curtailed other non–revenue-producing sports as well.

We can recall also that final quarter of the 20th century was the time after which one segment of the student population was protesting about many aspects of society. Intercollegiate athletics was at times included in their demands for reform. In their search for available funds, colleges and universities were seeking any economies possible and were occasionally courting agencies that were thought by some to be undesirable for financial assistance.

As expenses increased more rapidly than revenues, athletic associations found it necessary to increase ticket prices for sporting events whenever there was a steady demand (e.g., football). Whereas television contracts provided considerable assistance for the big-time sport colleges and universities, conversely, support from university regents, alumni, and students in a number of instances was declining. Also, university athletic departments often found it necessary to expand their facilities and related equipment supplies to keep up with the times and their competition. They soon realized that they were increasingly in competition for the entertainment dollar. In this way the problems steadily increased for those relatively few universities where the athletic programs had been quite sufficient traditionally. Officials at a number of these institutions argued that, unless cutbacks were made, it would be necessary to turn to state legislatures for funds--a situation that had not existed previously. Of course, many in intercollegiate athletics were anxious to maintain their independence and not take such assistance. At such times it was disturbing to hear the idea expressed by many publicly that "it is not responsible to devote public funds to sports programs." This type of statement is simply a continuation of the--in the writer's opinion--that intercollegiate (and interscholastic) athletics could never under any circumstances be considered sufficiently educational to justify financial support from public funds.

Marketing Environment of the 1970s and 1980s

As if these developments were not bad enough for competitive sport in educational institutions during the 1960s, the 1970s witnessed four different occurrences in the social and economic realm as follows: (1) slower economic growth, (2) emerging public concern over the physical environment, (3) dwindling raw material resources, and (4) changing social values. Considering these developments, it was apparent that each one of these occurrences would influence the marketing environment faced by intercollegiate/interuniversity sport thereafter.

First, with the slower growth in the economy at that point, it was expected that inflations would be minimal. This did not happen, however, and the term "stagflation" appeared to describe an unanticipated development. In addition to the market demand decreasing somewhat from an overall standpoint, the actual nature of the demand was changing as well. Obviously, we needed to improve our knowledge of the various changes in life cycles that took place, and how this may have altered the characteristics of consumption. It was simply not realistic, for example, to think that the gross national product (GNP) would rise forever in North America. We seem to have been proceeding somewhat blindly on the assumption that growth was guaranteed by an expanding and more affluent population. Instead of pursuing an accepted belief that there is no competitive substitute for its major product, a company that had been producing goods and services had to begin to think of itself as an organization that is buying materials, creating products, and satisfying customers." Question: How does this affect the possible demand to watch intercollegiate athletic competition? Further, what must educational athletics do to provide customer orientation? (The response to these questions will be offered below for consideration.)

Buell's second and third points (or occurrences) mentioned above-- emerging public concern over the environment and dwindling raw material resources--may be subsumed under one heading: the growing influence of ecology on the world (1978). There appears to be no doubt that environmental concerns will continue to affect the quality of life in North America and elsewhere. Whether we cite overcrowding, noise, safety, pollution, inflation, drugs, delinquency, vandalism, or dwindling raw-material resources, these types of hazards and concerns will plague and haunt the leaders of the world on into the indeterminate future. Those of us involved in the promotion of intercollegiate athletic competitions, sports club contests, intramural athletics, and physical recreational activities for the masses will of necessity be involved with the prevention of, and the possible solution for, these environmental challenges.

Finally, in relation to what happened in the 1970s and early 1980s, what should we keep in mind about the changing social values and norms? For example, many people were now challenging the quality of life that had developed in North America. Some were beginning to appreciate that a truly high quality of living does not necessarily require the application of technologic advancements to an ever-increasing, almost overwhelming extent. Keeping Veblen's theory of conspicuous consumption in mind, might it not be possible that in the process of creating a higher material standard of living that we may end up as well with a lower quality of life? These are fundamental questions to be considered from time to time. In addition,, from the standpoint of marketing, they point out that we must be aware of the extent to which changing social values affect market demands. With our own product, for example, do we really understand just what benefits may accrue to the participant from his or her respective type of involvement with competitive sport and/or physical recreation or exercise? What causes the fan to listen, to watch, or to actually attend the sport contest? What causes a person to undertake an exercise program or some type of physical recreation? The time is past due for more sophisticated market research along these lines.

It is interesting also to approach this topic tangentially by asking the question whether a business organization should *always* give people what they want whether it is good for them or not. Who among us is fully or even best equipped to make such a decision? In our free–market economy, should an organization selling goods or services exercise social leadership? If so, under what conditions should this occur? Buell had indicated that many responsible business leaders may now agree that "the purpose of a business is to create and serve customers in a socially responsible manner" (1978, p. 692). Should we not be able always to state a *minimum* but *high* standard for competitive sport within educational circles? This accedes to the thought that such a standard is not possible for all types of highly organized *professional* sport in our culture? There is evidence that a gradual elevation of the marketing concept should be ever present in our planning, and not merely a subject for future conjecture.

Marketing Management for Athletics & Physical Recreation

Everything stated to this point may be regarded as history. In addition, I admit the difficulty of gaining true historical perspective on the immediate past. However, present demands are confronting us squarely with a *quality imperative*. Hence, I will now offer some suggestions and recommendations that may be helpful as directors of athletics prepare to face the evolving internal and external environments of the 21st century. As we think of the total process of sport marketing (see Figure 1 below), keep in mind that there can be three categories of parameters and/or variables that influence the entire undertaking as follows: (1) environmental *non–controllable* parameters

213

(constraints or opportunities); (2) internal *controllable* variables; and (3) *partially controllable* variables (that may be external or internal). It is important that all concerned--athletic directors, sport managers, business managers, governing boards, etc.--understand how strong these factors may be.

The environmental *non-controllable* parameters may be viewed as external influences that must be considered seriously. They are such

Systems Analysis Applied to Sport Marketing

persistent historical problems as: (1) the influence of the society's values and norms; (2) the influence of politics (or the type of political state in which the organization is functioning); (3) the influence of economics (or the type and state of the economy); (4) the influence of religion; (5) the influence of ecology; and (6) the presence of competition (see bottom right of Figure 1 above). Not designated here, but often extremely powerful, is the influence of nationalism in one of several forms.

Initially, the business organization perceives certain societal demands and/or needs. Depending on the specific circumstances, the society and/or the organization's backer respond by making available (initially or potentially) material and human resources such as available capital, some level of market position or reputation, and a management team of good, bad, or indifferent stature. Of course, all of this is ultimately part of the total management process itself. After the initial *input* stage has been started, we are really describing functions that occur within the larger management process that is

214

typically characterized by such terms as planning, organizing, staffing, directing, and controlling.

What we are actually presenting here is a model of a systems approach to sport marketing. Marketing plans include such factors or elements as (1) the guidance of stated objectives or goals; (2) the infusion of monetary resources; (3) the availability of a production unit; and (4) the services of a research and development division. This is the first stage of the *thruput* phase of a systems approach and also the first set of *internal controllable variables*. If we relate a business model to sport marketing, however, it becomes obvious immediately that all of these factors have typically not been available to the manager of athletics in as sophisticated a form as they might be or should be (e.g., a research and development division).

As we move forward to the second stage of the *thruput* phase of this systems approach--the stage in which the marketing mix is developed--it is readily apparent that the administrator/manager is confronted with four major elements which are the same ones that must be considered in any business. They are (1) the product presented to the public; (2) the price charged for that product; (3) the ways the product will be distributed to the public (i.e., the athletics competition, the fitness club services, etc.); and (4) the means employed to promote the product. We can readily understand how the proportions of the marketing mix may necessarily change in order to produce the most profitable marketing mix. For example, an administrator could soon be priced out of the market by charging too much for tickets, or by charging the budget too heavily for advertising within the total promotional effort.

The *output* stage of our systems approach correlates with the distribution channels of a marketing system. These channels--which in connection with sport marketing are usually intercollegiate (or interscholastic) athletics, intramural sports and sport clubs, and recreational sports and developmental physical activity services, are designated as *output*. They may also be regarded as *partially controllable variables*. This variability is present because–in the final analysis–the athletics director or manager is confronted with output variables that he or she only partially controls.

Finally, then, we have arrived at the user or consumer stage of our systems approach. It is this point that the administrator soon discovers whether the distribution channels of his/her presumably educational business--whether public, semi-public, or private--are functioning poorly, adequately, or in superior fashion. Here we think initially of success from a profit-and-loss standpoint. However, in the control phase of the management process, it is absolutely imperative that the manager obtain various types of feedback from consumers as to their satisfaction with the entire process. This means that the administrator should measure and then evaluate the several products regularly and systematically (i.e., determine how the three channels of distribution (or program offerings are being received by the various consumer levels). In the case of a college or university, for example, these consumers would be the students, faculty, staff, alumni, higher administration, board of trustees or governors, and the general public. Further, at all points during the entire process, the sport and physical activity program--in total or in part--may encounter favorable, neutral, or unfavorable influences from the many external non–controllable parameters (e.g., state of the economy, competition, poor weather).

Concluding Statement

From many conversations with others who are also involved with the program management, and based on a careful analysis of the literature, we believe that few athletics and physical activity managers have ever had (or taken) the opportunity to invoke a systems concept that could help them to understand fully how such an involved process are (1) market planning, (2) the development of a marketing mix, (3) the careful arrangement of the distribution channels, and (4) the feedback from the users, could work in its entirety. Of course, we have all been involved in the various phases of our positions in a piecemeal fashion. However, unless the manager came to the position with a background in theory, he presumably did not have the knowledge and competencies to envision the entire process in the light of operations research. As stated above, who ever heard of a research and development unit for an intercollegiate athletic program before the time when such educational institutions found themselves running "business enterprises."

What should we do specifically to provide sufficient (potential) customer orientation with our several programs? How can we move ahead to meet the immediate demands of a North American *quality imperative*? The answer would seem to be that all of us should have an introduction to what might be called *strategic market planning* in which we learn specifically what steps must be taken to develop a sound, realizable plan for our respective organizations. Then, once we have achieved an overall conceptualization of the entire subject, each of us will be in a position to study the skeleton, theoretic *evaluation schedule* offered below in this chapter.

> (Note: As it happened this "theoretic model" was actually
> adapted to a real life situation in the Physical Recreation &
> Intramurals Program of The University of Western Ontario.

Proceeding from this point, the reader would be ready to adapt the evaluation schedule to his or her own needs in arriving at a decision as to long range aims and immediate objectives. From this assessment, the reader (as a prospective or present administrator/manager) can build an effective strategic marketing plan that will result in a customer-oriented program involving more than (1) an expression of good intentions, (2) a variety of promotional tricks, and (3) a program of good, bad, or indifferent quality. This will be difficult, especially at a time when it is urgent also that academic subject-matter be taught more effectively. However, it must be done because physical activity education & recreation are important in the education of all young people. As a manager, you may indeed respond that you already have a marketing plan in place. If this is true, that's fine. However, you may then wish to employ this Evaluation Schedule by adapting it to mesh with (or enhance) your present plan. There is always room for improvement as we strive for excellence in an ever more competitive environment.

Appendix
Program Evaluation Schedule
(Based on Strategic Market Planning)

The growing importance of the marketing concept as an aid to the development of sport, fitness, and recreation programs in the various aspects of our society led to the development of an evaluation schedule. This schedule is designed for use by an individual, a group of individuals, or other interested parties to evaluate the present status of an organization's marketing plan (including the marketing mix). Strategic market planning, as envisioned here, consists of five steps or stages as follows: (1) Definition of the organization, (2) Status of the organization (including present budget and resource allocation), (3) Evaluation of the present marketing plan, (4) Assessment of the present marketing mix, and (5) Determination of the future marketing plan (including a new marketing mix and subsequent budgetary implications).

At each stage of this evaluation or assessment, those concerned are asked to check off their reactions in regard to (1) general administration and (2) various aspects of their programs, thereby possibly detecting problem areas. (An individual rating omitted or added would change the divisor accordingly [up or down] in each step.) In addition to the evaluation of status, the schedule may also be used as an aid in setting up a marketing plan for the future.

The schedule is primarily a self-rating device for use by those in a position to respond *knowledgeably* to the questions asked. These queries have to do with facilities, personnel, program, and services. The overall program (and/or individual subunits or subdivisions ratings) provide both individual and/or group analyses depending on how the instrument is used. It will help determine whether any changes are required in the operation of your present marketing plan. The schedule proceeds sequentially through the five steps of strategic market planning as outlined above.

The schedule may be used with a numerical scoring system. Scoring for each item (i.e., Excellent = 5, Very Good = 4, etc.) is from the highest rating to the lowest. The adjectives or numbers you assign should correspond to the present effectiveness of that aspect of the organization or its subunits under consideration.

Instructions for Using the Evaluation

Since the evaluation schedule is a self-rating device, the director or chairperson, as manager, leader, and coordinator of the overall management team in the organization, may wish to have the different people holding a variety of duties and responsibilities fill out a checklist. Although he and the unit heads may wish to apply different weightings to the various sets of responses that are received, this is nevertheless a good way to receive a number of opinions on the success, mediocrity, or failure of the present (marketing) plan of operation being employed.

Each item should be rated separately. At the end of each STEP (of the total of five) is a space for the mathematical average of all items in that phase to be figured. Later these averages can be transferred to the summary section at the end. From this summary total, an overall average can be determined by simple arithmetic. The qualitative and numerical ratings are as follows:

EX---excellent.........................5
VG---very good......................4
AC---acceptable....................3
FA---fair...............................2
PO---poor............................1

Notes:

(1) The evaluation schedule has been set up with the Physical Recreation and Intramurals of one university of mind. *With a minimum of changes throughout the schedule, it may be very easily adapted to any program desired (i.e., college, university, commercial organization, non-profit agency, governmental agency, etc.)*

(2) Ratings of individual items may be averaged where and when this is desired. This point should be kept in mind since averaged ratings of all individuals items lumped together tend to move the overall averaged scores toward the midpoint of 2.5

(Please proceed to STEP ONE below)

STEP ONE: DEFINITION OF THE ORGANIZATION

Please indicate how well these statements reflect
your personal beliefs and opinions

Numerical
Score
(e.g., VG = 4)

A. PURPOSE (or overall program definition)

1. The Physical Recreation and Intramurals
   Program at The University of Western
   Ontario should be one of four programs
   within the Faculty of Kinesiology.   _____

2. PRIP should be supported by student
   activity fees, non-student membership
   fees, charges for special services, and,
   to a limited extent, by general univer-
   sity funding.   _____

3. It should maintain its administrative
   office in the University Community Centre
   with the Sports and Recreation Services
   Office in Thames Hall.   _____

4. The mission of PRIP should be to motivate
   members of the university community to be
   responsible for their own health and fitness, and to promote and facilitate their
   involvement in wholesome physical activity
   to carry out this responsibility.   _____

5. To do this PRIP should offer a balanced
   program of wholesome activities that involve
   learning and practising sport, physical
   fitness, and recreational skills in various
   settings ranging from casual to highly
   structured.   _____

6. PRIP's activities should be divided into
   the following units: (1) drop-in (casual)
   activities; (2) non-credit instruction; (3)
   intramural competitive sports; (4) physical
   fitness; (5) aquatics; (6) sport clubs.   _____

B. PRODUCT AND MARKET SCOPE

(from an <u>overall</u> standpoint)

1. Generally, how well have the target
    markets (i.e. clients) been defined
    within the University Community?   _____

2. Generally, have the services provided
    been sufficiently differentiated to meet
    the clients' needs?   _____

3. Has market segmentation been suffi-
    ciently achieved (i.e., by separating
    the market into categories and there-
    by developing an adequate market
    profile)?

    3.1 <u>Who</u>? Do we adequately under-
         stand whom we are dealing with
         in each category?   _____

    3.2 <u>Where</u>? Are we serving clients
         in the place where they want to
         be served?   _____

    3.3 <u>When</u>? Are we serving clients
         when they want to be served?   _____

    3.4 <u>How Many</u>? Are we serving a
         sufficient number of clients
         in the program offering with
         which they want to be involved?   _____

    3.5 <u>How</u>? Are we serving clients
         in the way they wish to be
         served (i.e., quality of
         service or instruction?   _____

    3.6 <u>Type of Client</u>? Are we reach-
         ing those clients who need to
         be served?   _____

C. AVERAGE RATING--ORGANIZATIONAL DEFINITION =   _____

220

<u>Note</u>: Please add up the NUMERICAL ratings the column above. Then divide the total by the <u>number</u> (DIVISOR) of ratings you felt qualified or able to make. For example, if you felt that you could answer 10 of the 14 questions, 5 of them with a rating of 3 and 5 with a rating of 4, your total would be 35. 35 divided by 10 = 3.5. Thus, you have evaluated the ORGANIZATIONAL DEFINITION of the PRIP with a 3.5 (or in the middle between Very Good [VG] and Acceptable [AC]).

STEP TWO: STATUS OF THE ORGANIZATION

<u>Note</u>: Be careful here to evaluate A here from the standpoint of your involvement with a <u>specific</u> unit (e.g., Fitness) and C based on your evaluation of the <u>overall</u> Program.

<u>Numerical</u>
<u>Score</u>
(e.g., AC = 3)

A. MARKET OPPORTUNITIES
(assessing your unit <u>specifically</u>)

_____

1. Market Share:

1.1 <u>Current</u>? Is my unit (interest area) serving the number of clients that it should in line with the PRIP overall program aims and objectives?

_____

1.2 <u>Potential for future</u>? What is the potential for the future growth of my unit (interest area)?

_____

1.3 <u>Client loyalty</u>? How loyal are the present clients in my unit (interest area)?

_____

2. Competition:

2.1 <u>Knowledge about competition #1</u>?
How adequate is my knowledge about

221

the <u>direct</u> competition that my unit
(interest area) is facing? (i.e., other
university-sponsored activities)   _____

2.2 <u>Knowledge about competition #2</u>?
How adequate is my knowledge about
the <u>indirect</u> competition that my
unit (interest area) is facing?
(i.e., non-university-sponsored
entertainment activities)   _____

2.3 <u>Time scheduling</u>? If direct or
indirect competition (i.e., other
programs) are scheduled at the same
time, how good are the chances that
my unit (interest area) will be chosen?   _____

3. Knowledge of societal and/or
environmental trends? How adequate is
my knowledge and understanding of
social, legal, political, and techno
logical trends, etc. in relation to the
present status of my unit (interest
area)?   _____

4. Present market situation? Everything
considered, how do I rate my unit's
(interest area's) share of the presently
available market?   _____

B. AVERAGE RATING--MARKET CAPABILITIES =   _____

C. ORGANIZATION'S (PRIP's) CAPABILITIES
(from an <u>overall</u> standpoint)

1. Financial status?

1.1 <u>Ability to meet costs</u>? Keeping
the present situation in mind, how
do I rate our ability to balance the
budget each year?   _____

1.2 <u>University funding #1</u>? How do I
rate the adequacy of University
funding based on what <u>should</u> be
made available?   _____

222

1.3 <u>University funding #2</u>? How do I
rate the adequacy of University
funding based on what is provided
by universities for other PRIP
programs within the OUAA?   _____

1.4 <u>Revenue generation #1</u>? How do I
assess the adequacy of the level
to which program participants
contribute through basic activity/
membership fees to the support of PRIP?   _____

1.5 <u>Revenue generation #2</u>? How do I
assess the adequacy of the level
to which program participants
contribute for special, expensive
program features and offerings?   _____

2. How do I assess PRIP's (Program's)
adaptability (i.e. to expand
or to make revisions)?   _____

3. How do I rate the overall PRIP
(Program) structure (i.e. its
balance and individual strengths)?   _____

4. Personnel:

   4.1 <u>Management personnel</u>? How
   do I assess the management
   of the overall program (i.e.,
   generally and specifically)?   _____

   4.2 <u>Support Staff</u> How do I
   evaluate the overall performance
   of the various members of the
   support staff?   _____

   4.3 <u>Part-Time Staff</u> How do I
   evaluate the performance
   of the part-time staff?   _____

   4.4 <u>Physical Plant Personnel</u> How do
   I assess the maintenance services
   provided by the staff in the

Physical Plant? _____

C. AVERAGE RATING--PRIP/PROGRAM STATUS = _____

       (Please add up the individual ratings you felt
       able to complete and then divide the total by
       the number of individual responses that you made
       [i.e., divide the total by the DIVISOR and enter
       the number obtained under C immediately above].)

STEP THREE: EVALUATION OF UNITS' MARKETING PLANS

       <u>Note</u>: In Step Three base your evaluation on your
       involvement with a specific unit of the entire
       Program (PRIP).

<u>Numerical
Score</u>
(e.g., EX=5)

A. MARKET PENETRATION
   (i.e., to what extent is my unit
   (interest area) under the PRIP
   working to increase the use of present
   services in the <u>current</u> markets?)

  1. To increase the use of services by:

   1.1 <u>Advertising</u>? Is the advertising
      for my unit (area of interest)
      sufficient quality and quantity   _____

   1.2 <u>Price cutting</u>? What is the
      adequacy of the price established
      for <u>special services</u> within my
      unit?   _____

   1.3 <u>Promotional devices</u>? How adequate
      are the promotional gimmicks or
      devices that are used in connection
      with my unit?   _____

1.4 <u>Enhancing the benefits of parti-
cipation</u>? Are we currently offering service in such a way that the
benefits of participation in an
activity are being steadily enhanced?
(i.e., striving to "give more bang
for the buck")

                                                         _____

2. Attracting participants from other
units? Are our current efforts as
described in #1 immediately above
of such quality and quantity that
participants from other units (interest
areas) are joining my particular unit?

                                                         _____

3. Attracting current non-users? Are
our current efforts as described in #1
above of such quality and quantity
that current non-users of any PRIP
services are getting involved?

                                                         _____

B. MARKET DEVELOPMENT
(i.e., to what extent are the several
units (sub-programs under PRIP)
working to increase the use of
current services in <u>new</u> markets)

1. Capability to expand? (i.e., To what
extent does my unit (interest area)
have the <u>capability</u> to serve any
untapped new markets for the program
I represent?)

1.1 <u>University</u>? To what extent
does my unit (interest area)
have the capability to expand
on campus?

                                                         _____

1.2 <u>Alumni</u>? To what extent does my
unit (interest area) have the
capability to expand to serve
alumni within the 11 counties
that the UWO serves basically?

                                                         _____

1.2 <u>Local community</u>? To what extent

225

does my unit (interest area)
have the capability to expand to
the Greater London Area? _____

2. Services that appeal to new segments
   of potential markets? If services were
   made available to new segments with
   appropriate advertising, to what extent
   might my unit (interest area) attract
   new segments of the "populations"
   mentioned immediately above? _____

C. PRODUCT DEVELOPMENT & DIVERSIFICATION
(i.e., to what extent am I expanding [1]
present services for current markets and/or
[2] new, dissimilar services within my
unit (interest area) to attract new
classes of participants?)

Present Product Development

1. Have I the potential to adapt or modify
   present services or activities within
   within my unit (interest area)?
   (e.g., fitness, intramurals) _____

2. Have I the potential to create
   different levels of services within
   my unit (interest area)? (e.g., novice,
   intermediate, and advanced levels) _____

3. Have I the potential to develop new
   services or activities for current
   markets within my unit (interest
   area)? (e.g., computerized stroke
   analysis in golf instruction classes)? _____

New, Dissimilar Services

4. Describe the availability of facilities
   for new, dissimilar, types of activities
   within my unit (interest area) to attract
   new participants? (e.g., competitive water
   wrestling within aquatics) _____

5. Could I obtain supervisory personnel to

develop new, dissimilar services? _____

  6. Could I obtain instructors for new,
     dissimilar services? _____

D. INTEGRATIVE GROWTH
(i.e., could I work to increase efficiency
or unit (interest area) use by expanding or
moving "backward, forward, or horizontally"
within the target market [examples below]?)

  1. Ability to control facility use? The
     extent to which I can control the use of
     facilities needed for my unit (interest
     area)? _____

  2. Ability to control activities and
     scheduling for my unit (interest area)?
     The extent to which I have the freedom or
     leeway to make such program adjustments? _____

  3. Ability to make input concerning other
     program units in the overall market area?
     The extent to which I can make input
     into the planning for other units
     within PRIP? _____

E. AVERAGE RATING OF GROWTH DIRECTIONS
OR FUNCTIONAL STRATEGIES WITHIN THE
OVERALL MARKETING PLAN DEVELOPMENT   =   _____

(Please add up the individual ratings you felt
able to complete and then divide the total by
the number of individual responses that you
made--i.e., divide the total by the DIVISOR
and enter the number obtained under E
immediately above.)

STEP FOUR: ASSESSMENT OF PRESENT UNIT MARKETING MIX

INSTRUCTIONS FOR DETERMINATION OF THE MARKETING MIX

The marketing mix can be regarded as the actual (recognized or unrecognized) marketing plan presently in existence for the overall program and its several sub-program components.

This Marketing Mix is the sum of the time, effort, and resources expended on the present implementation of any functional strategies currently employed.

It consists typically of four elements as follows: (1) PRODUCT, (2) PLACE, (3) PROMOTION, and (4) PRICE.

An analysis of each of the <u>four</u> elements of the Unit Marketing Mix (e.g., product, place) is a required step for future planning.

Once the weightings of the present aims, status, and functional strategies have been determined, the results should be discussed carefully.

Any relationship between the UNIT MARKETING MIX RATING (STEP FOUR) and the rating(s) determined in STEPS ONE, TWO, and THREE (including the OVERALL RATING AVERAGE) should be discussed <u>after</u> the latter rating(s) have been established.

In all probability, there will be a close correlation between the MARKETING MIX RATING and the OVERALL RATING AVERAGE!

Decisions concerning any <u>future</u> Marketing Plan in keeping with the desired Marketing Mix may then be made at the end of the planning process.

Assessment of the established UNIT <u>and</u> PROGRAM Marketing Mix should be carried out periodically for best results (e.g., annually, biennially). Fine tuning may be required even sooner.

> <u>Note</u>: Here you are asked to assess the present marketing mix of your unit in the overall PRIP program.

<u>Numerical Score</u>
(e.g., EXC=5)

A. PRODUCT

1. Overall quality of services offered?
   (including instruction)   _____

2. Number of services or activities
   offered?   _____

3. Variety in the program offerings? _____

4. General appeal to participants? _____

5. Quality of <u>non-program</u> services
   offered?

   5.1 Locker rooms / reservations _____

   5.2 Administrative / supervisory _____

   5.3 Sports & Recreational Services
   Office _____

B. PLACE

1. Locations of the services? _____

2. Access to services (e.g.,
   overcrowding)? _____

3. Planning of services offered? _____

4. Quality of equipment? _____

5. Availability of facilities? _____

6. General atmosphere? _____

7. Homogeneity of attendees
   (where services dictate a need)? _____

C. PROMOTION

1. Public relations?

   1.1 With undergraduate students? _____

   1.2 With graduate students? _____

   1.3 With faculty members? _____

   1.4 With staff members? _____

   1.5 With alumni & larger

community? _____

    1.6 With various media? _____

2. Personal selling of program? _____

3. Advertising (regular, <u>paid</u>)?

    3.1 Variety of media used? _____

    3.2 Timing? _____

    3.3 Amount of advertising used? _____

    3.4 Quality of advertising
        "messages"? _____

4. Advertising (<u>unpaid</u> exposure)? _____

5. Short-term promotions
  (e.g., special events)? _____

D. PRICE

1. Amount of fees charged for
  <u>ongoing</u> services? _____

2. Amount of fees charged for
  <u>special</u> services? _____

3. Collection procedures? _____

4. Discounts/allowances? _____

5. Refunding policies? _____

E. AVERAGE MARKETING MIX RATING   = _____

        (Please add up the individual ratings you felt able
        to complete and then divide the total by the
        number of individual responses that you made--i.e.,
        divide the total by the DIVISOR and enter the
        number obtained under E immediately above.)

STEP FIVE: DETERMINATION OF A FUTURE MARKETING PLAN
(including a Revised Marketing Mix with
Appropriate Financial Implications)

Note: At this point the entire group will become a
Committee of the Whole to facilitate ready input
and discussion.

The managers and the unit coordinators will be asked to form a panel of resource people at the front of the room. Others will be seated in a semi-circle facing the panel.

A marketing mix outline will be placed on a blackboard, and present finance and resource allocations in tabular or chart form will be made available to facilitate discussion.

The plan is to receive a variety of inputs from the various units and services (i.e., greatest strength and evident weakness) on the various headings under the Marketing Plan and the Marketing Mix as follows:

Marketing Plan	Marketing Mix
Market Penetration (increasing use of current services in present market)	**Product:** (quality, features, options, packaging, variety)
Market Development (increasing use of current services in new markets)	**Place:** (locations, timing, transport, coverage)
Product Development (developing expanded services for current markets)	**Promotion** (advertising, selling, media, special events)
Diversification (developing new dissimilar services for new markets)	**Price/Fees** (allowances, refunds, fee increases, payments)
Integrative Growth (increasing efficiency or program use within current market)	

EVALUATION SCHEDULE SUMMARY

Numerical

	Score

STEP ONE: Definition of the Organization
(OVERALL)   _____

STEP TWO: Status of the Organization
(UNIT & OVERALL)   _____

STEP THREE: Evaluation of the Present
Marketing Plan
(UNIT)   _____

STEP FOUR: Assessment of the Present
Marketing Mix
(UNIT)   _____

OVERALL AVERAGE RATING (FOR STEPS 1 THROUGH 4)   _____

> **Note:**   This final Overall Average Rating may be
> regarded in the same light as the individual ratings
> and average ratings of STEPS made throughout the
> evaluation process (from EX [5] down to PO [1]).
> (The entire process is still subjective, of course,
> but an evaluation adds rationality to this future
> planning exercise. Thank you for participating.

STEP FIVE: Determination of a Future Marketing Plan
(including a Revised Marketing Mix with
Appropriate Financial Implications)

Recommendations from a Committee of the Whole

A Final Note: You are not asked to sign your name to this evaluation.
However, it would be helpful if you would indicate the unit within PRIP
where you work. Please place an "**X**" alongside the appropriate unit. Thank
you for your involvement in the day's evaluation sessions.

_____ **Intramural Sports**   _____ **Casual Recreation**

_____ **Non-Credit Instruction**   _____ **Aquatics**

_____ Fitness   _____ Sport Clubs

_____ General Administration   _____ Sports and Rec. Services
                                                     (incl. locker room staff)

Instructions:
Please help us evaluate the effectiveness of today's
PRIP Retreat. Use the same numerical ratings that
were followed on the Evaluation Schedule.

<u>Evaluation</u>

1. Did you develop some understanding of
    strategic market planning?.....................   _____

2. Did you develop a better understanding
    of the entire PRIP program?.....................   _____

3. Did you develop a better understanding
    of your own special area of involvement?........   _____

4. Did you have an opportunity to express
    your feelings and beliefs about the
    overall program and/or your own unit?...........   _____

5. Do you think that PRIP's leadership
    will develop a better understanding
    about the program's future develop-
    ment after today's planning session?............   _____

6. Is leaving the campus for this planning
    session a good idea?...........................   _____

7. How do you rate Spencer Lodge for
    this purpose?...................................   _____

8. How do you rate the overall planning
    session?.......................................   _____

9. What other thoughts do you have on
    this subject?

_____

_____

References

Bole, R.A. *An Economic Analysis of the Factors Influencing Football Attendance at the University of Illinois, 1926-1968*. Ph.D. dissertation, Urbana, University of Illinois, 1970.

Buell, V.P. "Marketing, Concepts, and Systems." In *Encyclopedia of Professional Management* (Ed., L.R. Bittel). New York: McGraw-Hill, 1978, pp. 690-695.

BusinessWeek. "The Quality Imperative: What It Takes to Win in the Global Economy" (Special 1991 Issue), Oct. 25, 1991.

Levitt, T. "Marketing Myopia." In *Harvard Business Review* (The Editors). London: William Heinemann, 1976, pp. 176-196.

Rosenberg, J.M. *Dictionary of Business and Management*. New York: John Wiley & Sons, 1978.

Swift, E.M. "Why Johnny Can't Play," *Sports Illustrated*, 75, 13 (Sept. 23, 1991), 60-72.

Weinberger, M. and Worthing, P.M. "Positioning Strategy: Marketer vs. Consumer Reality." A paper presented at the Conference on Sport Management Art and Science, May 7, 1979, University of Massachusetts, Amherst.

Zeigler, E.F. "A Revised Marketing Orientation for College Athletics in the 1980s," *Athletic Administration*, 14, 4 (Summer 1980), 15-19.

Zeigler, E.F. and Bowie, G.W. *Management Competency Development in Sport and Physical Education*. Philadelphia: Lea & Febiger, 1983.

Selected Bibliography

Allen, Peter. *Marketing Techniques for Analysis and Control*. Estover, Plymouth: Macdonald and Evans Limited, 1977.

Bradway, Bruce M., Pritchard, Robert E., and Frenzel, Mary Anne. Strategic *Marketing*. Reading, MA: Addison-Wesley Publ. Co., 1982.

Buell, Victor. *Handbook of Modern Marketing*. NY: McGraw-Hill Book Co., 1970.

Crompton, John L. "Formulating New Directions with Strategic Marketing Planning." *Parks & Recreation*, 18, 7 (July 1983), 56-58, 61-63, 66.

Ellefson, Lynn. "A Marketing Approach." *Athletic Administration*, 12, 2 (1977), 18-19.

Gelb, Gabriel and Gelb, Betsy. *Insights for Marketing Management*. Santa Monica, CA: Goodyear Publishing Co., Inc., 1977.

Gilbert, R. Bruce. "The Marketing of a Sports Program. *Athletic Administration*, 13, 1 (1978), 16-18.

Hayden, Catherine. *The Handbook of Strategic Expertise*. NY: The Free Press,1986.

Hiebing, Roman G., Jr. and Cooper, Scott W. *How to Write a Successful Marketing Plan*. Lincolnwood, IL: NTC Business Books, 1990.

Joselyn, Robert W. *Designing the Marketing Research Project*. NY:

Petrocelli/Charter, 1977.

Kotler, Philip. *Marketing for Nonprofit Organizations*. Englewood Cliffs, NJ: Prentice-Hall, Inc., 1973.

Mullin, Bernard. *Sport Marketing*. An unpublished workbook, University of Massachusetts, Amherst, 1980.

Nickels, William. *Marketing Principles*. Englewood Cliffs, NJ: Prentice-Hall, Inc., 1978.

Palmisano, Michael. "The Right Kind of Promotion Can Mean Added Revenue." *Athletic Administration*, 16. 2 (1981), 13-14.

Phillips, Michael and Rasberry, Salli. *Marketing Without Advertising*. Berkeley, CA: Nolo Press, 1986.

Robicheaux, Robert, Pride, William, and Ferrell, O.C. *Marketing: Contemporary Dimensions*. Boston: Houghton-Mifflin Co., 1977.

Rolloff, Bruce. "Early Public Relations for Physical Education." *Journal of Physical Education and Recreation*, 50, 8 (1979), 84-85.

Ross, Alan. "Vanderbilt Football: A Marketing Success Story." *Athletic Administration*, 16, 2 (1981), 15-16.

Soucie, Daniel and Cantle, Rosemary. "Present Versus Preferred Public Relations Practices of Athletics Departments in Canadian Universities." *Canadian Journal of Applied Sports Sciences*, 4, 1 (1979), 178-186.

Stone, Bob. *Successful Direct Marketing Methods* (3rd Ed.). Lincolnwood, IL: National Textbook Co., 1986.

Weinberger, Marc and Worthing, Parker. "Positioning Strategy: Marketer vs. Consumer Reality." A discussion paper presented at the Conference on the Art and Science of Sport Management, Univ. of Massachusetts, Amherst, May 7, 1979.

Weinrauch, J. Donald. *The Marketing Problem Solver*. NY: John Wiley & Sons, 1987.

For Consideration and Discussion:

As an exercise at the end of this chapter, it is recommended that two students each make a 10-minute presentation, the first one explaining theoretically the historical background and status of sport marketing in relation to competitive sport in educational institutions. The other student should then explain the program evaluation schedule that has been developed based on strategic market planning. Then a third student should conduct a class discussion on the topic in a search for the way and means to bring such a project to fruition in a way that can serve the best interests of both groups concerned (i.e., those concerned primarily with varsity sport and those whose interest is primarily intramural sports for all).

CHAPTER 12

RISK-MANAGEMENT
IN
PHYSICAL ACTIVITY EDUCATION & ATHLETICS

Introduction

The object of this brief chapter is to provide the prospective manager with a preliminary understanding of legal liability and (what has been termed) risk management in relation to the management of a physical activity education and athletics program. Here we will only "scratch the surface" of this complicated subject by offering the management trainee with an opportunity to use the legal information provided as a basis for the development of a risk-management program.

The law and its effects on the world of physical activity education and athletics is becoming ever more important to teachers, coaches, administrators, and sports officials. This is because social change and certain events have increased the overall complexity of physical activity education and athletics including the interpersonal relationships within the field. In addition, one might say that an "unknown quantity has become more of a known one," a statement that could apply equally well to all parties and aspects concerned.

In addition to understanding something about the legal system in your state or province, an administrator needs to be familiar with the fundamental legal concepts involved in "the risk-management process." What should a professional manager know, and how should he/she act?

The Changing Situation

In the first half of the twentieth century, all sorts of legal problems and accompanying legal liability were not common in educational programs involving physical activity education and athletics programs. Policies and procedures were typically based on relationships characterized by trust that had been established among coaches and players, teachers and students, and administrators and parents. The number of people involved was smaller, and no one seemed to be regarded with great suspicion as a stranger. In addition, and this may have been more important than realized presently, relatively few people were familiar with their rights under the law in regard to liability.

The contemporary scene varies a great deal from the situation of even a few decades ago. In fact, it has somehow happened that the U.S.A. has become the most litigious country on the face of the earth (with Canada moving in this direction as well). This development is reflected as well in physical activity education and athletics programs that have become ever better organized as a result of steadily increasing commercialization. Like it or not, over-emphasized university athletics, professional sport, and commercial recreation have taken on the many attributes--the pluses and minuses, if you will--of a multitude of business enterprises.

Even local clubs operate with handbooks and rulebooks, all within a legislative framework. More people of all ages take part in sport, physical activity, and physical recreation, and the cadre of managers and staff has grown accordingly. Concurrently, individuals are now more aware of their rights and prerogatives. This means that we have an accompanying increase in legal disputes and wrangling. Thus, a manager of a sport organization, for example--whether it be a local skating club or an NFL or CFL football team--should be fully aware of the various and manifold legal aspects of his or her position. There is the basic question of possible negligence on the part of the manager and/or staff members. Further problems may arise in relation to (1) facilities, (2) personnel management, (3) equipment, and (4) medical care.

The situation is now such that risk-management with concomitant concern for legal liability must be a major concern for the sport manager. The goal here is to offer some basic information that will help the prospective manager develop a preliminary understanding of certain legal problems that may be encountered as a professional manager. However, there are many other aspects of "the law" with which the administrator should also be reasonably familiar. Here we are referring to such aspects as property-acquisition, copyright law, civil rights, legal authority to operate, land usage, use permits, environmental concerns, employment regulations, criminal law, etc. Obviously, the management trainee can't be an expert in any or all of these subjects, but a course experience--or at least a segment of such--that includes laboratory experiences is definitely needed.

The Basis of Effective Risk Management

From the standpoint of the insurance industry, the assumption of risk involves the possibility of an adverse event occurring to a client so that the organization may be effected in such a way that future operation may be hampered or eliminated. Hence, the organization needs to take steps to guarantee that risks to which it is exposed will not bankrupt it and prevent the continuance of its services. Effective risk management means that the organization has devised a plan whereby (1) it understands what can go wrong in its operation, and (2) what it can do to prevent such occurrences. Failing this, (1) how can the organization respond to loss or harm that occurs and–*very importantly if it is to blame*–and (2) has it the ability to pay for the damages?

The manager should understand, of course, that risks are not eliminated *even if* an effective risk-management is prepared to recognize them. However, they can be recognized and evaluated insofar as priority is concerned. People can be protected from harm–or further harm, for example. Liability might be reduced, and this would automatically help the stability of the organization.

The management trainee should be asked to use some of the information provided here to develop a preliminary risk-management program as a "first port of call." This need to understand legal responsibility does *not* mean, however, that the manager must become a lawyer with a specialization in all phases of (what is now called) sport law. It does mean that the manager must be fully aware of certain basics (i.e., disparities and commonalities) of the social and physical environment in which the organization is functioning. In addition, and fundamentally, managers should understand fully (1) what the organization's legal responsibility is, and--most important, also—(2) what legal responsibility the manager himself or herself has as programs of sport, exercise, and physical recreation are promoted.

Areas of Responsibility for the Manager

In this brief knowledge statement, we will not discuss an entire approach to the subject of sport and physical activity education law. We won't even have space to cover risk management and legal liability thoroughly. However, we will offer a brief outline of what we believe is absolutely necessary as a start. There are a number of aspects or sources of accountability and responsibility that a manager of an overall program of physical activity and sport must understand fully. This means that the manager:

> (1) must keep abreast of any changes in the law,
> (2) should have adequate overall planning,
> (3) must maintain the avenues of communication
>   with all concerned, and
> (4) must keep the concept of "planning for safety"
>   uppermost (Drowatzky, 1993, pp. 2-3).
>
> (Note, also, that the legal structure of the United
> States starts with a different background than that
> of Canada.)

We could argue that the principal legal responsibility for a manager is to avoid negligence. Negligence is part of tort law that exists within common and civil law. Tort law is somewhat difficult to define precisely because of continued social and accompanying change that has occurred within the broad scope of this area. Thus, it may be more accurate to view tort law as a large group of unconnected "wrongs" each with its own name (e.g., trespass, nuisance, negligence). Basically, we can say that a person exhibits negligence when he or she fails to act as a reasonably prudent person in a given situation. (This concept would accordingly carry over from the private citizen to the person practicing as a professional in some field.) Therefore, if a person is found by the courts to be negligent, that individual becomes liable for the action committed (or not committed) and may be subject to some kind of penalty.

The above definitions in regard to negligence would seem to leave considerable latitude to court officials who are in a position to make arbitrary decisions. Moriarty (1980, p. 13) provided four questions that can serve as a common basis for decision-making in cases where negligence is alleged to have taken place. These are:

(1) Did the defendant(s) owe the plaintiff a duty?
(2) Was there a breach of the duty that was owed?
(3) Was the defendant's breach of duty the proximate cause of the injury? and
(4) Was there actual loss or damage resulting to the interest of another?

Admittedly, these questions offer a degree of discretion. However, they do present a reasonably good idea of how an initial assessment of such a problem should proceed.

We might all agree that physical activity education and athletics programs should be challenging and interesting to the participant. Additionally, the safety and wellbeing of the participant is a basic priority that must not be neglected. As we pursue these objectives, to offer such physically active programs in a safe manner demands the institution of a planned risk-management program including (1) accident prevention, (2) accident investigation, (3) follow-up, and (4) appropriate insurance coverage. The following is an enlarged list of areas to be covered within the risk-management program:

1. Adequate supervision
2. Ongoing maintenance of medical records
3. Emergency care at times when accidents occur
4. Careful reporting of accidents
5. Attention to the posting of safety rules at points where needed
6. Regular information provided to all concerned about special danger areas
7. Ongoing system to obtain permissions and/or waivers in areas where accidents might occur

8. Careful attention to means whereby program
participants are transported to athletic events

What are some further some details about the "areas of responsibility"
that are listed above. For example, managers and their teaching and/or
coaching and maintenance staffs should understand the importance of acting
responsibly when supervising clients of all ages. Also, any exercise or sport
activity should be conducted in a safe environment including equipment and
apparatus provided. Further, the activities carried out in these areas must be
adequately supervised at all times. Additionally, a qualified trainer and
readily available medical assistance for accidents and possible emergencies
should be guaranteed. Finally, the organization should obtain appropriate
general liability insurance coverage. Moriarty (1980, p. 13) concurred largely
with the above strictures for managers and suggested further that risks
should be anticipated. He also stressed that, once an accident has occurred,
care should be taken not to increase the severity of any injury.

Of course, sound planning can save many subsequent "managerial
headaches" from ever occurring. Administrators must be certain that
instructors are thoroughly qualified in the sport or exercise skills that they
are teaching or administering. An instructor should know that individual
abilities and differences in size and skill should be considered so that suitable
competition and/or activity is carried out. In a wrestling class when practice
competition is scheduled, for example, matching the proverbial "96 lb.
weakling" with a rugged light heavyweight because all others are already
paired off could lead to disaster. Moving a student beyond his or her present
skill level in so-called "collision sports" must be avoided. There should be
clearly written rules for training and general conduct prominently posted as
well. To prevent the type of problem discussed here, Railey & Tschauner
(1993) recommend regular workshops for teachers and coaches where staff
competencies are evaluated and in-service training sessions are made
available.

A Transportation System. Railey & Tschauner (1993) stress also the
need to develop a system governing the transportation of participants in
physical activity-based programs. First, the state or provincial laws and
regulations concerning motor vehicle use should be reviewed. Then the local
situation should be assessed regarding the availability of buses and other
commercial carriers, unit rental possibilities, and the advisability of using
private vehicles. Keeping the budget in mind, after the appropriate authority
has made a decision, clearly written policies and procedures should be
developed. Subsequently, the manager must supervise ongoing
transportation to insure that sound practices have been followed (with
occasional evaluation for possible improvement where needed). For example,
Horine (1991, p. 121) stressed the need for the organization to have fully
adequate liability insurance, and such provision must extend to managerial

240

and staff personnel. The medical and hospitalization concerns of the participants must be cared for as well.

Medical and Training Practices. Another phase of a risk-management program that requires ongoing attention is that of establishing the best possible medical and training practices for all participants. It is essential to obtain adequate health data about all those who take part in programs of physical activity. This can be obtained through annual medical examinations prior to program participation with records kept about the results as a minimum. Proper conditioning for the type of activity is essential, as is the necessity for adequate equipment used. Trainers and teachers and coaches should be qualified to administer first aid, but should not provide what is considered medical treatment. A complete accident report form should be filled out after an injury requiring treatment occurs with witnesses' names when available (in triplicate). When a student or client has dropped out of regular participation because of illness or injury, written medical clearance must be required and filed before the person is permitted to return to action. A physician should be readily available (on call relatively close by!) when contact (collision!) sports competitions are held. Student trainers must be under the direct supervision of certified personnel (Horine, 1991, p. 125).

Law Court's Expectations. Coaches, teachers, and managers should understand what the law court's expectations are of them in the event of a suit for damages. The following are several questions that may well be asked. (1) Is there a relationship between the player's age and the nature of the activity? (2) Was adequate instruction given to the people involved in the activity insofar as the risk of danger was concerned? (3) Were there any previous accidents reported under similar circumstances?

Concluding Statement

All of the factors mentioned above must be considered when developing a sound risk-management program. This is why an overall program approach is needed, one that starts with capable, prudent instructors and coaches functioning in safe environments with sound equipment. Yet, no matter how much concern is shown, and how much care is taken, accidents will occur in the best of programs. The major responsibility and duty is to do one's best to avoid as many accidents as possible by careful planning, to be ready to cope with the situation in the proper way when they occur, and to be adequately insured in the event that there is negligence on the part of any one involved. Moriarty (1980, p. 5) stated that, when confronted with a lawsuit, the manager should "call his insurance carrier and your lawyer, in that order."

References

Drowatzky, J. N. (1993). Legal issues in sport and physical
  education management. (2nd ed.) Champaign, IL: Stipes.
Horine, L. (1991), Administration of physical education and sports programs.
  (2nd ed.). Philadelphia: Saunders.
Moriarty, R. (1980). Physical activity and legal liability. Ottawa,
  Canada: Canadian Association for HPERD.
Morford, W. R. (n.d.). Risk management in the fitness industry.
  (This is an unpublished manual developed expressly for the UBC
  Birdcoop Fitness Facility.)
Railey, J. H. & Tschauner, P. R. (1993). Managing physical education, fitness,
  and sports programs (2nd ed.).

For Consideration and Discussion:

As a possible "laboratory experience" for use with Chapter 12, it is recommended that the course instructor check to find out what arrangement has been set up at his/her college or university in regard to the whole question of risk management and concurrent legal liability. A presentation by the university's legal office representative might be one possibility for a class session. The athletic director could also be invited and asked to react in relation to his/her program. Then the course instructor could moderate a question-and-answer session involving the students enrolled in the management course.

Chapter 14

Balancing Life's Conflicting Aspects:
A Challenge for the
Sport & Physical Activity Administrator

(Author's Note: This background essay is intended to be synoptic in nature. It represents an evolving version of many of the ideas, opinions, and recommendations expressed by the author about management theory and practice as applied to physical education and sport in a variety of publications over a period of approximately 60years. Prior to a collaborative effort with Gary Bowie (Lethbridge) designed to introduce a management competency development approach to professional preparation in physical education and educational sport, the author had collaborated earlier, also, with Marcia Spaeth (retired from SUNY, Cortland) and Garth Paton and Terry Haggerty (now both at New Brunswick, but earlier at Western Ontario). Some of this material (i.e., that related to proposed areas of administrative research and that related to the professional preparation program) had been researched by Professor Spaeth and Professor Paton, respectively and appeared in Zeigler and Spaeth [1975]).

Introduction

In this chapter I hope to bring this dilemma down to the personal level. It is an effort to get you, the reader, to figure out--unless you are absolutely certain where you stand on the matter already–where you may be going in the years ahead in a field that is uncertain as well. Nevertheless, translating the disciplinary theory of "kinesiology" into generalizations about professional practice in physical activity education is fundamentally important to our society. The lives of people of all ages and conditions can be affected positively if this aim is carried out efficiently and effectively. Our task in the field today is to discover a host of young Canadians who will "make things happen" so that the field of developmental physical activity will prosper and thereby fulfill the potential for humankind that it inherently offers.

The purpose of this analysis was to outline how a sport and physical activity administrator (e.g., of physical activity education & athletics) might better comprehend the need to balance life's "conflicting aspects." These conflicting aspects are typically the broadening of one's professional vision while simultaneously seeking to maintain perspective as to his or her chosen aims and objectives in life. It was decided to employ a systems analysis approach to help explain what can be called "human and natural (or physical) ecologic interaction." The main problem of the analysis was first divided into five sub-problems (phrased as questions) for subsequent consideration:

1. Why should an administrator of physical activity education (including athletics) understand the various ramifications of ecology for humankind?
2. How can systems analysis coordinated with "human and natural ecologic interaction" apply to the *organizational* task? of such an administrator?
3. How can systems analysis coordinated with human and natural ecological interaction apply to the *personal* development of this administrator?
4. How can the two approaches be merged to achieve both *successful professional* life and a *fulfilling personal* life?
5. What may be reasonably concluded from this discussion?

A Physical Activity Administrator Should Understand the Ramifications of Ecology for Humankind?

For this analysis, ecology was defined as "the field of study that treats the relationships and interactions of human beings and other living organisms with each other and with their natural (or physical) environment" (Hawley, 1986, p. 2). Ecology, which is much more than so-called "environmentalism," is about truly understanding relationships with and/or interactions between humans and other organisms within the environment. This involvement has no doubt been with humankind over the centuries. In addition, the apparent continuing lack of understanding and full appreciation of it by leaders, not to mention almost all others, has still not been overcome. Further, the steadily increasing size of the world's population and the accompanying vast societal development has exacerbated the problem even further.

To put the matter more simply, the basic underlying issue of dwindling supply and increasing demand has never been brought home sufficiently to the world's leadership, much less to the majority of the people. And, in the relatively few cases where it has, urgent *present* need has almost invariably thrust the need for preparation to meet impending *future* disasters aside. In fact, that appears to be exactly what is happening at this very time.

Despite the ever-increasing importance of this subject to humankind, somehow the vital importance of the subject of ecology as a *fundamental social institution* such as economics, politics, etc. did not begin to receive serious attention by at least a segment of society until the early 1960s.

Today, however, selected countries and certain groups within these countries are striving to come to grips with the need to face up to the headlong collision looming between ecology and economics as conflicting social forces. For example, Epstein (1997) reported that "five years after 10,000 diplomats from 178 countries pledged to clean up the world at the United Nations-sponsored Rio Earth Summit, the first formal assessment of that pledge begins today" (March 13). At the same session, Maurice Strong, the 1992 conference chair, stated: "the process of deterioration has continued..."

Since 1970, many educators have gradually come to understand that the problem of ecology was here to stay. Zeigler (1989; 2003), for example, designated it as a persistent problem faced by the field of sport and physical education in the same way as he had identified the five other basic social forces (or influences) of values, politics, nationalism, economics, and religion back in 1964. No longer, as it had almost always been possible in the past, could people simply move elsewhere to locate another abundant supply of game to hunt, water to drink, or mineral resources to exploit when on-site resources are depleted. Today, as this problem is gradually being recognized globally with seemingly little response, the time is past due for the profession of physical education and sport to also pay special attention to this social force in the various aspects of its work.

More specifically, there are several very important reasons right now for the field to show ever-greater awareness of *human ecologic interaction* with its many ramifications for humankind. First, the promotion and subsequent development of such an awareness could soon result in the field's general acceptance of an overall human and natural (physical) ecologic orientation that could be designed to underlie all of its professional efforts. Such awareness and subsequent orientation would call the profession's attention to the fact that our basic concern as part-time and full-time administrators should be with the *total* life cycle of people considered both individually and collectively.

Second, the graduates of professional education programs, who subsequently serve as administrators or managers in organizations of all types functioning in culturally influenced environments, need to be so prepared they will understand and then commit themselves to the application of an overall ecological approach in their work. In this context this means that they, as professional managers serving as administrators, have a basic responsibility to develop and strengthen their particular institution or organization in which they serve so that it will have an ongoing capability *to adapt successfully to the changing (natural and cultural) environment in which it is located.*

They need to keep in mind that fundamental changes in society are continually taking place, and that they are accordingly influencing professionals in their administrative endeavor positively, negatively, or possibly not at all. This means that, at the practitioner's level, they should be (must be?) ever ready to meet such change (or lack of it) directly and adapt to it successfully if and when it occurs. For example, there appears to be an ever-present need to understand "cutback management" (or "management in decline," as it is often called. This, and other approaches are often called on in today's rapidly shifting environment. Another very important understanding that can serve all administrators well is a reasonably basic comprehension of change process itself, a development that is ever present and requires the ongoing attention of the administrator.

Coordinating Systems Analysis with Human and Natural Ecologic Interaction in the the *Organizational* Task of the Administrator??

The scope of the systems function in management today has gone far beyond the dreams of the "scientific management" pioneers such as Taylor, the Gilbreths, and Henri Fayol. Today the sport management profession should be fully aware of the potentialities of an ongoing systems analysis approach. Such an approach should be *coordinated with* the best type of overall human and natural (physical) ecologic interaction as the profession seeks to serve the public professionally through the medium of sport and physical activity. Concurrently, in this analysis of the *professional* function (i.e., organizational "task") of the manager, the same systems-approach concept can be merged with overall human ecologic interaction as applied to the sport manager's *personal* development.

The first consideration here is with the intricacies of a systems approach that give attention to *how* this can be done most efficiently. The assumption behind a systems approach to human and natural ecologic interaction is that the physical activity-delivery organization and its administrator(s)--and the people functioning within it as associates--should all understand the importance and ramifications of a complete ecological approach and be committed to its implementation in all aspects of their work. If this were understood fully, they would then strive to serve their clients and constituents in ways that help the organization grow and develop. (At this point there will not be an explanation of *why* the administrator should strive for *general* aims in an ever-changing human and natural environment, or *what* specific objectives might be subsumed under these long range aims.)

With such an approach to management, the managerial team and key associated personnel would seek to develop, employ, and maintain power and influence that lead to the achievement of planned (immediate) objectives en route to long-range aims or goals. In doing so, they should involve many people within the organization in one way or another in assisting with the implementation of the well-recognized, fundamental processes of planning, organizing, staffing, directing, and controlling the operation of the organization (Mackenzie, 1969, pp. 80-87). Throughout this series of experiences it is imperative that good human relations be employed by all through the use of effective and efficient communication techniques. The successful implementation of these various processes is extremely complex, of course. This is why a top-flight managerial team is becoming increasingly necessary to move a complex organization ahead.

The major responsibilities of physical activity administrators (in physical education and sport), presuming they live up a code of ethics, should include:

(1) the professional's obligations to provide services to all in society who want and need them;

(2) the professional's specific obligations to his/her students/clients as individuals;

(3) the professional's responsibilities to his/her employers/employing organization;

(4) the professional's obligations to his colleagues/peers and to the profession; and

(5) the professional's responsibility to overall society itself (as recommended by Bayles in (Zeigler, 1992, pp. 13-14).

All of these obligations should be deliberately included in a code of ethics along with a procedure for disciplinary action to guarantee the enforcement of these responsibilities. (The latter procedure rarely been enforced in any profession to date--with notable exceptions [e.g., medicine, law, psychology]. Several professions have at least made some effort to discipline those colleagues who are reported as having acted unprofessionally and

Figure 1

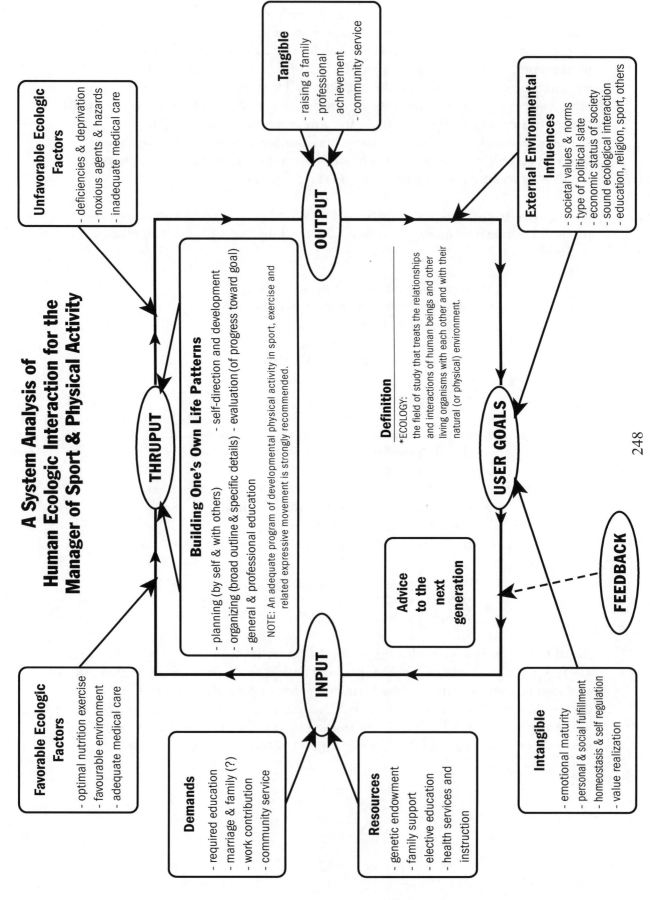

A System Analysis of Human Ecologic Interaction for the Manager of Sport & Physical Activity

Unfavorable Ecologic Factors
- deficiencies & deprivation
- noxious agents & hazards
- inadequate medical care

Favorable Ecologic Factors
- optimal nutrition exercise
- favourable environment
- adequate medical care

THRUPUT

Building One's Own Life Patterns
- planning (by self & with others)
- organizing (broad outline & specific details)
- general & professional education

- self-direction and development
- evaluation (of progress toward goal)

NOTE: An adequate program of developmental physical activity in sport, exercise and related expressive movement is strongly recommended.

OUTPUT

Tangible
- raising a family
- professional achievement
- community service

External Environmental Influences
- societal values & norms
- type of political slate
- economic status of society
- sound ecological interaction
- education, religion, sport, others

Definition
*ECOLOGY:
the field of study that treats the relationships and interactions of human beings and other living organisms with each other and with their natural (or physical) environment.

USER GOALS

Advice to the next generation

FEEDBACK

INPUT

Demands
- required education
- marriage & family (?)
- work contribution
- community service

Resources
- genetic endowment
- family support
- elective education
- health services and instruction

Intangible
- emotional maturity
- personal & social fulfillment
- homeostasis & self regulation
- value realization

248

unethically. If a professional acts *illegally* within a given legal jurisdiction, it can, of course, be expected that the political jurisdiction itself will judge the severity of such action and make an appropriate decision. Such a decision will subsequently give guidance to a professional society's committee on ethics as to any disciplinary action it should take.)

To meet these professional obligations, the physical activity administrator will be involved both professionally and personally in an ongoing struggle for recognition and accompanying status as he/she fulfills (1) those important obligations that relate to his/her *professional* life, as well as (2) those obligations that are required for optimum *personal* development. Moving on, it will now be considered first how a schematic, systems-analysis model could assist the manager to comprehend fully the scope and intent of these obligations and/or responsibilities in both "realms" of his or her existence.

A Schematic Model for the Administrative Process That Embodies a Systems Approach

A generation ago a schematic model for the management process was developed (the elements of the set, so to speak) that arranged the elements of a systems approach logically within a behavioral science perspective (Milstein and Belasco, 1973). The concern was with *input, thruput,* and *output,* and it was stressed that these three aspects must be strongly interrelated because any systems outputs "that result from transforming the human and material resources within the educational system must be at least minimally acceptable to environmental groups and organizations" (p. 81). If the outputs are not acceptable, the external groups and organizations will quite simply let it be known in short order that the "lifeline" of human and material resources will be sharply cut or eliminated.

A schematic model of such a systems model is offered here, in this case a systems model for managerial effectiveness with a professional training program for physical activity administrators. Here the goal or output for the purpose of this discussion is related to the education of people for various careers relating to our field. It is a substantive adaptation of the material available in both Milstein and Belasco (1973) and George (1972). (See Figure 1 above.)

One definition of administration states that it involves the execution of managerial acts by a competent person, including the application of personal, interpersonal, conceptual, technical, and conjoined skills, while combining varying degrees of planning, organizing, staffing, directing (i.e.,

Figure 2

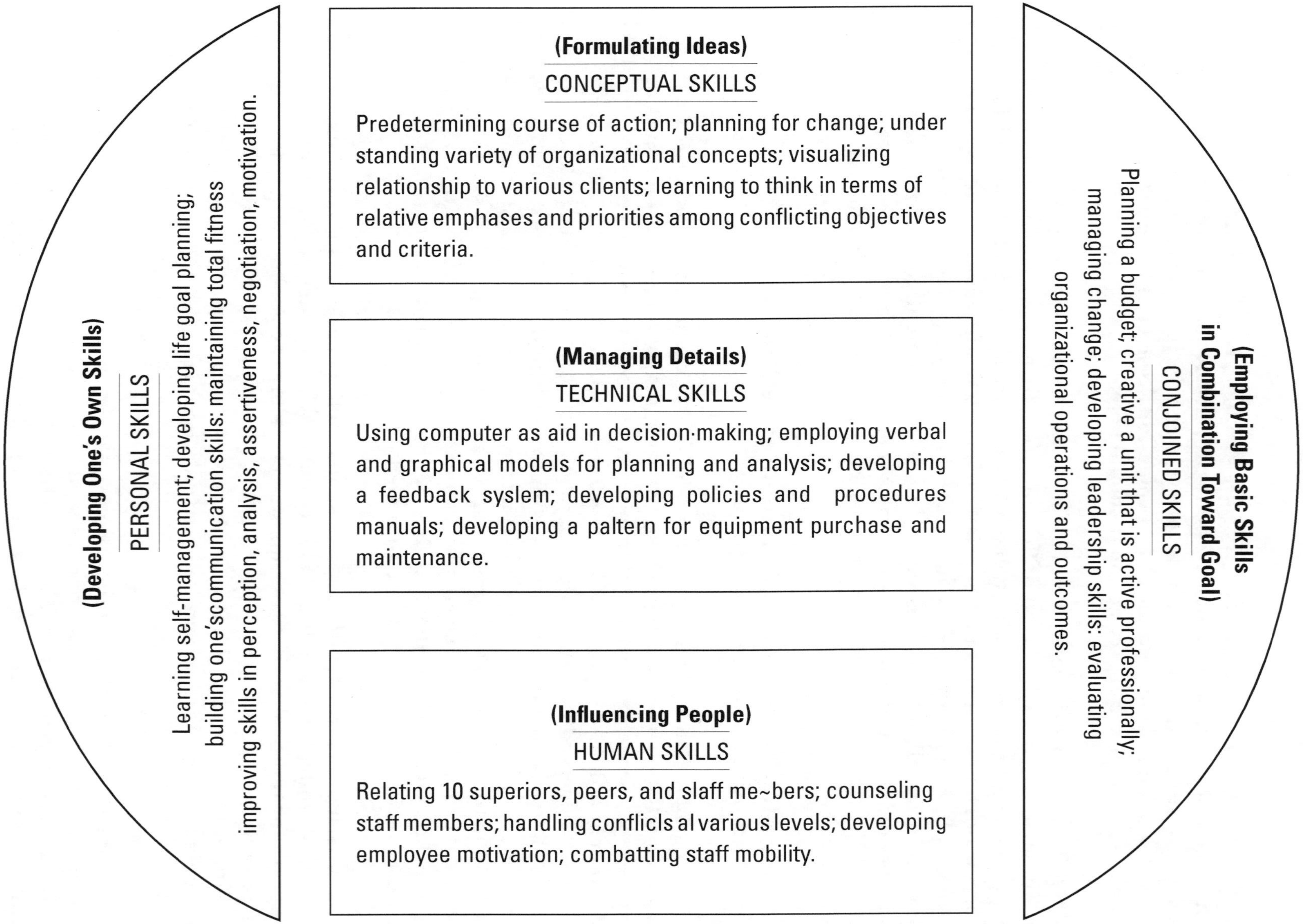

(Employing Basic Skills
in Combination Toward Goal)

CONJOINED SKILLS

Planning a budget; creative a unit that is active professionally; managing change; developing leadership skills: evaluating organizational operations and outcomes.

(Formulating Ideas)
CONCEPTUAL SKILLS

Predetermining course of action; planning for change; under standing variety of organizational concepts; visualizing relationship to various clients; learning to think in terms of relative emphases and priorities among conflicting objectives and criteria.

(Managing Details)
TECHNICAL SKILLS

Using computer as aid in decision-making; employing verbal and graphical models for planning and analysis; developing a feedback system; developing policies and procedures manuals; developing a paltern for equipment purchase and maintenance.

(Influencing People)
HUMAN SKILLS

Relating 10 superiors, peers, and slaff me~bers; counseling staff members; handling conflicls al various levels; developing employee motivation; combatting staff mobility.

(Developing One's Own Skills)

PERSONAL SKILLS

Learning self-management; developing life goal planning; building one'scommunication skills: maintaining total fitness improving skills in perception, analysis, assertiveness, negotiation, motivation.

The names of three of the categories were taken from Katz, M. L.: Skills of an effective administrator Harvard Business Review 52. 5: 90-102. 1974

Management Development and Process (The knowledge and skills obtained through a competency-based approach).

leading), and controlling (i.e., evaluation) within the management process to assist an organization to achieve its goals effectively and efficiently (Zeigler and Bowie, 1995, p. 115).

Further, the assumption is that such managerial acts will be directed toward individual and group goals within both the internal and external environments of an organization. In this example (Fig. 1), those directing the professional preparation program within a college or university perceive certain societal demands and/or needs (e.g., a societal demand for various types of physical activity administrators). Depending on the specific circumstance, the university and its alumni and supporters respond by making available (initially or potentially) (1) material and human resources such as available capital, (2) some level of achievement in sport competition and fitness promotion, and (3) a management program staff of good, bad, or indifferent stature. All of this initial development is, of course, ultimately part of the total administrative process itself. After the initial input stage has been started, we are really describing functions that occur within the larger management process that is typically characterized by such terms as planning, organizing, staffing, directing, and controlling (Mackenzie, 1969). For the administrator to execute these functions adequately, he or she should have acquired the necessary knowledge, competencies and skills (adapted from Katz, 1974, with advice from William Penny).

Thinking of the total administrative or managerial process in this example of a system analysis model for maximum effectiveness, keep in mind that there can be three categories of parameters and/or variables that influence the entire undertaking, as follows: (1) environmental *non controllable* parameters (constraints *or* opportunities), (2) internal *controllable* variables, and (3) *partially controllable* variables (that may be external and/or internal). It is important that physical activity administrators understand how strong these variables (influences) may be and accordingly be ever ready to factor their impact into the overall administrative process. Too often it appears that when such a non controllable or partially controllable parameter looms suddenly on the horizon, "internal panic" results because administrators--and thus their organizations, of course--have not planned ahead and typically are *in no way* ready for its appearance.

The environmental *non–controllable* parameters should be viewed as external influences that must be considered seriously. They are such persistent historical problems as (1) the influence of the society's values and norms; (2) the influence of politics (the type of political state and the "stance" of the party or person in power); (3) the influence of nationalism (or whatever powerful "chauvinistic" influence might develop); (4) the influence of the prevailing economic situation (including depressions, tax increases, inflation, etc.); (5) the influence of prevailing religious groups (including boycotts, conflicting events); (6) the influence of ecology (as discussed above in this paper); and (7) the influence of competition (from other attractions, etc.).

To understand the concept of "administrative effectiveness" generally, as diagrammed in the model (Figure 1), it is necessary to consider specifically the relationship of managerial acts (ACTS) and the external and internal environments (Ee and Ei, respectively) of the organization to the eventual accomplishment of *at least a certain percentage* of the organization's goals (pGg) as well as *at least a certain percentage* of the (total of) individual's goals (pGi) realized.

In other words, an effective administrator would be a person who strives successfully to accomplish the organization's goals to the greatest possible extent, while at the same time giving adequate or ample consideration to what percentage of the goals held by individual employees is achieved. At this point, then, the concept of managerial effectiveness (Me) is added to our ongoing equation as that percentage (p) of the organization's and the (total of) individuals' goals that are realized.

(Note: Initially, the percentage of an individual's goals achieved would be a collective percentage; however, where individual goal achievement exists with a differentiated reward system and a varying pay scale exists, the effectiveness of any one person could be evaluated as well.)

Thus

$$Me = (pGg) + (pGi)$$

Similarly, if we accept that managerial acts (Aplanning, Aorganizing, Astaffing, etc.) are a function of a percentage (% of the attainment of) of Gg and Gi, then

$$M = F (<pGg + (pGi>)$$

Further, if G (Gg + Gi) is known, it follows that Gi) is a function of it.

(Note: For those interested, a much more detailed analysis of this mathematical model seeking to explain the administrative process is available in Zeigler and Bowie, 1995, pp. 115-120.)

(See Figure 3 below)

Figure 3

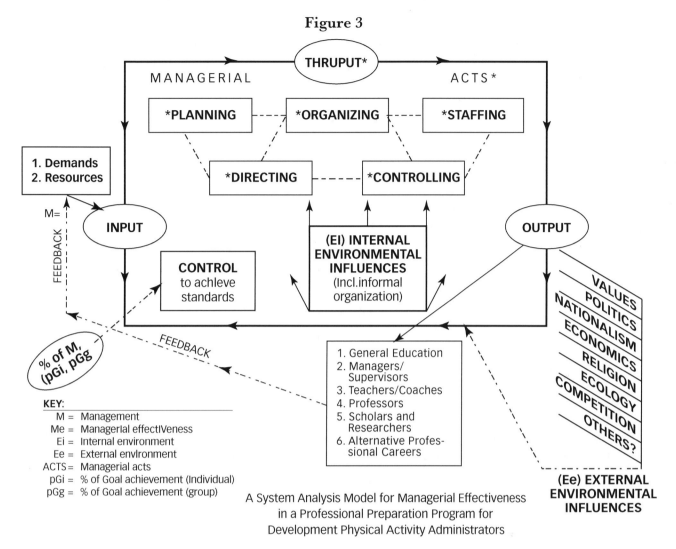

A System Analysis Model for Managerial Effectiveness in a Professional Preparation Program for Development Physical Activity Administrators

Coordinating Systems Analysis with Human and Natural Ecologic Interaction in the *Personal* Development of the Administrator

But what of *the individual* who is involved professionally in the managerial task itself--i.e., the first-level, second-level, etc. administrator? Adoption of this approach mandates that this person should have regular opportunities for *both* personal and professional growth. This can be accomplished by implementing a similar plan for the administrator, also, one that outlines a system analysis of the administrator's own human ecologic interaction as he or she strives *to achieve a life purpose in this profession* while concurrently serving the organization's clientele and the larger community.

If this is to be carried out successfully, such a plan should also be based on a model that includes (1) *input* factors such as demands and resources; (2) *thruput* factors such as planning, evaluation, general & professional education, and evaluation; (3) tangible *output* factors such as (possibly) raising a family, professional achievement, and community service, and (4) intangible *user goals'* factors such as emotional maturity, personal and social fulfillment, homeostasis and self-regulation, health & fitness, and personal & social value realization.

253

Basically, the discussion at this point outlines how physical activity administrators can use a systems analysis approach to achieve optimal health (so-called wellness) for an effective personal and professional life within a reasonably balanced lifestyle. The idea of achieving optimal health within one's lifestyle has been equated with, and compressed in recent years by many to, the concept of "wellness":

> Wellness can be described as a lifestyle designed to reach one's highest potential for wholeness and wellbeing. Wellness has to do with a zest for living, feeling good about oneself, having goals and purposes for life . . . This concept is far more than freedom from symptoms of illness and basic health maintenance, but reaches beyond to an optimal level of well-being (*ERIC Digest* 3, 1986).

These thoughts and ideas are really not new, but they have been placed in a more modern perspective here. Many years ago Jesse Feiring Williams defined positive health as "the ability to live best and serve most." The wellness movement has similarly recommended a balanced lifestyle. It has encouraged people to assume more responsibility for their health and to view health in the same light as Williams did earlier--that is, in a positive light in which the person's "wellness" involved all aspects of a unified organism.

In this light, at the input stage the physical education and sport administrator will typically acquire a better understanding of the *demands* (e.g., required education) made upon him or her, as well as an understanding of the *resources* (e.g., genetic endowment) necessary for a satisfactory response. (See the left section of Figure 3.)

Next, at what is called the thruput stage, the manager will appreciate more fully what steps should be taken as the individual plans, organizes, and carries out life plans. At this stage these steps should be carried out optimally through self-direction with evaluation at several strategic points along the way. (See the middle section toward the top of Figure 3.)

While all of this is taking place, there are a number of external, natural and social environmental influences impinging upon the manager's development (e.g., changing societal values, declining economic status; see bottom right of Figure 3.) An administrator may have control over some of these influences, but others are often beyond control. These include both favorable and unfavorable ecologic factors. (See top right and left of Figure 3.) In the final analysis, the administrator must make a number of crucial decisions throughout life. Such decisions may be made before the fact, so to speak, while others are made as best possible in response to natural and social factors that may often be completely or partially beyond the manager's ability to control them.

In the third or output stage of an administrator's life viewed through a system analysis perspective, the manager will be asked to consider what she or he wants both her/his extrinsic, measurable and her/his intrinsic, non-measurable life goals to be. The administrator will need also to seek some sort of relationship between these measurable goals and what may be called intrinsic (i.e., typically less measurable life goals).

> (Note: See "tangible" output at right of
> Figure 3 and "intangible" output stated as
> "user goals" at the bottom left of Figure 3.)

In the first case, the tangible output, this refers to the person's achievement in his or her chosen career or occupation, as well as family life (however defined) and community service. In the second instance, he or she will need to assess the matter of achievement of personal and social fulfillment through the possible self-realization of those values that are felt to be most important.

> (Note: A more detailed outline of this
> analysis of a desirable life cycle is offered
> below in the Appendix.)

Finally, toward the end of this system loop, provision should be made for feedback resulting in advice to the next generation. This lifelong process for the individual is typically influenced by (1) such *external environmental influences* as (e.g.) the economic status of the society; (2) such favorable ecologic factors as (e.g.) adequate medical care; and (3) such unfavorable ecologic factors as (e.g.) the presence of noxious agents & hazards.

Merging the Two Approaches to Achieve Both: A Successful *Professional* Life and a *Personally Fulfilling* Life

Turning attention away from self-management (i.e., the personal life pattern of the individual physical activity administrator) and back to the overall organizational administrative task itself, it becomes apparent that these two managerial techniques can be merged successfully. Whether these techniques will be in any particular organization involved with the administration of sport and physical activity depends on the overall administrative philosophy prevailing. On the surface an ecological orientation merged with a systems analysis approach to management would almost necessarily result in an "organizational management climate" that is eclectic in nature.

An "eclectic" administrative style may be needed because of the increasing number of situations today where a managerial team is responsible for the direction in which the organization is heading. This means that it may include, where possible and when desirable, any or all aspects of the traditional, behavioral, or decision-making patterns of administrative behavior. Thus administrators may find themselves functioning with an amalgam of traditional principles, cooperative behavioralist ideas, and decisionalist competitive strategies (Gibson, Ivancevich, and Donnelly, 1997, pp. 433-439).

Conclusion

In the twenty-first century, such an "amalgamated" approach to professional *and* personal management behavior as discussed here may indeed become both necessary and desirable. This would be true so long as the original formulation of aims and objectives has occurred democratically. And, as it has happened, in Western culture people have been increasingly involved in the decision-making process in all aspects of life. As a result, an organization that fails to prepare its people adequately (i.e., both theoretically and emotionally) for the introduction of change could well find its seemingly realizable goals to be thwarted--or at least temporarily blocked--by (1) human conflicts, (2) natural or cultural barriers within the general (external), or (3) changing interpersonal and/or situational circumstances within the immediate (internal) environment (Mikalachki, A., Zeigler, E.F., & Leyshon, G.A., 1988, pp. 1-17).

In respect to the organization itself and its achievement of predetermined group and individual goals, it should be borne in mind that such organizational "growth" does not necessarily mean growth in size. This is especially important where an "ecological-oriented" business strategy has been adopted on the basis of an overall philosophical stance. It does mean that the adaptive behavior of those involved in the administrative task who (1) subscribe to an "ecological orientation" philosophically and (2) employ a systems approach functionally should be in a strong position to help the organization to remain viable, to be stronger, to remain competitive, and to be increasingly more effective and efficient in the accomplishment of its long range aims and immediately realizable objectives.

Finally, similar problems or obstacles of varying nature and intensity may arise within the broader general (external) environment. Of course, the hope is that such situations would serve as challenges to physical activity administrators and their teams. The response to problems or obstacles should be heuristic in nature in the sense that a particular management team would be prepared to react to the prevailing demands and needs by adapting or possible adjusting means, behavior, and even ends at some point along the line. Developmental physical activity administrators should proceed only on the basis that the future belongs to those who manage effectively and efficiently in the pursuit of planned organizational goals.

References

Bayles, M.D. (1981). *Professional Ethics*. Belmont, CA: Wadsworth.

Epstein, J. (1997). Rio Summit's promises still unfulfilled. *The Globe and Mail* (Toronto), March 13, A12.

George, C.S. (1972). *The history of management thought (2nd Ed.)*. Englewood Cliffs, NJ: Prentice-Hall.

Gibson, J.I., Ivancevich, J.M., & Donnelly, J.H., Jr. (1997). *Organizations (9th Ed.)*. Chicago, IL: Irwin.

Hawley, A.H. (1986). *Human ecology: A theoretical essay*. Chicago: Univ. of Chicago Press.

Katz, R.L. (Sept.-Oct. 1974). Skills of an effective administrator. *Harvard Business Review*, 51, 5:90-112.

Mackenzie, R.A. (1969). The management process in 3-D. *Harvard Education Review*, 47: 80-87.

Mikalachki, A,, Zeigler, E.F., & Leyshon, G.A. (1988). *Change process in sport and physical education management*. Champaign, IL: Stipes.

Milstein, M.M. & Belasco, J.A. (1973). *Educational administration and the behavioral sciences: A systems perspective*. Boston: Allyn.

Prevention (July 1988). High health in the middle years. 40: 7: 35-36, 38-47, 100, 105-107, 110.

Zeigler, E.F. (1964). *Philosophical foundations for physical, health, and recreation education*. Englewood Cliffs, NJ: Prentice-Hall.

Zeigler, E.F. (1989). *An introduction to sport and physical philosophy*. Carmel, IN: Benchmark Press.

Zeigler, E.F. (1992). *Professional ethics for sport managers*. Champaign, IL: Stipes.

Zeigler, E. F. (2003). *Socio-Cultural Foundations of Physical Education and Educational Sport*. Aachen, Germany: Meyer and Meyer.

Zeigler, E.F. & Bowie, G.W. (2007) *Management competency development in sport and physical education*. Victoria, BC: Trafford.

APPENDIX

EMPLOYING A SYSTEMS ANALYSIS APPROACH, COORDINATED WITH HUMAN AND NATURAL ECOLOGIC INTERACTION, IN A QUEST FOR OPTIMAL HEALTH AND EFFECTIVE LIVING

INPUT Stage A: What *Demands* Are Made on a Person in Today's World?

1. Early Family Membership
2. Education
3. Marriage & Family
4. Work Contribution
5. Community Service

INPUT Stage B: What *Resources* Are Typically Provided?

1. Early Family Support
2. Educational Opportunities
3. External Social Influences
4. Employment Opportunities
5. Health & Community Services

THRUPUT Stage A: What *Steps* Should Be Taken in Developing One's Own Life As Fully As Possible?

1. Planning for the Long Haul Ahead
2. Organizing the Required Factors & Details
3. Implementing Life Stages Through Self-Direction
4. Evaluation of Progress Made in Goal Achievement
5. Modifying or Redirecting One's Developmental Pattern
6. Planning for Retirement

THRUPUT Stage B: What *External Environmental Factors* Might Be Encountered?

1. Favorable Ecologic Factors:

   a. Good Heredity; No Disabling Disease
   b. Healthy Environment; No Debilitating Factors
   c. Safe Living; No Careless Risk
   d. Optimal Nutrition, Exercise, & Rest
   e. Challenges; Satisfying Work & Recreation
   f. Commitment to High Values
   g. Competent Medical & Dental Care
   h. Homeostasis & Self-Regulation; Emotional Maturity

i. Personal & Social Fulfillment; Freedom & Privacy

2. Unfavorable Ecologic Factors

    a. Poor Heredity; Disabling Disease
    b. Unhealthy Environment; Noxious Agents & Hazards
    c. Unsafe Living; Careless Risk
    d. Inadequate Nutrition, Exercise, & Rest
    e. Little Challenge; Unrewarding Work & Recreation
    f. Lack of Commitment to High Values
    g. Inadequate Medical & Dental Care
    h. Deprivation; Excesses; Immaturity
    i. Low Level of Achievement & Personal Fulfillment;
       Restraints & Overcrowding

3. Improved Health in the Middle Years (40-49)

    a. Assessment of nutritional intake
    (including reasonable coffee intake, compensating
    for "metabolic slowdown"; watch amounts of alcohol,
    desserts, and fat consumed; pare diet down &
    exercise)

    b. Body conditioning
    (work with weights; stretch; watch for "middle-age
    spread"; strive for consistency, not intensity;
    exercise will burn off fat)

    c. Circulo-respiratory conditioning
    (regular, moderate exercise within "threshold zone"
    will keep heart healthy--serves to lower high blood
    pressure and blood cholesterol)

    d. Contraception
    (continue birth-control methods for one year post-
    menstrually; barrier contraceptives still recommended
    for middle years; check new methods available care-
    fully; consider clip sterilization)

    e. Good sex
    (sexual interest peaks for women in late 30's or
    early 40's; males better lovers at this stage;
    communication of feelings; stay healthy; maintain
    strength of PC and/or vaginal muscles; vaginal
    lubricants; remain active sexually; women may
    consider HRT.

f. Healthy relationships
(beware of burnout and boredom; involvement in shared
tasks and interests; cultivation of friends)

g. Job transition
(change positions only for the right reasons; be more
concerned about fulfilling needs and interests than
before building size of bank account or stock
holdings; your age is biggest asset; experience
brings ability to solve practical problems)

h. Brainpower
(stay mentally active and even work for improvement;
try not to act your age; limit TV viewing time;
strive to be productive creatively; boost memory
power and pay attention.

(Note: This section above is based on "High
Health in the Middle Years, *Prevention,* July
1988).

OUTPUT Stage A: Tangible (Extrinsic) Life Accomplishments

1. A Family Raised Successfully
2. Achievement in Chosen Career
3. Record of Community Service
4. Plan Developed for Successful Retirement

OUTPUT Stage B: Intangible (Intrinsic) Life Accomplishments

1. Personal & Social Fulfillment
   Through Value Realization
2. System Feedback: Advice to the Next Generation

THE OVERALL GOAL: Optimal Health, Effective Living,
                  and Personal & Social

For Consideration and Discussion:

As an exercise at the end of this chapter, it is recommended that two
students each make a 10-minute presentation, the first one explaining
theoretically the *organizational* task of the administrator. Then the other
student should explain the personal development of the maturing
administrator. Finally. a third student should conduct a class discussion on
the topic in a search for ways to strike "a happy balance."

CHAPTER 14

APPLIED ETHICS
FOR THE
MANAGER OF PHYSICAL ACTIVITY EDUCATION
(INCLUDING ATHLETICS)

Introduction

The entire educational system seems to be challenged constantly in one or more ways more than ever before in memory. We hear that the pendulum seems to be swinging back to the teaching of values in U.S. schools. Next colleges and universities are being told that they face loss of governmental aid if race is a criterion for admission. These same institutions of higher learning are also examining their core curricula because their relevance has been challenged. Students are viewed as bureaucrats, because they soon get tend to lose interest when they enter school and soon discover that their teachers are telling them what to learn, how to learn it, when to learn it, and in what form to "regurgitate" those gems of wisdom when testing time comes around.

But worst of all in some people's eyes is the fact that other students in comparable societies are going to school longer, studying harder, and obtaining higher scores on standardized tests. What shall be done? The obvious answer to this question, at least as far as most parents, many teachers and administrators, and public-conscious politicians, is to stress the time-proven "educational essentials," lengthen the school year, and set national standards while introducing national standardized tests to measure how much learning occurs at the various levels of the educational system.

Much of what has been said above may be true, but not always for the same reasons that have been given. In the first place, some of the problem may be laid at a different doorstep. For example, there is no evidence that tells us that children in North America today are less intelligent. What is happening is that the electronic media, faster-paced life-styles, environmental hazards, unstable family patterns, poverty, stress, and current educational practices are changing the way children think--and perhaps even the very structure of their brains. Also, as usual, the typical cry for an educational revolution typically stresses dubious goals and inadequate ways of achieving what is really needed. Students need to be motivated to achieve desirable knowledge, skills, and competencies that will prepare them both for fine personal living and successful careers in professions and related occupations in the 21st century.

Over and above all this, it doesn't appear that the pendulum hasn't swung back far enough yet in regard to the study of values and norms in a democratic society. Moreover, in addition to inadequate training in personal ethics in the public schools, North American society is now "playing catch-up" in the matter of including upper-level course experiences in ethics in professional curricula. This chapter on professional ethics for physical activity education and athletics managers begins at this point by explaining the need for an improved approach--any systematic approach for that matter--to ethical understanding in the management of this educational enterprise.

This short chapter can only introduce the reader to the presently inadequate way that people make ethical decisions generally. Recommendations for improvement are offered because personal ethics are explained as being foundational to professional ethics. Then criteria for sound professional status are necessarily introduced, because it appears that physical activity education (including athletics) management is playing "catch-up" in regard to its professional status, a condition shared to a degree with the entire profession of education. You will be introduced to the subject of professional ethics generally, and then specifically to one specific approach for the development of a code of ethics.

Despite certain present inadequacies, an ethical creed was approved by the North American Society for Sport Management. Then, with advice from Prof. Garth Paton, developed a detailed code of ethics was enacted by the membership. (This has since been updated.) The only conceivable bone of contention since that time has been the failure to implement a discipline system for those committing ethical misdeeds! My argument is still that it can be said that a profession "has arrived" when it regularly polices itself in this regard. The field of education has much room for improvement.

Lest prospective sport and physical activity managers be unduly worried, the same statement about past lack of attention to ethics and ethical decision-making can be made for our entire culture. Perhaps this lack of a systematic approach to ethical understanding can be blamed on the doctrine of separation of church and state, but who would wish to imply that this should be otherwise? There is no doubt, however, but that those associated with physical education, competitive sport, and physical recreation have allowed themselves to go along with the drift. Now all of society, and sport and physical education as a field within society, has to "play catch-up" in troubling times. (This despite the fact that pioneers within the allied professions gave some thought to ethical professional behavior as long ago as the 1930s.)

How is it then that the North American culture, and sport and physical activity management in this instance, is now facing a need for an improved approach to ethics as we approach the beginning of the 21st century? A possible response relates to the fundamental condition of men and women in the world. Throughout their existence humans have been confronted with the difficulty of establishing wholesome human relations within a harsh physical environment. In the developed nations at least a recognizable semblance of adaptation has been made to these problems.

However, it has not yet been possible to remove much of the insecurity evident so that people can live together peacefully and constructively in a world with sharply increasing population, manifold wars often occasioned by conflicting politico/religious groups, and seeming steadily increasing expectations for human life in social settings. In considering humankind's basic problem, Burtt (1965, p. 311) believed that the human's "disturbing emotions and destructive passions" represent the greatest danger for the future. Accordingly, the application of a sound ethical approach--whichever one of a number available is chosen--to both personal and professional living can be of inestimable assistance to people who are truly seeking a "sensitive understanding" of themselves and their associates.

Today there is abundant evidence from a variety of sources that many other professionals (e.g., medicine, law, business) have seen the need for study about ethics. There has been a subsequent rise in enrollment in established ethics courses and a spate of new applied ethics courses have been established, a trend that somehow "went right over the heads" of the large majority of faculty working in professional programs in sport and physical education. Whether such a trend can be shown to have a relationship with the earlier social consciousness felt in the 1960s and early 1970s is debatable, but somehow in the 1990s there is now every evidence that interest in values and ethics will be maintained.

What is being recommended, therefore, is that those working in professional training should now give serious consideration to the matter of professional ethics, while not forgetting the importance of the underlying personal ethics of individual concurrently. It is simply not possible to argue at present that an aspiring sport manager, or a sport and physical education teacher/coach, typically receives any significant course experience along these lines? Whether the provision of such experience would result in a more ethical person and/or sport manager cannot be shown objectively. However, the odds are that a solid course in applied ethics with accompanying laboratory experiences would provide additional pause for an individual to think seriously when situations involving ethical decision-making arise in personal and professional living.

How Ethical Instruction is Handled in North America Today

Unfortunately, the child or young person typically learns to make *rational* ethical decisions poorly and inadequately, a tragic condition because personality development is so important. An interesting analysis of what occurs before any semblance of a rational philosophy develops has been offered by Rand. The human possesses a 'psychological recorder" that is truly the person's subconscious, integrating mechanism. This so-called sense of life "is a pre-conceptual equivalent of metaphysics, an emotional, subconsciously integrated appraisal of man and existence. It sets the nature of a man's emotional responses and the essence of his character" (Rand, 1960, p. 31).

Granting the apparent truth of what I have just described, we who are interested in the entire educational process must hope that all young people in our society will have the chance to develop *their own* rational powers through the finest possible educational experience. Reason should soon begin to act as the programmer of the person's "emotional computer." Thus, our concern must be, therefore, to help this young person develop conscious convictions in which the mind leads and the emotions follow. The person gradually learns what values are important; thus, "the integrated sum of a person's basic values is that person's sense of life" (Ibid., p. 35).

Finally, what the young person really needs at this juncture of his or her development is an "intellectual roadbed" that provides a "course of life" to follow. The eventual goal should be a fully integrated personality, a person whose mind and emotions are in harmony a great deal of the time. When this occurs, there is a situation where the individual's sense of life matches his or her conscious convictions. It is fundamental, of course, that the young person's view of reality is carefully defined by himself or herself and is reasonably consistent. If ethical instruction were planned more carefully and explicitly, the quality of living would probably be greatly improved for all.

From Personal to Professional Ethics

If there is agreement that a young person in our society should be so educated that there is ample opportunity for him or her to develop rationality as a life competency, it is essential further that such ability be available for use with the many ethical problems that arise in all phases of daily life. Thus a more basic concern in this discussion is that the young adult be able to apply such competency to the ethical problems that arise in the course of professional service to the field.

I am not arguing that we as a field within education are any better or any worse that most other fields in regard to the application of professional ethics to our endeavors. Perhaps it would simply be best to state that our entire culture is confused in this matter, and it has just happened that way in North American development. This tangle of ethics has developed because of a diverse inheritance of customs and mores from the other lands, and we have simply added our own brand of confusion to this ill-suited mixture of moral systems.

Where does that leave the profession of physical activity education, and specifically those concerned with its management (including athletics)? The answer at this point must be, "In trouble!" Nevertheless, if our field is to survive and to continue to grow, it must serve society more effectively in the years immediately ahead. To do this, our field, along with all other fields within the education profession, must be attuned to the all-important values and norms that have been established within the culture.

It is obvious that we need to take a hard look at ourselves--admittedly a difficult assignment. Responding to current heavy criticism of highly competitive athletics is indeed a humbling experience. Further, we are part of the teaching profession, and yet ideally physical education and sport has a broad mission that extends from infancy to our oldest citizens be they "normal," "special," or "accelerated."

We do have many of the attributes of a profession (e.g., extensive training period; significant intellectual component to be mastered; and some recognition that the trained person can provide a basic important service to society) (Bayles, 1981, p. 7). However, physical activity education has not done as well as some of the highly recognized fields in developing and enforcing carefully defined professional obligations that the practitioner must follow to remain in good standing with his or her fellows and with society.

What Is Currently Available in Sport and Other Physical Activity Education?

In considering what we have in the field that might be considered to be professional ethics, initially we must be careful to distinguish between a *creed*, or "statement of professional beliefs" and a *code*, or "set of detailed regulations of a more administrative nature" (Bayles, 1981, p. 24). In competitive sport, for example, the National High School Athletic Coaches Association has developed what might be called an embryonic code. A similarly brief code, with some overlap, was adopted by the Minnesota High School Coaches Association.

In physical activity education, which is unfortunately usually viewed only within the domain of the education profession, several efforts have been made over the years to define what our ethical concerns should be. However, at present there appears to be no concerted effort underway to rectify a situation that is glaringly inadequate. Several textbooks have been made available by Shea (1978), Fraleigh (1984), Zeigler (1984), DeSensi amd Rosenberg (1996), and Kretchmar (2007). However, there are relatively few courses in physical activity education ethics offered in our field.

A Recommended Approach

In response to the question, "Where do we go from here?" I suppose the best answer is, "There's nowhere to go but up!" I strongly believe that there should be a required course in professional ethics for all teachers, managers, and coaches in their programs of professional preparation. A strong case can be made for this recommendation if we but remind ourselves that without ethical behavior a teacher/manager/coach could be "nothing" overnight. Just one mistake in regard to accepted ethical behavior could put a large dent in--*or even ruin*--what was fast becoming a fine professional career.

To become more specific, I have argued that we need something that is not too complicated. Despite the fact that I was not a trained moral philosopher or ethicist, I was determined to bring this area to the forefront because of the urgency of the matter. I finally decided to offer an approach recommended to me by a Dr. Richard Fox, professor of philosophy and departmental chairman at Cleveland State University, a person who has taught in this aspect of philosophy for several decades. His advice was that, for the teaching of ethics to undergraduates in this culture, we would do well to amalgamate three great ideas about ethics that Kant, Mill, and Aristotle promulgated into a progression that may be used for the determination of what's good or bad, or right and wrong.

This "trivium approach" to ethical decision-making moves from the application of Kant's test of "<u>universalizability</u>" or *consistency*, to Mill's test of *consequences*, and then to Aristotle's test of *intentions*. The ethical dilemma begins when the athlete or the physical activity educator/coach or the so-called sport manager is faced with an ethical choice. The question is, "What should he or she do about such-and-such a problem that has arisen?"

Step #1, Kant's test of consistency, asks the question, "Is it possible to universalize the action that we are judging to all people on earth?" Kant said, "So act that you could wish the maxim of your action to become a universal law of human conduct." This approach is similar to the Golden Rule and other maxims and, of course, does have some imperfections.

When the professional person have determined if he or she can answer the question posed by Kant either affirmatively or negatively, move to Step #2, Mill's test of consequences. Here Mill would say something like this: "Have you acted so as to bring about the greatest (net) good or happiness that is possible in this situation?" Accordingly, the professional educator should be able to say that she (for example) acted on the basis of the best evidence available at the time of acting, and that such-and-such an action is right because it produced the maximum amount of *net,* not *gross* happiness. It helps at this stage in making a judgment to keep such principles as autonomy, justice, and beneficence firmly in mind. Step #3 derives from the philosophic thought of the legendary Aristotle of ancient Greece, the man who tutored Alexander the Great. This step is called the test of intentions. It serves to take the focus away from the results of the action itself by reverting to what the perpetrator of the act had in mind when he or she carried it out. In his *Nicomachean Ethics* (1943, Book III, Chapter 1), Aristotle asked the question, "What were the conditions under which the act was performed?"

Merging with a Jurisprudential (Law-Court) Argument Format

Once the tests of consistency, consequences, and intentions have been applied in sequential order to confront a problem in ethical decision-making, an athlete, physical educator/coach, or sport manager may determine that the answer to the ethical problem is quite clear to him or her. In fact, I suppose we ought to be happy generally if we can get most people to proceed to this point in all phases of life.

However, there will be many people who will wish to introduce additional substantiation for any decision made. Thus I am recommending further that the steps already taken (1, 2, and 3) be superimposed on what Stephen Toulmin called his "layout for a jurisprudential argument" (1964, p. 95). This is a formally valid argument in proper form that is similar to arguments employed daily in jurisprudence (law-court) and mathematics. (See Figure 1 below.)

With this approach the person can move forward gradually, steadily, and reasonably from D to C, from the *data* to what seems like a reasonable *conclusion*. The next step (#2) in the Toulmin argument layout (the *warrant* or W) involves the creation of a general hypothetical statement that acts as a bridge to lend support to the (tentative?) conclusion that has been reached. It typically answers the question, "How did you get there?" (See Figure 1 above)

The third step (#3) in Toulmin's argument layout has two parts: (1) the introduction of *modal qualifier* followed by consideration of possible *conditions of exception* (or rebuttal). Thus depending upon the intensity or force of the warrant, the qualifying term (Q) may be "necessarily," "presumably," "probably," etc. This leads directly to the second part of Step #3, the condition(s) of exception or rebuttal that can introduce particular circumstances of greater or lesser import that might negate or even refute the authority of the warrant (W). (See Figure 1 again.)

The final step to be discussed, the introduction of *backing* (B) into the layout, in the rounding out of the argument presented in Figure 1 above takes us back to the nature of the warrant (W). The backing (B) serves the purpose of strengthening or supplementing the warrant (B) even further. Happily, it is

FIGURE 1

MERGING OF "TRIVIUM" APPROACH AND JURISPRUDENTIAL ARGUMENT FORMAT

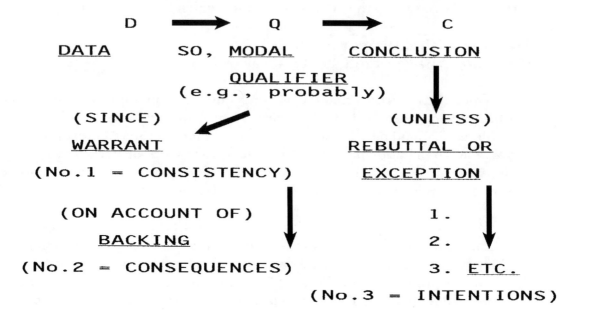

KEY TO JURISPRUDENTIAL ARGUMENT TERMS:

D = DATA (A STATEMENT OF A SITUATION THAT PREVAILS, INCLUDING EVIDENCE, ELEMENTS, SOURCES, SAMPLES OF FACTS)

Q = MODAL QUALIFIER (ADVERB EMPLOYED TO QUALIFY CONCLUSION BASED ON STRENGTH OF WARRANTS (E.G., NECESSARILY, PROBABLY)

C = CONCLUSION (CLAIM OR CONCLUSION THAT WE ARE SEEKING TO ESTABLISH)

W = WARRANT (PRACTICAL STANDARDS OR CANONS OF ARGUMENT DESIGNED TO PROVIDE AN ANSWER TO THE QUESTION, "HOW DO YOU GET THERE?")

B = BACKING (CATEGORICAL STATEMENTS OF FACT THAT LEND FURTHER SUPPORT TO THE BRIDGE-LIKE WARRANTS)

R = CONDITIONS OF EXCEPTION (ARGUMENTS OR REBUTTAL OR EXCEPTION THAT TEND TO REFUTE OR "SOFTEN" THE STRENGTH OF THE CONCLUSION (C) now possible to merge or blend the two phases of this plan of attack for ethical decision-making in athletics. It can readily be seen that Toulmin's argument layout can be used to assist in the resolution of just about any type of argument, theoretical or practical, in any field of endeavor. However, keeping in mind that the primary concern here is with ethical decision-making, we must be certain to determine the ethical *merits* or *demerits* of the situation at hand. To help us in our deliberations, I will now introduce a sample case situation, a true-to-life situation that occurred recently in a large university.

A Sample Case Situation: "Drug-Taking at Midwestern University"

This case situation is one in which we see graphically how a head coach has been confronted with a truly difficult predicament. Moments before his team is scheduled to take the field for the final game of what has been a most successful season, he learns that his co-captains may have been involved with drug-taking during the course of the season. What should he do?

Toulmin's jurisprudential argument layout offers one approach to a type of analysis. (See Figure 2 below.) However, it could be argued that with this layout sufficient emphasis is not being placed on the ethical aspects of the situation. This is why I am recommending that the three tests of the triple-play approach (i.e., consistency, consequences, and intentions) may now relatively simply be superimposed upon the argument layout of Toulmin to serve as a double-check, so to speak, for the warrant, backing, and rebuttal, respectively. For example, if the warrant and the test of consistency (universalizability) clash violently or "contradict" each other, further rationalization seems required. What we are looking for, one might say, is the best possible "fit" between the argument layout and the three tests.

In this situation, then, the following points may be made:

1. *Consistency (Universalizability)*--we certainly would not wish to universalize a situation where drug-taking in athletics is condoned, since society expects its so-called amateur athletes to appear like paragons of virtue.
2. *Consequences*--indiscriminate drug-taking has become a significant problem threatening the nation's health and well-being. This situation would become worsened, because all youth tend to copy practices of athletes.
3. *Intentions*--if the athletes have some sort of an acceptable explanation for their action (if the report is true), then the coach must assess their present attitude while deciding upon the severity of the claimed infraction of established rules.

FIGURE 2

DRUG-TAKING AT "BIG-TIME" UNIVERSITY
(based on a jurisprudential argument layout)

(D)

JUST PRIOR TO A FINAL
GAME OF WHAT HAS BEEN
A SUCCESSFUL FOOTBALL
SEASON, THE HEAD COACH
LEARNS THAT A NEWSPAPER
REPORTER CLAIMS TO HAVE
EVIDENCE THAT THE CO-
CAPTAINS HAVE BEEN
OBTAINING DRUG PRESCRIP-
TIONS FROM A NEARBY
DRUGSTORE

(Q)
SO, PRESUMABLY

(C)

THE COACH MUST DECIDE
--BASED ON HIS EARLIER
STANCE--WHAT ACTION HE
WILL TAKE AGAINST THIS
RULES INFRACTION (IF
PROVEN)

BECAUSE
(W)

WHEN THIS INFORMATION
BECOME PUBLIC KNOWL-
EDGE, SOME DISCREDIT
WILL BECOME ATTACHED
TO ALL CONCERNED
SINCE SOCIETY EXPECTS
ITS ATHLETES TO APPEAR
LIKE PARAGONS OF VIRTUE

(UNIVERSALIZABILITY)

UNLESS
(R)

THE CO-CAPTAINS HAVE AN
ACCEPTABLE EXPLANATION
FOR THEIR ACTION

AND/OR

THE MEN CONCERNED
APOLOGIZE FOR THEIR
ACTIONS AND REQUEST THE
CHANCE TO PLAY IN THEIR
FINAL COLLEGE GAME

AND/OR

THE COACH DECIDES THAT
THE SEVERITY OF WHAT
THEY HAVE DONE IS ONLY
A MINOR INFRACTION AND
RULES THAT SUSPENSION
AT THIS POINT WOULD BE
UNREASONABLE
ETC.

(INTENTIONS)

ON ACCOUNT OF
(B)

DRUG-TAKING OF A GREAT
VARIETY OF SUBSTANCES
HAS BECOME A SIGNIFICANT
PROBLEM THREATENING THE
THE NATION'S HEALTH AND
WELL-BEING, AND YOUTH
TEND TO COPY PRACTICES
OF TOP ATHLETES

(CONSEQUENCES)

What is happening here, of course, is that we are again seeking the "best fit" between the originally determined argument layout and the three "tests" as explained above (Zeigler, 1984, p. 117).

The following has been adapted to offer one example of how the above schemata could work for a code of ethics in sport management:

(1) *Standard of Virtue or Vice* (for the practitioner): a professional in sport and physical education management should be unselfish and beneficent (i.e., desirable virtues) in his/her dealings with a student or client.

(2) *Principle of Responsibility* (this allows for a degree of individual discretion): a professional should use his/her power over a student/client carefully and with discretion--not as a means to some personal end that the professional person might have in mind for himself or herself.

(3) *Rule of Duty* (this must be followed): a student/client should never be forced (i.e., made to feel) that he/she must do something because a third party's reputation is at stake (i.e., the manager). An example here could be a situation where the manager directly or indirectly let a student/client know that he/she should lie to higher administration or the press about a situation where unfavorable publicity might hurt the overall sport program.

The Major Areas of Concern
When Developing a Code of Ethics
for Managers of Athletics?

One way to learn about some of the major areas of concern that ought to be in a profession's ethical code is to examine other such codes in existence. For example, there is the code titled "Ethical Standards of Psychologists" as developed originally and revised by the American Psychological Association (1977). There is no denying that this is an excellent statement with a fine preamble. It was prepared carefully over a considerable period of time with numerous revisions along the way. This code contains nine principles to which the members of the Association have subscribed. These principles relate to the following aspects of the profession: (1) responsibility, (2) competence, (3) moral and legal standards, (4) public statements, (5) confidentiality, (6) welfare of the consumer, (7) professional relationships, (8) utilization of assessment techniques, and (9) pursuit of research activities (Ibid.).

As good as the prevailing APA code is, it does not appear to clarify sufficiently among standards, principles, and rules as Bayles has recommended. His plan (i.e., the format of standards, principles, and rules) represents a significant improvement over the prevailing arrangement. The APA's code simply lists nine excellent principles, but makes no effort to categorize or arrange them as sequentially as could (should) be done. Also, the APA has not sufficiently delineated among standards, principles, and rules. The result is a lack of clarity as to where one leaves off and the other begins. In other words, the ethical standards that have been developed make an effort to "throw a covering blanket" over the entire discipline and profession. This is fine, but the task should be designed more specifically to cover the duties, obligations, and responsibilities of each of the sub-professional groups concerned (i.e., management, teaching, clinical, research). As the code stands with its lack of specificity (i.e. specific rules that must be adhered to), it makes it unusually difficult to enforce compliance--as truly difficult as this seems to be whatever the case may be.

The listing of nine "principles" by the APA's ethics committee in a random order without categorization into major areas of concern is perhaps a satisfactory beginning. Nevertheless, as stated above, such a statement can be strengthened by further clarification. Analysis indicates that these APA "principles" listed can be subsumed under the five major areas of concern (as recommended by Bayles and applied to sport management situations):

(1) Bases upon which professional services are made available.

(2) Ethical nature of professional/client relationship.

(3) Conflict-resolution when conflicts arise between professional's obligations to clients or student/athletes, and to third parties (e.g., his or her employer, or the state or province).

(4) Professional obligations to society and to his or her own profession.

(5) Ensuring compliance to the profession's ethical code.

Examples of Provisions That Could Be Included Under Each of the Major Areas of Concern

The following are some examples of provisions (i.e., standards, principles, and rules) that could well be included under each of the major areas of concern in a developing code of ethics:

TABLE 1

Examples of Provisions for a Code of Ethics for Sport Managers

Categories	Standards	Principles	Rules
a. Bases upon which professional services are made available	A prof. should be <u>fair</u> and <u>just</u> in providing his/her services	A prof. should ensure that all students receive adequate instruc.	A client needing help should receive it as soon as possible

Example: A professional manager shows bias toward a client and offers him/her poor or inadequate management service in a way that might cause the individual to lose interest and to look elsewhere for such service.

Categories	Standards	Principles	Rules
b. Ethical nature of prof.-client relationship	A prof. should be <u>honest</u> in his/her treatment of a client	A prof. should never treat a client as a means to an end	A client must never be forced to take an illegal or unethical action because of fear of loss of status

Example: In sport management, an athletic director urges an athlete to act in a harmful or dishonest way by stating that a scholarship will be lost otherwise.

Categories	Standards	Principles	Rules
c. Conflict resolution when conflict arises between prof.'s obligations to clients and third parties	A prof. has an obligation to be <u>truthful</u> in dealing with third parties	In checking eligibility of a team member, a manager should be most careful not to permit an inaccurate statement to be entered	A manager must never knowingly sign an eligibility form in which an athlete has committed perjury

Example: A manager knows that an athlete's eligibility has been used up elsewhere, but signs the form nevertheless in which an athlete has perjured himself/herself.

Categories	Standards	Principles	Rules
d. Professional	A prof. should	A prof. has a	A prof. has

obligations to society and to profession (i.e., duty to serve the public good)	be _loyal_ to societal values and those of the profession	duty and responsibility to preserve and enhance the role of the sport management profession	a duty to upgrade and strengthen his/her knowledge by attending one or more conferences or symposia annually

Example: A professional gives the profession a bad name by obviously falling behind on the knowledge of his/her area of expertise.

e. Ensuring compliance with the established obligations of the professions code of ethics	A prof. should practice his/her profession with _honesty_ and _integrity_	A prof. should encourage his/her students to be honest within the letter and spirit of the established rules	A prof. who permits his/her client to lie or cheat shall be reported and should be excluded from the profession if found guilty

Example: A manager guilty of flagrant unethical practice shall be reported to the ethics committee of the professional society and subsequently to his/her employers.

Ethical Implications: Items a-e immediately above relate directly to the meeting of professional obligations to both society and the developing profession. These obligations should be met as the professional society moves steadily and deliberately toward the development of a sound code of ethics. In addition to the meeting of designated professional obligations, a code of ethics should include provisions for (1) the ready availability of services to all who desire them, (2) the maintenance of a sound professional-client relationship, (3) the fair and reasonable conflict resolution when the professional encounters conflicts between clients and third parties, and (4) the guaranteeing of compliance with the profession's code of ethics.

A specific *creed* for the sport management profession has been approved, and that this should be followed by a subsequent expansion to a detailed code of ethics as soon as possible to promote sound, long range development.

Programs of mandatory *licensing* at the state/provincial level and voluntary *registration* at the national level should be developed as soon as possible. Future development of such required or mandatory licensing for all practitioners (both in the society at large and within education) will necessarily have to take place on a state-by-state or province-by-province basis.

In the development of such national registration and state/provincial licensing procedures, every effort should be made to avoid narrow discrimination on the basis of "professional/disciplinary labels" and training (i.e., unwillingness to accept obviously comparable course experiences from another profession/discipline as part of certification requirements). What must be guaranteed, of course, is that an acceptable level of knowledge, competency, and skill has been determined, and that all who practice professionally possess such ability on a continuing basis.

Concluding Statement.

The main concern of this chapter has been to present an approach to ethics in sport management. This approach involved a discussion about "professionalization" within the field with specific reference to ethics. After ethical creed became available for the profession through the North American Society for Sport Management, the society followed through with the task of developing a code of ethics while working cooperatively with the National Association for Sport and Physical Education (a division of the American Alliance for Health, Physical Education, Recreation, and Dance). Everything considered, this is assuredly the time to move in the direction of a sound, inclusive, enforceable code of ethics as the field of sport management strives to improve its professional status on the North American continent.

References and Bibliography

American Psychological Association. (1977*). Ethical standards of psychologists*. Washington, DC: American Psychological Association.

Aristotle. (1943). *Nichomachean ethics* (Book III, Chapter 1). In Aristotle (L.R. Loomis, Ed.). NY: W.J. Black. (Translated by J.E.C. Welldon).

Asimov, I. (1970). The fourth revolution. *Saturday Review*, Oct. 24, pp. 17-20.

Bayles, M.D. (1981). *Professional ethics*. Belmont, CA: Wadsworth.

Branvold, S. (1991). Ethics. In B.L. Parkhouse (Ed.), *The management of sport: Its foundations and application* (pp. 365-378). St. Louis, MO: Mosby-Year Book.

Callahan, J.C. (1988). *Ethical issues in professional life*. NY: Oxford University Press.

DeSensi, J. T. & Rosenberg, D. (1996). *Ethics in sport management*. Morgantown, WV: Fitness Information Technology.

Fox, R.M. & DeMarco, J.P. (1990). *Moral reasoning: A philosophic approach to applied ethics*. Fort Worth, TX: Holt, Rinehart & Winston.

Fraleigh, W.P. (1984). *Right actions in sport*. Champaign, IL: Human Kinetics.

Glasser, W. (1972). *The identity society*. NY: Harper & Row.

Goldman, A.H. (1980). *The moral foundations of professional ethics*. Totowa, NJ: Rowman & Littlefield.

Healy, J.M. (1990). *Endangered minds: Why our children don't think*. NY: Simon & Schuster.

Kaplan, A. (1961). *The new world of philosophy*. Boston: Houghton Mifflin.

Kretchmar, R. S. (2007). *Ethics in sport*. (2nd Ed.). Champaign, IL: Human Kinetics.

Kultgen, J. (1988). *Ethics and professionalism*. Philadelphia: University of Pennsylvania Press.

McIntosh, P. (1979). *Fair play*. London: Heinemann.

Northrop, F. S. C. (1946). *The meeting of east and west*. NY: Macmillan.

Rand, A. (1960). *The romantic manifesto*. NY & Cleveland: World.

Shea, E.J. (1978). *Ethical decisions in physical education and sport*. Springfield, IL: C.C. Thomas.

Skinner, B. F. (1971. *Beyond freedom and dignity*. New York: Alfred A. Knopf.

Toulmin, S. (1964). *The uses of argument*. NY: Cambridge.

Zeigler, E.F. (1983). Strengthening our professional arsenal. In *Proceedings of the Nat. Assoc. for Phys. Educ. in Higher Educ.* Champaign, IL: Human Kinetics.

Zeigler, E.F. (1984a). *Ethics and morality in sport and physical education*. Champaign, IL: Stipes.

Zeigler, E.F. (1984b). Applied ethics in sport and physical education. *Philosophy in Context*, 13, 52-64.

Zeigler, E.F. (1985a). Sport ethics in world perspective. A paper presented at the Ethics and Athletics Conference, Louisiana State University, April 7.

Zeigler, E.F. (1985b). The development of an ethical code for sport psychologists. A paper presented to the Sport Psychology Academy of the Amer. Assn. for HPERD, Atlanta, Georgia, April 18.

Zeigler, E.F. (1986). Dimensions of an ethical code for sport coaches. In *Coach education: Preparation for a profession* (pp. 79-90). London/NY: E. & F.N. Spon.

Zeigler, E.F. (1987). Rationale and suggested dimensions of a code of ethics for sport psychologists." *The Sport Psychologist*, 1, 2 (June), 138-150.

Zeigler, E.F. (1988). The dimensionality of an ethical code for the Canadian Association for Health, Physical Education and Recreation. *CAHPERD Journal*, 54, 1 (Jan.-Feb.), 15-21.

Zeigler, E.F. (1989a). Proposed creed and code of professional ethics for the North American Society for Sport Management. *Journal of Sport Management*, 3, 1 (Jan. 1989), 2-4.

Zeigler, E.F. (1989b). Sport and physical education ethics in world perspective. *Journal of the International Council for Health, Physical Education, and Recreation*, XXV, 4 (Summer), 4-8, 37.

Zeigler, E.F. (1989c). A professional responsibility: The promotion of sport ethics globally, *Journal of Comparative Physical Education and Sport (Cross-Cultural and International Studies)*, XI, 1, 3-5.

For Consideration and Discussion:

As an exercise at the end of this chapter, it is recommended that two students each make a 10-minute presentation, the first one explaining the merging of the "trivium approach" with the law-court jurisprudential argument. Then the second student should explain how this "merger" can be applied to the drug-taking case at a university. Finally. a third student should conduct a class discussion on the topic of the possible effectiveness of a code of ethics for the sport manager.

CHAPTER 15

SUCCESSFUL MANAGEMENT FOR THE FUTURE

Note: The reader will find some repetition in this summarizing chapter that contains the essence of the information that the author had hoped to convey to the reader

Introduction

The phenomena of (1) organized physical activity education within education, (2) organized athletics (as part of physical activity education) also within education, and (3) a great variety of public agency, private agency, and commercial programs of developmental physical activity of all types in sport, exercise, dance, and play for all ages and all abilities that have taken place in North America for more than the past 100 years flourish today in any direction one looks. Physical activity has blossomed into an unbelievably large and complex enterprise worldwide that demands a multitude of wise and skillful managers.

The situation is now such that the appointment of a director of physical (activity) education, or an athletic director, or a manager of a fitness club, or a private agency physical director, or a supervisor of physical recreation, etc. is a very ordinary and expected occurrence. These men and women within the education establishment are professional *educators* who teach a subject: physical activity education! Those who function in similar posts in society at large are not uniformly organized in the sense that they may be considered as members of a unified national profession promoting physical activity. For example, in referring to the "physical trainer" that a business person might visit in a fitness establishment twice a week, he or she might well be known as a "physical activity educator"–just as his or her counterpart within education could be designated. Then *together* they could be members of the "National Physical Activity Association" (or whatever title might be agreed upon).

Having said this, we should keep in mind that a recognized profession needs an organized body of knowledge based on research. A profession that is fully worthy of the name must, of course, meet certain other criteria (e.g., have a code of ethics that is enforced). For now, however, keep the criterion of an organized body of knowledge based on research firmly in mind. Hence, the perpetuation of our "species"--the instructor or manager of some type of developmental physical activity as it relates to our field--requires that some effective and efficient organizational structure be developed through which the body of professional knowledge may be transmitted to those who follow.

278

(Of course, this deficiency looms also as a concern for those functioning with either public or private education.

If we grant the above statements concerning one of the primary criteria of a true profession, as well as the continuing need to prepare new managers professionally through some sort of experience in which this background knowledge is transmitted both theoretically and practically, then let us consider very briefly how administrators and managers within all educational levels and those in the business world received their preparation for this demanding position in the past. The answer to this question is immediately obvious: Generally speaking, many, if not all, of these men and women worked their way up through the ranks in some sort of an apprenticeship scheme (no matter how ridiculous some of these schemes may seem when examined in the light of subsequent demands made upon the individual).

One basic prerequisite seems to be that they themselves were interested and active in physical activity education (including sporting activities). Quite often, as well, they were physical education majors and took several courses of an administrative nature at the undergraduate or master's levels, either within physical education or in educational administration. In some cases, and this was especially true for men, they were (1) not physical education majors at college, but later decided to cast their lots with our field because of successful competitive athletic experience; or (2) they were physical education majors at college, but initially had really not planned to stay with the field. Whatever the case may have been, the fact has been that these people demonstrated many fine personality traits and leadership traits. They knew how to get along with people; they made good appearances; they wanted to get things done; they were willing to work hard; and they believed strongly in the benefits of competitive sport.

Such a method of "preparing" managers or administrators is not unique in the field of physical activity education (including athletics). In mid-20th century, Halpin explained that a similar circumstance was evident when one examined the professional programs in schools of education, business, public administration, hospital administration, and social work (1958). Still further, he stated that the more mature professional schools of medicine, law, and engineering exhibited a similar pattern in earlier stages of their development. This was in contrast, of course, to the recognized academic disciplines, where administrators were picked typically on the basis of scholarly and research endeavor (and perhaps because they possessed certain desirable personality traits as well). In the latter case, this method of selection is still practiced quite generally today, and the very large majority of this group may have never taken even one course in management theory and practice. One is tempted to state that what has happened in higher education generally over past several decades shows it!

Despite the inadequacies in professional preparation for management in our field that have existed for decades, it must be confessed that courses in the organization and administration of physical education and athletics have been offered in our field since 1890 (Zeigler, 1951)! By 1927 they were typically included in professional curricula throughout the United States (Elliott). Since that time there has been a proliferation of similar courses relating to administration and supervision at both the undergraduate and graduate levels. In addition, literally thousands of master's theses and doctoral dissertations have been deposited on the shelves of our libraries. Most of these studies involve the descriptive method of research, or some technique thereof, and there is undoubtedly a body of knowledge "of sorts" about practice of an administrative nature. Relatively speaking, however, there is still very little research in management theory. What we have is an endless stream of articles, theses, dissertations, monographs, and texts on the subject-matter area, but what it all adds up to is anybody's guess.

Indeed, what *can* be said at the present? If those working in the area are searching for academic respectability, management theory in this field must steadily and increasingly strive for a sound theoretical basis. Writing about the subject of management in the business community, Matthew Stewart titled his effort The Management Myth (2009). His criticism about the professional preparation of prospective business managers in MBA programs is absolutely devastating. The subtitle to his book is a question: "Why the Experts Keep Getting It Wrong." Obviously the author has exaggerated by taking such a stark position. However, the actual situation does seem to need further examination.

In regard to professional preparation of managers in physical activity education (including athletics), the fact is that– even though organization and administration have a long history in our professional preparation programs–investigation into these topics has nowhere nearly achieved the recognition that has been accorded to research in (for example) sport and physical activity education physiology or psychology. How can we improve this situation? The answer to this question was available to us as early as mid-20th century! First, the terms and concepts used must be clear, and they must be related to systematic theory. Second, the theory that we are able to develop should be "generalizable" (and therefore abstract). Third, the research endeavor should be as value-free as possible; if we want to introduce values, they should be treated as variables in the investigative methodology. Fourth, such scholarly endeavor will undoubtedly be based on the social (and primarily the behavioral) sciences. Finally, five, correlations are interesting and also significant, but adequate theory should, in the final analysis, clarify processes that will produce quality performance (J.D. Thompson, in Halpin, 1958, pp. 29-33).

A Plan for Progress

We really don't have much choice at the present other than to make all possible efforts to place professional preparation for administrative or managerial leadership within our field on an academically sound basis. At present the need for vastly improved leadership comes at us from a number of different directions. We simply do not have enough fine leaders in any field--and our field is no exception to this statement. If we don't have good leadership, an organization or enterprise soon begins to falter and even to stumble. Our field needs fine people who will take charge in the behaviorally oriented work environment of today's world. We've all heard that management involves the accomplishment of an objective through the enlistment of others to work closely with you. However, as Zoffer (1985) stated: "But I would add to that the need to achieve a certain excellence–accomplishing goals efficiently, cost-effectively and imaginatively, while respecting the lives and welfare of the broader community." There is no doubt but that physical activity education (including athletics) has achieved greater recognition within educational circles on this continent than in any other geographical area of the world. Such achievement is an accomplished fact, but we now have to continue in the direction of upgrading professional preparation for administrative or managerial leadership so that the field of physical activity education will consolidate those gains made. As should be the case with the successful basketball team–continue to "move strongly down court on balance toward the goal" (Rothermel, 1966).

Looking back, in the area of research Spaeth (in Zeigler and Spaeth, 1975) recommended strongly that we must strive in future research to examine management as a process or group of processes rather than as an area of content (the old "nuts and bolts" approach, or "this is how you organize a round-robin tournament"). There is nothing wrong with the execution of studies related to the various technical concerns, but we do need to investigate the more fundamental, broader processes of management that might be designated as decision-making, communicating, activating, planning, evaluating, etc.

Similarly, Paton (in Zeigler and Spaeth, 1975, p. 14) suggested a significantly broader approach to the teaching of administration courses in physical activity education. This is an approach that he and a number of his Canadian colleagues subsequently followed with significant success (e.g., Jackson at Victoria, Soucie at Ottawa; Moriarty, Olafson, Boucher, and Weese at Windsor; Chelladurai and Haggerty at Western Ontario, Daniel at Toronto, Maloney at Dalhousie, Paton at New Brunswick (after the UWO), Parks at Bowling Green State University, to name some of those who have been involved the longest).

Proposed Content for Management Courses
in Physical Activity Education (Paton)

Paton recommended a broadened approach to the teaching of the administration or management course in physical activity education (including athletics). The area of content specifically related to physical activity education, he urged, should depend increasingly on a body of knowledge developed through administrative research and theory in our field.

Educational institutions provide the setting within which many physical activity education (including athletics) programs are administered. Current efforts to develop managerial research and theory within the educative setting are directly relevant to our field. The fact that management is practiced in a specific setting has tended to obscure the fundamental similarities of the administrative process. The study of management as management will eventually provide a sounder theoretical base for understanding the entire administrative process.

Underlying all management or administrative theory are the social sciences (and still more specifically, the behavioral sciences). Concepts and theories related to the behavior of people in organizations have much to offer to an understanding of effective management. Obviously, this approach is characterized by an emphasis in which the area of content specifically related to physical activity education (including athletics!) should depend increasingly on a body of knowledge developed through management research and theory in *our* field. Further, educational institutions provide the setting within which the many physical activity education programs are managed. Current efforts to develop management theory and research on the broad administrative process mentioned above within the educational setting are directly relevant to our field. The fact that management–administration is practiced in a specific setting has tended to obscure the fundamental similarities of the managerial process. The study of administration *as* administration should eventually provide a sounder theoretical base for understanding the management process. Finally, and last but not least, underlying all management theory and research are the social sciences (and still more specifically, the behavioral sciences). Concepts and theories related to the behavior of people in organizations have much to offer to an understanding of administration or management.

Professor Garth Paton, University of New Brunswick, has been a keen analyst of the prevailing situation insofar as professional preparation for management in physical activity education is concerned. It is his opinion that:

. . . in the classroom, course instructors have not

282

have not adequately overlaid these approaches with what appears to be the appropriate theoretical framework. That is: they have not shown how theory applies to a particular situation or case competency. In case analysis, for example, the focus tends to be on a *"rational"* analysis and solution *only* as opposed to the inclusion as well of an adjunct explaining how theory might apply, or simply asking: "What theory applies here?" (2010).

A Competency-Based Approach to Management Development

I am now absolutely convinced that the field of physical activity education and sport should be moving as rapidly as possible to introduce a comprehensive management competency development approach as a requirement in all professional preparation programs. (I was originally convinced about this subject when I introduced the case method approach to the teaching of human relations and administration to the field in 1959, the idea being that almost anything represented an improvement over the stereotyped approach in use in the 1950s and earlier.)

A true competency–development approach should be adopted *as soon as possible* so that our graduates will be basically equipped to cope with the managerial demands of their positions (whatever those positions may be). There is no question but that bureaucratic forms of organizations are being challenged by the varieties of organizational upheaval that are occurring. We are told that the combined demand for *more* at *faster* speeds is working to undermine the great vertical hierarchies that have characterized our public and private institutions in the past (Toffler, 1970, 1980, 1992). Undoubtedly these emerging patterns and models are bringing about definite changes in managerial practice.

We really don't comprehend fully what these changes will mean to the management of physical activity education and sport. Interestingly, we do know that more than 50 years ago Snyder and Scott (1954) recommended the implementation of a problem-solving approach in our professional preparation programs. This recommendation has been re-asserted many times, but it still has not been implemented! It would seem that we now have a professional obligation to see to it that our professional preparation programs, as well as our in-service training as it emerges through the work of our professional associations, are so organized that people will be as ready as possible for change when it occurs. This statement has obvious implications for management training.

It was for this reason basically that I became concerned with what might be called the dimensions of management competency as it applied to the management of physical activity education and athletics. Concurrently I began to make a solid effort, working with others (like Marcia Spaeth, William Penny, Garth Paton, and John Baker), to pull together from any reliable source available what might be called the body of knowledge on this aspect of our field's endeavor. (King McCristal, David Matthews, and Laura Huelster, all of the University of Illinois, Urbana-Champaign, were all most helpful and supportive in this endeavor.) In full appreciation of the aphorism "better late than never," I am nevertheless somewhat embarrassed to confess that--probably because of other intervening "challenges and hurdles"--it took me somewhat longer than 25 years to arrive at the point where a *model* for a competency-based approach to management development was offered to the field (Zeigler & Bowie, 1983). Actually, the final steps might not have been taken yet if it were not for Gary Bowie's (Univ. of Lethbridge) urging in the late 1970s that such was truly needed as soon as possible.

Permit me to retrogress time wise a bit further to the later 1960s when the matter of what should be (or what might be) the actual components of physical activity education became clearer as a result of reading, discussion, and reflection. Cyril White, an Irish sociologist with a deep interest in physical activity education and sport argued in 1968 that the field had many of the characteristics of a multidiscipline and some of the aspects of what might be called a cross–discipline. He postulated that our future development to so-called interdisciplinary status would require a greater degree of sophisticated research abilities and orientation than the field possess at that time. However, as Phil Sparling (Georgia Tech) pointed out in 1978, the field seemed to be moving in an opposite direction to that postulated by White. White's original idea made sense to me, and it still does today and could become true eventually. This will not occur, however, unless a solid, conscious effort is made by the field *to define what it is we do, and then do it!*

In the early 1970s, therefore, I made an effort to help resolve a controversy in the field as to the relationship between what have been called (by some) the sub-disciplinary aspects and those aspects that have been designated as "sub-professional" in nature (e.g., management theory and practice). This analysis resulted in the construction of a taxonomic model for "optimum professional development in a field called 'X'" (Zeigler, 1972). The model included the following five sub-divisions: (1) operational philosophy, (2) a theory embodying assumptions and testable hypotheses, (3) professional preparation, (4) professional practice, and (5) disciplinary research and scholarly endeavor (see Figure 1 below).

The inclusion of *operational philosophy* (of "X") as an overarching entity in the model is based on the social theory (Parsonsian Action System)

Figure 1

A Model for Optimum Development of a Field Called "X"

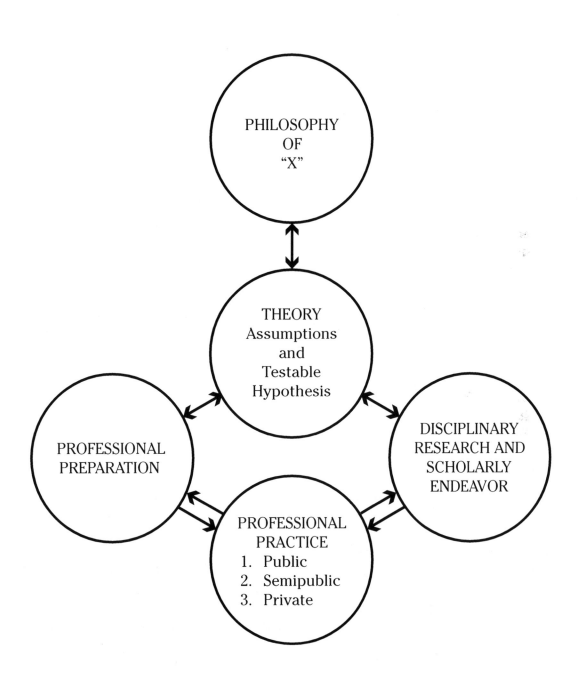

Earle Zeigler, Ph.D.

285

that the values and norms of the social system will be realized eventually within the society if all goes well. Put simply, this means that decisions regarding the development of a profession are based on the prevailing values and norms over and above any scientific evidence that may be available to create, strengthen, or broaden existing theory. Thus, there is a hierarchy of control and conditioning that operates within the system that exerts pressure downward affecting the society, the social systems, the structure of collectivities, and the structure of roles. In addition, we should not forget that such pressure may be exerted upward as well (i.e., that's how <u>gradual</u> change occurs--and even revolutions if the demand for change is strong enough!).

The second phase of the model is *theory*, or the systematic arrangement of facts or knowledge about a subject or field. From such theory we can also derive assumptions and testable hypotheses that should soon amplify and clarify a developing (and presumably coherent) group of general and specific propositions that can be used as principles of explanation for the phenomena that have been observed. Obviously, any profession must have a sound body of knowledge to serve as under–girding if it hopes to survive with its professional status fully recognized in society.

Professional preparation, the third division of the model, should be designed to educate the practitioner, the teacher of practitioners, the scholar and the researcher, and the administrator. Professional practice, the fourth entity in the model, relates typically to service provided for (1) the public, (2) the semi-public (or semi-private) agency, and (3) the private agency.

Disciplinary research and related scholarly endeavor, the fifth division, involves those individuals from the specific profession (or closely related disciplines and/or professions) who contribute in one way or another to the body of knowledge on which the professional practice is based. We have classified such knowledge into sub–disciplinary and sub–professional knowledge (e.g., in sport and physical education, the tenable theory about how best to administer programs of developmental physical activity to be made available to promote the full dissemination of such knowledge, respectively). I believe that this model (i.e., an explanation of "how it works") can be adapted for the purposes of any profession. We have classified such knowledge into sub–disciplinary and sub–professional knowledge (e.g., in sport and physical education, the tenable theory about the functional effects of physical activity and the tenable theory about how best to administer programs of developmental physical activity to be made available to promote the full dissemination of such knowledge, respectively). I believe that this model (i.e., an explanation of "how it works") can be adapted to any profession.

Adaptation of the Model of a Profession to the Competency Development Model

While the model of a profession as it presumably should function was being fashioned, another development was occurring that I did not at first relate to the work I had been doing. To paraphrase Lloyd E. McCleary, then at Illinois (UIUC) but subsequently at Utah, had worked closely with us at Illinois and helped a number of us to relate what he and his associates were doing in educational administration to our work in sport and physical education administration. As we moved along in the 1970s, it became steadily and increasingly apparent that definite, urgent measures were needed in sport and physical education to prepare people more carefully and thoroughly than previously for the "assumption of the administrative risk" in the years immediately ahead. And so, convinced that positive steps were needed to improve professional preparation for *managers* in our field, a number of people teaching in this area decided that it was time to introduce a management stream or minor into undergraduate and graduate curricula. To accomplish this for myself, I spent a portion of sabbatical-leave time analyzing the literature of management, with special reference to that which applied to the knowledge, competencies, and skills required by the manager. Shortly thereafter, Gary Bowie (Univ. of Lethbridge) and I united our efforts in the firm belief that an experiential approach to management competency development was indeed urgently needed in sport and physical education (Zeigler and Bowie, 1983).

To assist me with the classification or categorization of more than 100 competencies described in some form or other in the literature, I decided to employ one of the more highly regarded taxonomical models, that promulgated initially by Robert L. Katz in 1954 and then updated with slight modification 20 years later (1974). In addition to Katz's division of the task of management into three basic skills (conceptual, technical, and human), I felt it to be advisable to add a mixed-skill or conjoined category, as well as one in which personal skills could be placed (the total then becoming five instead of the original three).

The next step was to adapt the model for the (any!) profession described above (Figure 1) to the quasi-discipline–profession of management science (or theory). As anticipated, this adaptation was readily accomplished (see Figure 2 below). From this point it became apparent that the model for competency-based management education in educational administration developed by McCleary and associates could be merged readily and successfully to my model. My position was reinforced when I discovered that McCleary had also employed Katz's taxonomy (1973). Thus it was possible to adapt his recommendations to my own purposes in keeping with the fivefold classification (adapted from Katz). My debt to the work of McCleary and associates (1972) is obvious. The culmination of our work along these lines

287

Figure 2

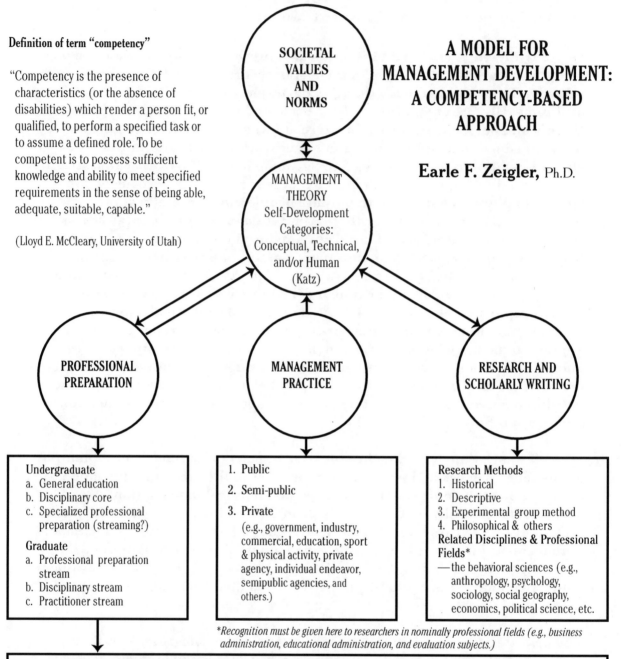

Definition of term "competency"

"Competency is the presence of characteristics (or the absence of disabilities) which render a person fit, or qualified, to perform a specified task or to assume a defined role. To be competent is to possess sufficient knowledge and ability to meet specified requirements in the sense of being able, adequate, suitable, capable."

(Lloyd E. McCleary, University of Utah)

SOCIETAL VALUES AND NORMS

A MODEL FOR MANAGEMENT DEVELOPMENT: A COMPETENCY-BASED APPROACH

Earle F. Zeigler, Ph.D.

MANAGEMENT THEORY
Self-Development
Categories:
Conceptual, Technical,
and/or Human
(Katz)

PROFESSIONAL PREPARATION

MANAGEMENT PRACTICE

RESEARCH AND SCHOLARLY WRITING

Undergraduate
a. General education
b. Disciplinary core
c. Specialized professional preparation (streaming?)

Graduate
a. Professional preparation stream
b. Disciplinary stream
c. Practitioner stream

1. Public

2. Semi-public

3. Private
   (e.g., government, industry, commercial, education, sport & physical activity, private agency, individual endeavor, semipublic agencies, and others.)

Research Methods
1. Historical
2. Descriptive
3. Experimental group method
4. Philosophical & others
Related Disciplines & Professional Fields*
—the behavioral sciences (e.g., anthropology, psychology, sociology, social geography, economics, political science, etc.

Recognition must be given here to researchers in nominally professional fields (e.g., business administration, educational administration, and evaluation subjects.)

A Plan for Competency-Based Management Education (Including the Teaching/Learning Process)

1. Ascertain professional functions & needs.
2. Specify competencies (including self-development and those under conceptual, technical, human, and "conjoined" categories).
3. Determine performance levels.
4. Specify program content & instructional, methodology (involving a problem-solving approach in achievement of performance levels: what needs to be known; where obtained; organization of the learning experience; probable results, and others.
5. Identify and evaluate competency attainment.
6. Validate process periodically.

Teaching/Learning Techniques
(e.g., lecture, discussion, case, role-playing, action research, pure and applied research, independent study, debate, computer-assisted or programmed instruction, internship, game theory, panels, forums, and others—depending upon technique's applicability to learning of a competency)

(Adapted from McCleary & McIntyre 1973)

was the publication of a text for undergraduates in which an experiential approach is featured. Students are provided with an opportunity to evaluate themselves in relation to the five aspects of managerial skill through the employment of a series of laboratory experience as part of a formal course.

Managing the Enterprise: Looking Ahead

Up to this point, in addition to some introductory and background material, I have argued essentially (1) that the world is changing and becoming increasingly complex with each passing day, a development that has obvious implications for the field of physical activity education (including athletics); (2) that physical activity education needs managers who function effectively and efficiently on the basis of tenable management theory to organize and administer its far-flung programs; and (3) that we have done quite poorly in preparing our people to manage, an inadequacy that we should correct as soon as possible by implementing a management competency development program of high quality.

Let us assume that we can agree on the need for improving the quality of physical activity education management in the near future. This need is not peculiar to our field, however, since we are hearing pleas from all over North America about a broader need for a higher quality in managerial performance than may have been present in the past. To meet the challenge to North American industry and business, for example, we were exhorted in the 1980s to consider "Theory Z" as wisdom coming from our Japanese colleagues (Ouchi, 1982)–actually a debatable assumption as it has turned out. In addition, there has been a spate of books with the world "excellence" in the title. For example, in the book titled *Creating excellence* (Hickman and Silva, 1984), we were presented with a list of "new age skills" that management executives should cultivate for the long term: (1) creative body of knowledge on which the professional practice is based. We have classifiedsuch knowledge into sub–disciplinary and sub–professional knowledge (e.g., in sport and physical education, the tenable theory about how best to administer programs of developmental physical activity to be made available to promote the full dissemination of such knowledge, respectively). I believe that this model (i.e., an explanation of "how it works")insight: asking the right questions; (2) sensitivity: doing unto others; (3) vision: creating the future; (4) versatility; anticipating change; (5) focus: implementing change; and (6) patience (pp. 99-246). After these achievements, you begin to "walk on water!"

Toward the goal of alerting present and prospective managers of physical activity education about they may be facing as they assume the role of "managing the enterprise" in the present societal climate, I will now "freewheel" a bit to offer a variety of opinions, suggestions, and recommendations as to what (prospective) professional leaders might expect to find when they assume a managerial post--and what they might possibly do about any such discoveries or unexpected findings.

An Ever-Changing Society. First, changing social influences have brought about various types of organizational upheaval. As a result our present bureaucratic forms of organization--although often "struggling on doggedly"–seem to need drastic change in both the structure of the operation and in the way managers function within it. We have had our "organization men and women," but are we ready for what Toffler has called "associative man or woman"–i.e., people who are not immobilized by concern for economic security (1970, pp. 125-134)?

The Matter of Individual Freedom. Second, even within our evolving democracy, we still encounter persistent attempts of some basically domineering (and often at heart fearful because of insecurity) individuals to deny people the freedom they have a right to expect in this culture. As managers we should be asking ourselves to what extent the individual in North American society should be able to choose his or her own goals in life and then have the opportunity and means to attain them to a reasonable degree. How crucial is individual freedom for a person as we all strive to improve the quality of life, or are we inevitably moving toward a social system (somewhat more like present oligarchic communism) that Skinner would characterize as "beyond freedom and dignity?" In other words, what is the best or ideal route whereby we may possibly reach a high level of excellence? Do we want a more pyramidal, depersonalized bureau–technocratic society or one that seems to be working <u>for</u> the best interests of individual man and Woman (Tesconi & Morris, 1972)? Questions like these are, in my opinion, especially important for managers functioning in some aspect of physical activity education and athletics, a group not noted in the past for the implementation of creative models of democratic administration.

Managing by Objectives. Third, one of the areas of concern most neglected by managers has been that of the determination of the organization's objectives. Everyone gives lip service to the need for "managing by objectives" as espoused by Drucker as long ago as 1954, but the moment one tries to pin down a practicing manager in this regard the result is typically an empty recital of words and phrases that displays "the lack of a well-developed language of organizational purpose" (Gross, 1965). One of the best responses to such a deficiency would seem to be a plan based on systems analysis that could quite quickly help an organization to develop a workable general-systems model. One of the great advantages of MBO, of course, is that it provides middle managers and employees an opportunity to plan together for the achievement of common objectives–objectives for which *all* will ultimately be responsible. Odiorne (1965) has promoted MBO as strongly as anyone and, according to Filly, House & Kerr (1976), it has subsequently been employed more widely than any other similar technique.

Positive Approach to Management. Fourth, if a person decides to throw his or her hat in the ring by applying for an administrative post and is then selected, the subsequent approach taken to the task should be a highly positive one. This is especially true in academic situations where one is somehow still expected to keep up with scholarly writing and research (and then may make light of the need to make time for solid human relations). Admittedly the dual responsibility is difficult, but it is by no means impossible if a person is willing to work hard and plan carefully. Of course, this is why a limited term of managerial service (e.g., five years) in such situations is highly desirable.

Half-hearted commitment of time to managing clashes sharply with the duties and responsibilities that the managerial revolution has thrust upon us. As Gross stated, "It provides the people of this planet with their first opportunity of discovering their vast potentials for self-development." Viewed in this light, management is a social skill that will have to be employed wisely to help the inhabitants of this earth work their way out of the predicament into which they have gotten themselves. Transferred to the educational setting, who will not admit that an inadequate administrator of physical activity education and/or athletics can soon bring a department, division, or school down to a level where the program is barely subsisting (i.e., "semi-planned mediocrity")?

Hence, considering the importance of the role of manager, and the steadily increasing complexity of the organizational management task, it is my contention that young men and women in the field should be encouraged to prepare themselves *adequately for* the vital task of managerial leadership. Further, the assumption of this challenge does not mean that the individual must automatically put scholarship and research aside (although it typically has happened that way in the past). The manager should be equipped by word and deed to promote the idea of management as an emerging social science, as one of the sub–professional aspects of our work that demands continued scholarly research.

Need for an Action-Theory Marriage. Fifth, what has just been stated above provides some substantiation for the gradual emergence of management science. Many say that management thought is too practical, while others avow that it is usually too theoretical. This may seem to be true, but I believe it can be said more accurately that really practical administrative thought will simply have to be based on far more tenable knowledge and theory than is yet available. Scholarly investigation on this topic should be carried out to the greatest possible extent on the "observable facts of real-life administration" (Gross, 1964). A manager on the job is typically confronted with a real-life situation to resolve. To resolve the problem effectively and efficiently, something better than trial and error is needed in our increasingly complex social environment. That "something" should be the most <u>tenable</u> theory available. In other words, a research strategy is needed that is characterized by a "theory-research balance" between theoretical and applied investigation.

The Current Theory Debate. Sixth, the mushrooming of the behavioral sciences has made it literally impossible for a scholar to keep up with the vast quantities of literature in many languages being produced all over the world. As a result those preparing for the profession of management have found themselves facing an impossible task--keeping up with an information overload, as well as retrieving a great deal of knowledge that helps to form a sound human behavior inventory. Also, the conflicting approaches to management (i.e., the different theories as to "how it should be done") that compete for the attention of the manager in the many books, monographs, and journals are very puzzling. Forty-five years ago Gordon (1966) defined these historical, actually overlapping approaches as (1) the traditional, (2) the behavioral, (3) the decisional, and (4) the ecological. He concluded by recommending that a flexible framework should be employed as a synthesis of the four approaches enabling the student of administrative theory to build a conceptual framework that provided a much fuller perspective and a "working model" of the management process.

The idea of such a flexible framework emerged from a recent discussion by Hodgetts (1979) in a slightly different manner. He explained that there is one line of thought that envisions three schools of management thought (i.e., (1) the management process school, (2) the quantitative school, and (3) the behavioral school) merging into a <u>systems</u> school. However, a second point of view holds that we already have a well-established systems school of thought and that it, along with the three approaches just mentioned, are moving in the direction of an overarching *situational* or *contingency* school. This has been called a *general contingency theory of management* by Luthans and Stewart (1977) in which management problems can be encompassed in a theoretical framework that integrates and synthesizes the various schools of thought into a workable research design that has three dimensions--management variables, situational variables, and performance criteria variables. The objective is to integrate tenable management theory into a composite system for ongoing study and investigation.

The Complexity of Any Administrative Situation. Seventh, years of involvement as a manager/administrator, as well as 60+ years of experience with the case technique or approach to the teaching of human relations and administration, has led me to include a few thoughts here about the complexity of any administrative situation (Zeigler and Bowie, 2007). This is so because of the large number of factors that may be involved in any case situation (e.g., past experience, one's present situation, economic incentive, personal attitude). The work situation itself and any changes that are occurring add to the mix. The group code within the organization, which in turn is affected by community standards and societal values and norms, are fundamental factors as well. Management <u>says</u> one thing, but management <u>does</u> another--this too can have an impact (Hower in Andrews, 1953). In some circumstances certain factors indicated above could be the most important determinants of behavior; in others they might well be relatively insignificant. As you analyze a problem, the task is to gain as much perspective as possible. However, while responding to the facts, half-facts, and opinions as you see, hear, and assess them, you should keep in mind that each person views a situation differently. Such a realization in itself should often cause managers to hold back at least temporarily before initiating strong, direct action to meet a problem.

Leadership in Organizational Settings. Eighth, in this changing (internal and external) organizational environment that we have been discussing, the interpersonal skills of the leader(s) need further examination and study. Certainly the leader must know self and know those with whom direct or indirect association is established. I have believed very strongly that the executive needs to establish an open climate. By this is meant that (a) associates can collect information about a problem accurately, (b) bring these data back to the decision-making group, and then (c) take part in the planning and execution of future actions (Bennis & Slater, 1968).

The concept of 'leadership,' however, has been an elusive one down through the years. For a long time what was called "trait theory" was in vogue--that is, we were concerned about the prospective manager's personal characteristics, ones that presumably made him or her a fine leader. In the 1940s, however, trait theory declined because investigations along this line produced no clear-cut results. Thus, even though this approach had, and still has, some descriptive value, it has been supplanted to a large degree by so-called "situational theory." With this approach it is argued (a) that there are situational factors that can be delineated in a finite way and (b) that they vary according to a number of other factors (Filley, House, & Kerr, 1976). Some of these factors, for example, are the leader's age and experience, the size of the group led, the cultural expectations of subordinates, the time required and allowed for decision-making. Chelladurai (1985), in his discussion of leadership, refers to charismatic leadership and organizational leadership, the latter being "just one of the functions of a manager who is placed in charge of a group and its activities, and is, in turn, guided by superiors and organizational factors" (p. 139).

Further, I should state my personal interest in a leadership spectrum (or perhaps a continuum) in which, as one moves from left to right (i.e., from anarchy to dictatorship), the manager gradually exercises greater authority and the staff members have lesser areas of freedom. I have found through long experience that I have a distinct aversion to one-person, arbitrary, authoritative decisions--especially in educational settings or anywhere else. I have personally eventually walked away from such positions of employment on four occasions. (Of course, I appreciate that in certain lines of work, such as the military or fire-fighting, there typically isn't sufficient time to have a lengthy discussion in an effort to achieve agreement or to take a vote before action is taken.) Nevertheless, I want staff members to be involved in the decision-making process to the greatest possible extent--*if they are willing to make serious efforts to be well informed on the matter at hand.* Further, once unformed members of a group make a decision democratically, the organization can and should demand loyal support from all members of the group. (The assumption here is that opportunities will be provided subsequently for people to be convinced in democratic fashion at a not-too-distant future date that a contravening decision should be made.)

Constants and/or Generalizations. Ninth, even though I have been emphasizing that the manager is being faced with a relatively fast-moving social system, a condition from which managers of sport and physical education cannot (and probably should not wish to) escape, change for us has somehow not occurred as rapidly as in certain other segments of society. However, managers in our field must now recognize the fact that they too are being put on notice about the fluid nature of their environments. Managers simply must take advantage of every opportunity to prepare themselves to keep ahead (or at least abreast) of their associates intellectually. This is necessary because they must be ready to meet change head-on and make the alterations and modifications necessary so that growth (if desired and/or desirable) and survival will be ensured (the ecological approach, if you will).

The above momentary digression is not meant to imply for an instant that there are not a great many constants and/or generalizations that carry over from yesterday to today and thence to tomorrow which help to maintain the structure and vitality of sport and physical education. This means, for example, that much of what is known about human nature today will be identical or quite similar tomorrow. It forewarns the manager that he or she shouldn't throw the baby out with the bath water just because many changes seem to be taking place. The great problem seems to be the urgent need to both strengthen and focus the body of knowledge available to the management profession so that the literally astounding development in the area of technology is reasonably approximated by the understanding and knowledge available about effective and efficient administrative behavior. While such a balance is being established, the tried-and-true constants or "principles" from the past should be used daily and only discarded or modified when there is ample evidence (scientific or normative) available to warrant any change.

Other Recommendations for Managers. *Tenth,* I would like to make several final recommendations for managers to consider as they look to the future (revised from Zeigler & Spaeth, 1975):

1. The manager, in addition to relying on the wisdom of the past, should make it a habit over the years to increase his or her theoretical and practical knowledge. (This is especially true if at any time an area of weakness in managerial knowledge, competencies, or skills is discovered-- e.g., personal computer capability.)

2. The manager should strive to improve his or her communication skills. (Generally speaking, it is reasonable to assume that people will work more enthusiastically with a manager who communicates with them in terms that they can readily understand.)

3. The manager should be prepared to invest himself (or herself) in the external environment. (Here I take the position that the manager does have a definite community responsibility that, even though ours is a strongly service-oriented profession to begin with, the manager should still be prepared to "invest himself or herself" in the community *at least to a reasonable degree.)*

4. The manager should work to strengthen organizational democracy. (With this recommendation, I am reiterating my ongoing concern that managers should continually be aware of both the responsibilities *and* rights of the people working with them in the achievement of mutually agreed-upon goals. If individual participation and self-development are promoted, the organization itself will be better for having shown such concern.)

5. The manager should recognize that he or she is taking part in the development of a management profession. (This implies that there is an obligation to live up to the various requirements of a true profession--e.g., service without undue concern for pecuniary reward, ongoing commitment, mastery of a body of knowledge, adherence to a (code of ethics.)

6. The manager should do whatever possible to expand and improve the quality of management education that is available. (The position being taken here is that, despite some improvement, the field of sport and physical education is still not placing enough emphasis on a reasonable amount of professional preparation for the management task. Such professional preparation should be under–girded initially by a sound general education. We are especially vulnerable here from the standpoint of management competency development through laboratory and internship experiences.)

Concluding Statement

Finally, then, what can be said in brief summary about managing the physical activity education enterprise? *First*, I believe that the field still has an opportunity to relate significantly to the developing social science of management—and specifically the behavioral sciences within that division of education. However, we can't dally much longer! I say this with a full understanding that most professionals in our field are still only dimly aware of the scientific development that has occurred in this field. I appreciate that scholarly endeavor has been labeled largely as a myth by Stewart (2009). Nevertheless, Wren (2005) insists that management "is more than an economic activity in the *sixth* edition of his historical endeavor. It is a conceptual task that must mold resources into a proper alignment with the economic, technological, social, and political facets of its environment" (p. 489).

Second, the vast enterprise that is sport in world society—and physical activity education within both education and society at large must for its very survival as a recognizable entity relate more effectively to the urgent need for qualified managers. The North American Society for Sport Management can make a significant contribution to this development and fulfillment of this need. Additionally, such development should be carried out in full cooperation with the National Association for Sport and Physical Education within the AAHPERD and PHE Canada (formerly the Canadian Association for Health, Physical Education, and Recreation).

Third, each present or future manager has a responsibility for self-examination in an effort to construct a personal philosophy that can be of inestimable assistance in becoming a more effective professional person. In addition to recommending that a manager "look inward" in an effort to develop an explicit personal philosophy, it is also absolutely imperative today that the manager "look outward" at both the immediate *and* the general environment in an ongoing attempt to analyze the social forces that impinge daily on the leader, his or her leadership group, and the organization. Sport, dance, play, and exercise have infiltrated our social environment to an enormous extent. Our evolving profession cannot succeed without highly qualified, dedicated people to manage this most important cultural enterprise.

Note

The reader should appreciate that this chapter was intended to be synoptic in nature. Hence, what is contained here represents an updated, revised (presumably improved) version of many of the ideas, opinions, and recommendations expressed by me about management theory and practice as applied to physical activity education and athletics (sport) in a variety of publications over a period of approximately 50 years.

References and Bibliography

Andrews, K. R. (Ed.), *Human relations and administration* (pp. 94-111). Cambridge, MA: Harvard University Press.

Baker, J. A. W. & Collins, M. S. (1983). *Research on administration of physical education and athletics 1971-1982: A retrieval system*. Reseda, CA: Mojave.

Bennis, W. & Slater, P. E. (1968). *The temporary society*. New York: Harper & Row.

Chelladurai, P. (1985). *Sport management*. London, Canada: Sport Dynamics.

Chelladurai, P. 1999. *Human resource manageent in sport and recreation*. Champaign, IL: Human Kinetics.

Drucker, P. F. (1954). *The practice of management*. New York: Harper & Row.

Elliott, R. (1927). *The organization of professional training in physical education in state universities*. New York: Columbia Teachers College.

Filley, A. C., House, R. J. & Kerr, S. (1976). *Managerial process and organizational behavior*. (2nd Ed.). Glenview, IL: Scott, Foresman.

Goodwin, M. (1986). When the cash register is the scoreboard. *The New York Times*, June 8, pp. 27-28.

Gordon, P. J. (1966). Transcend the current debate on administrative theory. *Hospital Administration*, 11, 2 (Spring), 6-23.

Gross, B. M. (1964). *The managing of organizations*. New York: The Free Press of Glencoe (Macmillan).

Halpin, A. W. (1958). The development of theory in educational administration. In A.W. Halpin (Ed.), *Administrative theory in education*. New York: Macmillan.

Hickman, C. R. & Silva, M. A. (1984). *Creating excellence* (pp. 99-246). New York: New American Library.

Hodgetts, R. M. (1979). *Management: Theory, process and practice*. (2nd Ed.). Philadelphia: Saunders.

Hower, R. M. (1953). Final lecture, advanced management program. In Katz, R. L. (1974). Skills of an effective administrator. *Harvard Business Review*, 52 (Sept.-Oct.), 90-112.

Luthans, F. & Stewart, T. I. (1977). A general contingency theory of management. *Academy of Management Review*, p. 182 & p. 190.

McCleary, L. E. & McIntyre, K. (1972). Competency development and the methodology of college teaching: A model and proposal. *The Bulletin (NASSP)*, 56 (March), 53-59.

McCleary, L. E. (1973). Competency-based educational administration and application to related fields. In *Proceedings of the Conference on Administrative Competence*. Tempe, AZ: Bureau of Educational Research, Arizona State University, pp. 26-38.

Odiorne, G. S. (1965). *Management by objectives*. New York: Pitman.

Ouchi, W.G. (1981). *Theory Z*. Reading, MA: Addison-Wesley.

Parsons, T. (1958) Some ingredients of a general theory of formal organization. In Halpin, A.W. (Ed.), *Administrative theory in education*. New York: Macmillan.

Paton, G. A. (with Zeigler, E. F. & Spaeth, M. J.). (1975). Theory and research in the administration of physical education. In Zeigler, E. F. & Spaeth, M. J., *Administrative theory and practice in physical education and athletics*. Englewood Cliffs, NJ: Prentice-Hall.

Paton, G. A. (2010). This reference refers to Prof. Paton's reaction (by e-mail on Jan. 5, 2010 after reviewing chapter 16 of this text.

Rosenberg, J. M. (1978). *Dictionary of business and management*. NY: John Wiley.

Rothermel, B. L. (1966). Conversation with the author, Oct. 3.

Spaeth, M. J. (1967). *An analysis of administrative research in physical education and athletics in relation to a research paradigm*. Doctoral dissertation, University of Illinois, Urbana-Champaign.

Snyder, R. A. & Scott, H .A. (1954). *Professional preparation in health, physical education, and recreation*. New York: McGraw-Hill.

Stewart, M. (2009). *The management myth: Why experts keep getting it wrong*. NY: W. W. Norton.

Tesconi, C. A., Jr. & Morris, V. C. (1972). *The anti-man culture*. Urbana, IL: University of Illinois Press.

Thompson, J. D. (1958). Modern approaches to theory in administration. In Halpin, A.W., *Administrative theory in education*. New York: Macmillan.

Toffler, A. (1970). *Future shock*. New York: Random House.

Toffler, A. (1980). *The third wave*. New York: William Morrow.

VanderZwaag, H. J. (1984). *Sport management in schools and colleges*. NY: John Wiley.

Wren, D. A. (2005). *The history of management thought*. NY: John Wiley & Sons.

Zeigler, E. F. (1951). *A history of professional preparation for physical education in the United States, 1861-1948*. Eugene, OR: Microfiche Publications, University of Oregon.

Zeigler, E. F. (1959). *Administration of physical education and athletics: The case method approach*. Englewood Cliffs, NJ: Prentice-Hall.

Zeigler, E. F. (1972). A model for optimum professional development in a field called "X." In *Proceedings (pp. 16-28) of the First Canadian Symposium on the Philosophy of Sport and Physical Activity*. Ottawa, Canada: Sport Canada Directorate.

Zeigler, E. F. & Spaeth, M. J. (Eds.). (1975). *Administrative theory and practice in physical education and athletics*. Englewood Cliffs, NJ: Prentice-Hall.

Zeigler, E. F. (1982). *Decision-making in physical education and athletics administration*. Champaign, IL: Stipes.

Zeigler, E. F. & Bowie, G. W. (1983). *Management competency development in sport and physical education*. Philadelphia: Lea & Febiger.

Zeigler, E. F. & Campbell, J. (1984). *Strategic market planning: An aid to the evaluation of an athletic/recreation program*. Champaign, IL: Stipes.

Zeigler, E. F. (1984). One decision-making strategy: The case method approach. *CAHPER Journal*, 50, 3 (May-June(, 30-32.

Zeigler, E. F. (1985). A proposed model for competency-based management development. In *Proceedings of the VII Commonwealth and International Conference on Sport, Physical Education, Recreation, and Dance* (M. L. Howell and K, Moore, eds.), University of Queensland, Australia, pp. 3-10.

Zeigler, E. F. (1985). Marketing our product. *CAHPER Journal*, 51, 4 (March-April), 36-37.

Zeigler, E. F. (1985). Understanding the immediate managerial environment. *Quest*, 37, 2, pp. 166-175.

Zeigler, E. F. (Feb. 1987). Sport management: Past, present, future. *Journal of Sport Management*, 1, 1, 4-24.

Zeigler, E. F. (Jan.-Feb., 1987). Appraisal Guide for the Administrator–Manager. *CAHPER Journal*, 53, 1:32-34.

Zeigler, E. F. & Haggerty, T. ((1987). Improving managerial decision-making through spreadsheet modeling. In *The organization and administration of sport* (T. Slack and C. R. Hinings, eds.). London, Canada: Sports Dynamics, pp. 229-243.

Zeigler, E. F., Mikalachki, A., & Leyshon, G. (1988). *Change process in sport and physical education management*; Champaign, IL: Stipes.

Zeigler, E. F., Bowie, G. W., & Paris, R. (1988). *Competency development in sport and physical education management*. Champaign, IL: Stipes.

Zeigler, E. F. (Fall, 1991). Managing physical education's corporate image. *The Physical Educator*, 48, 3:114-118.

Zeigler, E. F. (1992). *Case analysis in sport and physical education management (Including ethical implications). In Applied ethics for sport managers.* Champaign, IL: Stipes. (R. L. Case and S. Timewell assisted with the case collection and analysis.)

Zeigler, E. F. (1995). *A selected, annotated bibliography of completed research on management theory and practice in physical education and athletics to 1972 (including a background essay).* Champaign, IL: Stipes.

Zeigler, E. F. (Jan. 2000). Sport management enters the third millennium (C. E.). *International Journal of Sport Management*, 1: 1:1-3.

Zeigler, E. F. (April 2003), Sport's plight in the postmodern world: Implicatons for the sport management profession, *International Journal of Sport Management*, 4, 2:93-109.

Zeigler, E. F. (2007). Sport management must show social concern as it develops tenable theory. *Journal of Sport Management*, 21, 3: 297-318.

Zeigler, E F. & Bowie, Gary W. (2007). *Management Competency Development in Sport and Physical Education*. Victoria, Canada: Trafford. (This is a laboratory manual developed to go along with this 2010 text.)

Zoffer, H.J. (1985). Training managers to take charge. In *Business* (Section 3, 2), *The New York Times*, Oct. 20.

APPENDIX A

USING A CASE-METHOD APPROACH
FOR ETHICAL DECISION-MAKING

In this appendix, since I believe that it might be useful to you with your personal or professional decision-making, you will be introduced gradually into Phase Four of this overall approach recommended for ethical decision-making. You will find here one example (a case situation) with a case-method (human relations) approach to ethical decision-making that can be understood and applied by any reasonably intelligent person.

As we can all appreciate, applying the case method technique with an "ethical orientation" to the analysis of an ethical problem in no way resembles an exact science. I do believe, however, that many more find such a "deficiency" desirable and wholesome. The inexactitude of the results of a case analysis of an ethical problem in this ever more complex world is inevitable. Yet, as a way to further the making of the "best possible" decision, we really need some reasonably sound basis upon which to formulate an answer to the myriad of ethical problems that arise daily. This is why I began about 35 years ago to look into the subject of personal ethics and then gradually developed the overall sequential approach recommended here--i.e., from Phase One to Phase Two to Phase Three of this technique..

In an effort to improve prevailing, unsatisfactory situation for my undergraduate and graduate students, I sought earlier to provide them with an opportunity to develop rationality as a "life competency." I set out to place before them the prototypical, major ethical routes to decision-making that are available to undergraduate students today. Obviously, analysis of current sources may result in great variations in emphases and terminology. So I decided to organize these routes in tabular form under specific headings and took pains to present this material to my students in some detail.

In the process, admittedly not executed in great depth (see Table 1 and 2 below)), I emphasized (a) the underlying presuppositions, (b) the criteria for evaluation, (c) the method for determining ethical decisions, and (4) the probable result of each of six approaches (i.e., authoritarianism, relativism [arguably an approach], situationism, scientific ethics, the "good reasons" approach, and emotivism).

It became apparent that I could not get the students to learn every one of these approaches to ethical decision-making in a first course of this type. Nevertheless I was determined to help students approach (both personal and professional) ethical decision-making in as explicit a manner as possible as a point of departure. I wanted this to be an approach that could be useful to

Table 1
Comparative Aspects of Major Philosophical Approaches to Ethical Decision-Making (Part 1)

Decision-Making Approach	Underlying Presupposition	Criterion for Evaluation
I. Authoritarianism (or Legalism)	Absolute good and rightness are either present in the world, or have been determined by custim, law, or code	Conformity to rules, laws, moral codes, established systems. and customs.
II. Relativism (or Antinomianism)	Good and bad, and rightness and wrongness, are relative and vary according to the situation or culture involved.	Needs of situation there and then in culture or society concerned.
III. Situationism (with certain similaritity to #1 above)	God's love (or some other summum bonum is an absolute norm; reason, revelation, and precedent have no objective normative status.	"What is fitting" in the situation is based on application of agapeic love; subordinate moral principles serve to illuminate the situation.
IV. Scientific Ethics (scientific method applied to ethics)	No distinction between moral goods and natural goods; science can bring about complete agreement on factural belief about human behavior.	Ideas helpful in solving problematic situations are true; empirical verification of hypothesis should soon bring union of theory and practice.
V. "Good Reasons" (the "moral point of view")	Implies that ethical action should be supported by best reasons (good) reasons--i.e., facts superior to others; *moral* reasons superior to other types.	Same rules must be for good of everyone alike; unselfish decisions to be made on principle that can be universalized.
VI. Emotivism (analytic philosophy's response to ethical problems that arise)	Ethics is normative (i.e., moral standards) and therefore cannot be a science; the term "good" appears to be indefinable.	An ethical dispute must be on a factual level; value statements must be distinguished from factual ones.

Table 2
Comparative Aspects of Major Philosophical Approaches to Ethical Decision-Making (Part 2)

Decision-Making Approach	Method for Determination of Ethical Decision	Probable Result
I. Authoritarianism (or Legalism)	Application of normative standard (or law) to resolve the ethical dilemma or issue.	The solution to any ethical dilemma can be readily determined and then implemented
II. Relativism (or Antinomianism)	Guidance in the making of an ethical decision may come either from "outside"; intuition; one's own conscience; empirical investigation; reason, etc.	Each ethical decision is highly individual since every situation has its particularity; there are no absolutely valid principles
III. Situationism (with certain similarity to #1 above)	Resolution of ethical dilemma results from use of calculating method plus contextual appropriateness; act from loving concern; benevolence = right.	The best solution, everything considered, will result when the principle of God's love is applied situationally
IV. Scientific Ethics (scientific method applied to ethics)	Use of scientific method in problem-solving; reflective thinking begets ideas that function as tentative solutions for for concrete problems; test hypotheses experimentally.	Agreement in factual belief will soon result in agreement in attitude; continuous adaptation of values in the culture's changing needs will result in social change.
V. "Good Reasons" Approach (the "moral" point of view)	Two stages: (1) determining which facts are relevant; (2) weighing facts to determine relative weight for consideration; a hierarchy of reasons needed.	Assumption is that person can reason way through to a satisfactory method of ethical decision-making using a class of good reasons
VI. Emotivism (analytic philosophy's response to ethical problems that arise)	Involves logical analysis of ethical (normative) standard) terms; factual statements referred to social scientists; analyze conflicting attitudes to determine progress.	Ethical dilemma can be resolved through the combined efforts of the moralist and the scientist; common beliefs may in time change attitude.

them as developing young people as well as subsequently throughout their adult lives. Of course, it had to be one that they could build upon as required or desirable as well. Hence, I decided to arrange the information about the six different approaches to ethical decision-making in tabular form (see Table 1 and Table 2 above) so that you could make some comparisons as to (1) the underlying suppositions, (2) the criteria used for evaluation, (3) the method used for determination of an ethical decision, and (4) the probable result of any deliberation.

Thus, I explained earlier that, over a period of approximately five years, based on the early recommendations of Prof. Richard Fox, I gradually incorporated an overall four-phase plan of attack for ethical decision-making in my work with my own students. As I made clear to them, also, this was just one basic approach with which they were being asked to experiment as they move toward greater sophistication in this subject within their lives. As we have seen--a quick review again!--this plan of attack in its entirety includes the following four phases:

Phase One. Determine through the employment of a "three-step approach"--from "Kant to Mill to Aristotle"--what the ethical or moral issue is in the specific case at hand. That is, the person analyzing an ethical problem proceeds from a test of universalizability (Kant) to one of (net) consequences (Mill/Bentham), and finally to a test of intentions (Aristotle).

Phase Two. Once Phase One has been carried out, if you wish to "reinforce" (or "strengthen"), proceed with Phase Two, or the lay-out of the argument (recommended as a jurisprudential argument in S. Toulmin. *The uses of argument.* NY: Cambridge University Press, 1964).

Phase Three. Then, in Phase Three, if you wish to strengthen your potential decision still further, seek to compare Phase One and Phase Two by superimposing (a) the "universalizability" maxim (Test 1) onto Toulmin's warrant, (b) the net consequences result (Test 2) onto the presumably unethical action for the backing, and (c) the intentions analysis items (Test 3) as possible conditions of exception or rebuttal. With this type of comparison, you will quite soon discover whether you have a "good" or a "bad" fit. If your comparison (i.e., Phase One on Phase Two) seems to mesh poorly, you can readily see where you may have possibly gone awry.

Now I will move on to the main purpose of this appendix--that is, the introduction of the case method technique (Phase Four) as a possible tool to assist you still further--in confronting either personal, professional, or social/environmental problems--with the making of a decision in a situation with ethical ramifications.

Phase Four:
Adding a Case Method Technique
To Ethical Decision-Making

With the introduction of Phase Four, therefore, I am recommending that you consider the use of the case method technique that has been employed extensively in legal and medical training since the turn of the twentieth century. It is also true that the case method has been used as a teaching technique by business schools dating back to the 1920s. Notable examples of this are the Harvard Business School in the United States and the Ivey School of Business Administration at The University of Western Ontario in Canada.

Teachers in various professional training programs know that the need to develop knowledge, competencies, and skills on the part of students in such programs is obvious and ever-present. A common complaint of students in these programs is that adequate laboratory and/or field experiences are typically not available. And yet, somehow, this approach within professional preparation programs was not introduced to the field until the 1950s. Furthermore, oddly and interestingly, due mainly to several social influences (e.g., onrushing science and technology) and subsequent, prevailing educational essentialism, it is not used as extensively as it should be presently).

Experience and past literature have shown that people react most favorably to this teaching technique. Accordingly, a sample case (an actual situation that occurred), along with a recommended, detailed analysis is presented below. This particular case and analysis includes ethical implications, a topic that is also being considered widely in professional training at this time. (However, this approach to the case method technique of decision-making can be used very well also without special consideration being given to the ethical aspects of any given case.)

This is the reason why I have recommended that the person fundamentally concerned with a problem of ethical decision-making, along with significant "others," work their way through an even more detailed, overall approach (see Phase Four below) to ethical decision-making (as adapted (a) from my own investigation related to case analysis (see Zeigler, 1982), and (b) from P.T. Manicas, and A.N. Kruger, Essentials of logic. NY: American Book Company, 1968.)

The Seven Steps of Phase Four

Note: Upon the completion of Phases One, Two, and Three, if there is time--and I suggest that you make time if the opportunity and/or need arises--

discuss the ethical problem at hand in detail with "significant others." I believe this approach is vital whether the problem has arisen in either your personal or your professional life. There is simply no escaping the fact that *human relations* play a significant part in our lives. It may seem to be a truism to state, but more people lose jobs because of inadequate human relations than because of the quality of their work. Additionally, as we all recognize, maintaining solid friendships of all types revolves around the question of human relations once again.

The seven steps to this overall approach of Phase Four, steps that I gradually refined through hundreds of case method discussions over the years, are as follows:

a) Determine the main ethical problem after considering all conceivable sub-problems Take care to denote which of the latter have definite ethical implications,

b) Explication of any "knowledge base carry-forward" that may exist already in the mind of the participant(s) in connection with this sort of case problem (including pertinent ethical implications).

c) Analyze the main ethical problem keeping in mind employing the application of the "three-step approach" above (Fox), as blended with or superimposed on, the four-step layout of the argument (Toulmin).

d) Analyze carefully the various personalities and their relationships with others involved.

e) Formulate only those alternative solutions to the ethical problem that appear to be relevant, possible, and meaningful. (A certain amount of subjectivity is inevitable at this point.)

f) Elaborate the proposed alternative solutions involving the framing of warranted predictive statements (i.e., both pro's and

con's). (Here an effort is made to look at both
sides of the various alternative solutions deemed
worthy of further consideration before a final
decision is made.)

g) Select the preferred alternative
solution (including initial tentative postulation
of the ramifications of the proposed solution prior
to its actual implementation). This is especially
important if the case is actually a true one to be
resolved as soon as possible.

h) Assess and determine currently useful
generalizations for possible future use in similar
ethical situations as "knowledge base
carry-forwards" in subsequent case discussions.

What I am recommending here, therefore, is that typically the person
primarily concerned with the ethical problem at hand serve as the
"chairperson" of a small group of relatives & friends if the problem is a
personal one. If the problem is a *professional* one, then try to bring a small
group of close associates together for a similar discussion, once again serving
as the chairperson of a group (seated preferably in a circle or around a square
table so that a more open and democratic discussion will result).

I believe it would be wise for you, as the chairperson of the discussion
group (and as the person primarily involved in the situation), to write up the
case situation beforehand in as factual a manner as possible. This may take
some time--and it is most important to outline the facts at hand of the case
carefully and sequentially (as they occurred)--before you begin to write (see
the case problem below as written by William Sanders, a fictitious name).
Try to avoid introducing your (or any!) prejudices into the case--or at least
"confess" openly to having or sensing this or that prejudice. Or, if you believe
you made a tactical and/or ethical mistake at any point as a case participant,
say so in your case write-up. Basically, however, keep in mind that you are
striving to be a good "reporter" telling the facts--the "who, what, where,
when, and (possibly) why"--to the potential readers who will be helping you
through analytic discussion to arrive at a decision.

Thus, as you sit down with your friends or associates to discuss the
ethical problem at hand, hand each person your very carefully prepared,
space-and-a-half summary of the situation to be discussed. Try to keep the
length of the case situation to approximately (no more than!) four pages.

Note: The case situation below (explained by William Sanders
in Section I below) is followed by a written summary and

306

analysis of the discussion about the problem that subsequently took place. The aspect of "ethical implications" was added for the purposes of this book.

A CASE METHOD APPROACH TO ETHICAL DECISION-MAKING: COACHING ETHICS AND THE TENDERED ATHLETE

by

Earle F. Zeigler, The Univ. of Western Ontario
Robert L. Case, Sam Houston State University
Steve Timewell, The Univ. of Western Ontario

SECTION I--A Case Situation: Grading Practices
   for Athletes at Midwestern University

Note: William Sanders is an instructor working on his doctoral degree at Midwestern University. On February 1, 1997, he sent the following letter to Prof. T.C. Collins, Chairperson, Department of Sport and Physical Education, Midwestern University:

Dear Dr. Collins:

As you know, Head Coach Tom Courtney and I have just completed the teaching of PE 156 (Wrestling), a course that we have handled jointly for the past few years. This year I had developed a new grading scheme that we presented to the students at the first class period. We agreed that I would determine the written work to be completed, and the skills we were to teach were those that Head Coach Tom stresses typically.

Both of us graded students at various times during the semester on their achievement with the skills. Tom asked me, as usual, to grade all of the written work. This I did, and all grades, including attendance, were listed on a large chart kept in Mr. Courtney's office. (Near the end of the term, incidentally, a number of the students were complaining to both Tom and me that he [Tom] had been marking them absent incorrectly.)

While grading the written work, I noticed that one student, a prominent Midwestern athlete, turned in someone else's class notebook (a regularly assigned project) under his own name. I actually remembered grading this particular notebook over Xmas vacation a year ago. He also handed in several other assignments at this time, ones that were actually due at the middle of the semester. He explained that injury during the fall season had prevented him from getting them in on time. As it happened, this was not his own work either. I notified Coach Courtney immediately since he is, of course, technically my superior (holding professorial status). He suggested that I give him the papers and the notebook, and that he himself would confront the student and his coach together.

The following day Coach Tom informed me that, despite the young man's plagiarism, Courtney and Slaughter (the student's coach) agreed that the athlete should re-work his notebook and assigned papers. As punishment he would be asked to complete an extra assignment recommended by me. In this way his failing grade could be raised sufficiently so as not to make it impossible for him to get off academic probation. The student came to see me; received the extra assignment; and was to return everything to me when it was completed. Then I would change the grade if his work merited such revision.

My complaint is that I never saw the results. I asked Coach Tom about it, and he explained that he had received the work, graded it, and had misplaced it at home. I decided to check out the grade submitted and learned that this person, and many other varsity athletes, received a grade of A in the course, while others more deserving received B's and C's.

Regretfully, as a result of this experience, I must charge Coach Tom with dishonesty and a lack of professional ethics.

Very sincerely yours,

William Sanders, Asst. Coach

SECTION II: Analysis of a Case Situation
          (Including Ethical Implications)

(Step 1. Determination of the main problem after consideration of the various sub-problems denoting those sub-problems that have ethical implications.)

Step 1. Sub-Problems & The Main Problem:

   a. The seemingly evident plagiarism of the athlete
       athlete--ethically wrong.
   b. Courtney, despite pre-determined grading agreement
       with Sanders that the latter would grade written
       work, grades Sanders' written work himself and
       doesn't even allow Sanders to see the submission
       --ethically wrong.
   c. Athlete evidently was using his "athletic profile"
       for a special privilege (i.e., to be able to get
       away with handing assignment in late)--ethically wrong.

d.   The fact that upon examination Sanders discovered that various varsity athletes received A's in the course, while others that Sanders felt actually did better received only B's and C's--ethically wrong.

e.   The fact that Courtney initially went to the athlete's coach to discussed the athlete's predicament (a person who was already on academic probation) and seemingly took his plagiarism so casually; one wonders whether they (Courtney and Slaughter) ever even intended that he should complete his work for the course--ethically wrong.

f.   The fact that Coach Courtney granted a truly unfair advantage to a varsity athlete, allowing him to escape any punishment for an offense that some other student might be severely punished for doing, or even dismissed from the university for such conduct ethically wrong.

g.   Sanders may have erred by accepting the "substitute plan" recommended by Courtney after the initial plagiarism had been detected and reported by Sanders to Courtney.

The Main Ethical Problem was determined to be Sub-problem #f above (Courtney's Ethical Conduct)

(Step 2. Explication of any knowledge base carry-forward that may exist already in the mind of the student in connection with the analysis of this sort of case problem, including ethical implications.)

Step 2.   Knowledge Base Carry-Forward (Prevailing Principles or Generalizations)

a.   Plagiarism is cheating, an unacceptable practice in higher education.

b.   Unless there are truly extenuating circumstances, we must live up to commitments we agree upon with others.

c.   Granting "special" privileges to some people and not to their peers is unfair and will create problems.

d.   Athletics is but one of many aspects of university life, and should be kept in proper perspective with the overall educational function of higher education.

(Step 3. Analysis of the main problem through application of the "three-step approach"   [i.e., the three tests listed above as recommended by R. Fox]; this is integrated with a layout of the argument [based on Toulmin's approach].)

Step 3. Employment of the Three-Step Approach:

a. Universalizability or Consistency (Test No.1)
    Based on society's values and norms, and that
    universities are regarded as pattern-maintenance
    organizations where honesty and integrity are
    absolutely essential, proven plagiarism is most
    serious.
b. (Net) Consequences (Test No.2)
    Proven dishonesty by teachers and coaches that
    is somehow not punished could seriously damage
    the university's reputation and place the
    institution's future in jeopardy
c. Intentions (Test No.3)
    The voluntary and/or involuntary nature of Coach
    Courtney's actions must be ascertained, and then
    appropriate action should be taken based on the
    findings (e.g., dismissal for cause)

Step 4. Integration of Triple-Play Approach with Argument Layout

Data (D)	So (Q necessarily)	Conclusion (C)
Head Wrestling Coach Courtney is reported by his teaching assistant as having extreme favoritism to a tendered athlete from another sport, a man who is on academic probation and who has evidently committed plagiarism		The department head should make every effort to learn the true facts of the situation, and then should take appropriate action based on his findings (e.g. ,dismissal for cause).

	Since Warrant (W)		Unless Rebuttal or Exception (R)
	Based on society's values and norms, and that universities are regarded as pattern-maintenance organizations where honesty and integrity are absolutely essential, an		It turns out that Courtney actually did forget and did grade the manual himself, and it was excellent in all regards

offense such as proven
plagiarism is most serious

        Universalizability
        (Test No. 1)

        Because
        Backing (B)

Proven dishonesty by teachers
and coaches that is somehow
not punished could seriously
damage a university's reputation and place the institution's future in jeopardy

        Consequences
        (Test No. 2)

        and/or

Courtney was under some
external pressure; felt
that he simply had no re-
course other than to help
the athlete who was on
academic probation

        and/or

Courtney was old, near retirement, had an excellent
record otherwise, offered
an apology; corrected the
well-intentioned error;
thus, clemency was felt to
be in order

        and/or

It turned out that the
whole problem has been
greatly exaggerated by
Sanders who had it in for
Courtney & perhaps hoped
to succeed to the position
if Courtney were dismissed

        Intentions (Test No. 3)

Key: Argument Layout (Toulmin, 1964)

D = data (a statement of a situation that prevails,
    including evidence, elements, sources, samples of facts)
C = conclusion (claim or conclusion that we are seeking to
    establish)
W = warrant (practical standards or canons of argument
    designed to provide an answer to the question. "How do
    you get there?")
Q = modal qualifier (adverbs employed to qualify con-
    clusions based on strengths of warrants--e.g., neces-
    sarily, probably)
R = conditions of exception (conditions of rebuttal or

exception that tend to refute the conclusion)
B = backing (categorical statements of fact that lend
    further support to the 'bridge-like" warrants)

(Step 5. Analyze the various personalities and their (ethical and working) relationships with others involved.)

Step 5. Personalities and Ethical Relationships:

  a. There appears to be a difference in the way which the coaches at Midwestern University regard academic work and offenses and infractions that might occur. Courtney evidently felt it was more important for a top athlete to be eligible than to be honest, as did Slaughter--but Sanders obviously didn't agree.
  b. At least some athletes at Midwestern figured you could get away with handing in someone else's work-- or else this one wouldn't have tried it. If this is true, this could affect a professional program most seriously.
  c. Even if everything that Courtney said was true (e.g., he had found it to be worth an A grade), what about the other varsity athletes who Sanders felt were receiving grades that were too high (relatively speaking, that is).
  d. If Courtney had been under some external pressure to see to it that the athlete became eligible again, one would think that Sanders might be aware of this--but perhaps not.

(Steps 6 & 7. Formulation of only those alternative solutions to the ethical problem that appear to be relevant, possible, and meaningful.)

Steps 6 & 7. Relevant Alternatives Open
            to One of the Case Participants:

(Note: In this instance, we chose to view the matter from the standpoint of Wm. Sanders, the Asst. Coach who faced this difficult situation.)

  a. Initially, Sanders should have taken a stand against Courtney when he first learned how the matter was to be handled (i.e., he should have asked to go along with Courtney when he discussed the matter with the athlete's coach). It could be argued that he had a responsibility (ethical?), also, to challenge Courtney

312

"immediately" when he somehow did not see the
results of the assigned work designated as
"punishment."

> Pro--maybe he could have convinced Courtney to quickly retrace his
> steps and change what he had just done (i.e., submit a false grade,
> etc., without showing the material to Sanders according to the
> arrangement).
> Con--Courtney might have been angry at being challenged and would
> have attempted to somehow "cover his tracks".

b. After Sanders discovered the plagiarism, he should
    have quietly referred it to Collins and not become so
    openly involved.

> Pro--by "playing it safe" his position might have been more secure.
> Con--his conscience might have bothered him because somehow in
> this culture an (unethical) "sneaky Judas" is especially condemned
> when an action becomes generally known.

c. Before taking any action (i.e., writing the letter),
    Sanders should have confronted Coach Courtney about
    this matter; he should have also asked him to justify
    the especially high grades for all the tendered athletes
    (with lower grades for others). This would have been
    somewhat more ethical than "going over his head"
    immediately.

> 1. See pro's and con's in Question No.6 below
>   (Preferred Alternative Solution).

d. Sanders could have contacted Coach Slaughter to
    discuss the situation. Slaughter's reaction might
    have provided additional evidence (one way or the
    other).

> Pro--this would have to be handled most carefully. It could have
> caused him to get back to Courtney rapidly to call the whole affair
> off. It would also have given Sanders a stronger case either way it
> turned out.
> Con--Sanders would have been "sticking his neck out" even further,
> and this might cause a violent reaction from the authorities in the
> Athletic Association directed at injuring Sanders' job-standing and
> his future.

e. Sanders could check grades over the most recent
    years to see if there had been a pattern indicating
    that athletes were consistently being treated in a
    special manner.

> Pro--this might also have strengthened Sanders' case, or it might
> have dissuaded him from writing the letter if nothing seemed to have
> been wrong. It could also have been used in connection with "c"
> above to help convince Courtney of the error of his actions.
> Con--it might have been difficult to get the former grade books
> without arousing suspicion on Courtney's part.

f. Once the complaint has been filed, Sanders should
    have left the matter at that and removed himself as
    far as possible from having anything to do with it
    (ethical?).

> Pro--one is tempted to do this if possible, and it does leave the
> accuser somewhat less tainted by the whole affair.
> Con--this possibility rarely develops, mainly because the accuser is
> needed as a witness and thereby is forced to take a stand.

g. Sanders should somehow have sent the information to
    Dr. Collins anonymously; in this way he might
    conceivably have escaped from any responsibility in
    the matter.

> Pro--this could really be playing it safe, and it might work.
> Con--Sanders' conscience would probably have bothered him, and
> also receipt of such an anonymous accusation might well be
> ignored.

Step 6 & 7 (cont.). The *Preferred* Alternative Solution

> **Note:** A difficulty with the recommended "preferred
> alternative solution" is that it is *retrospective*--that is, we
> know already what Sanders did do. He reported the matter
> directly to the department head. Typically, however, we
> are recommending that the person concerned with the
> making of a decision might wish to employ Phase Four
> before taking action.

Recommendation:

**Confront Courtney before reporting him
to departmental chairperson (Alternative "c" above)**

Pro's	Con's
i. Would have gone through proper channels	By confronting Courtney there might have been some "backlash"
ii. Courtney would have known that Sanders was aware of his unethical practices and might be reporting his unfair practices to the administrator	Improper grading might have led to punishment of Courtney and his dismissal anyhow
iii. Sanders would have given Courtney a chance to explain what he had been doing by offering some rationale for his having doe what he did	If Courtney could not have explained, he would working be working mightily to harm Sanders by having him "black-balled" by the Athletic Association.
iv. If Sanders could have convinced Courtney that his grading practices were grossly unfair, then something might have been worked out before the chairman was notified	If an investigation had taken place, and Courtney somehow was innocent. Sanders would have been in a most precarious position to say the least

8. Currently Useful Principles or Generalizations

> **Note:** These are recommended typically as a result of the present case analysis, being added to the Knowledge Base Carry-forward in No.2 above for possible use in future analyses that are similar in nature.

a. Keep in mind that there is a considerable range of opinion in this culture as to how ethical conduct is perceived

b. It is vitally important that teachers/coaches set

high ethical standards for themselves, as well as for their charges

c. Every effort should be made to keep the lines of communication open with colleagues in a work situation

d. When team teaching is being carried out, it is especially important to have the policies and procedures in use spelled out most carefully in advance of the actual teaching situation

REFERENCES

Aristotle. *Nicomachean ethics* (Book III, Chapter 1). In *Aristotle* (L. R. Loomis, Ed.) (1943). New York: W. J. Black. (Translated by J. E. C. Welldon).

Brubacher, J. S. (1978). *On the philosophy of higher education.* San Francisco: Jossey-Bass Publishers.

Commager, H. S. (August 27, 1976) The nature of academic freedom. *Saturday Review*, 13-15, 37.

Manicas, P.T., and Kruger, A.N. (1968). *Essentials of logic.* NY: American Book Co.

Rand, A. (1960). *The romantic manifesto.* N.Y. and Cleveland: The World Publishing Co.

Shils, E. (1983). *The academic ethic.* Chicago: The University of Chicago Press.

Smart, J.J.C. (1986). Utilitarianism and its applications. In J.P. DeMarco & R.M. Fox (Eds.), *New directions in ethics* (pp. 24-41). New York and London: Routledge & Kegan, Paul.

Toulmin, S. (1964). *The uses of argument.* N.Y.: Cambridge University Press.

Zeigler, E. F. (1982). *Decision-making in physical education and athletics administration: A case method approach.* Champaign, IL: Stipes.

Zeigler, E. F. (2007). *Applied Ethics for Sport and Physical Activity Professionals.* Victoria, BC: Trafford.

APPENDIX B

APPRAISAL GUIDE FOR THE ADMINISTRATOR/MANAGER

developed by
Earle F. Zeigler, Ph.D.
The University of Western Ontario

Note: Appreciation is expressed to Terry Haggerty, Ph.D. for advice.

Instructions (General)

It is quite common for faculty or staff members in educational institutions and other agencies to be evaluated in one or more ways by those who are selected to administer or manage. However, the converse--rating of administrative or managerial performance by faculty or staff--is not the case nearly as often. Why this continues to be so would make an interesting study in itself. Of course, it is quite possible that many public, semi-public, and private agencies are still not ready for the implementation of a plan of evaluation for managers (by workers) as well as for workers (by managers).

However, we do know that the organizational climate has been changing; thus, this appraisal guide is offered for consideration and possible use. Obviously, a concept of 'organizational democracy' should prevail for the institution of an appraisal such as this on a trial basis. Many administrators and managers, as well as many faculty and/or staff members, now agree that some mechanism should be devised to appraise the administrators/managers with whom they are *primarily* associated. (The investigator, when serving as an administrator in the mid-1970s, experimented with the idea of evaluation for all managerial personnel with good results.)

With any testing device or instrument, questions arises immediately as to the test's validity, reliability, and objectivity. Efforts are being made to answer these questions in the best way possible.

In considering the performance of the individual administrator or manager, the following characteristics, traits, execution of functions, etc. have been included:

1. Job Knowledge
2. Planning and Organizing Work
3. Supervisory Functions
4. Working with People
5. Personal Traits

6. Drive and Initiative
8. Cooperation and Team Play

As you begin this evaluation, please keep in mind that the administrator is typically required (expected?) to have the following types of *knowledge, competencies, and skills*: personal, conceptual, human, and technical (Katz). Also, the administrative <u>process</u> is typically viewed as involving planning, organizing, staffing, directing, and controlling (i.e., ensuring that all is progressing normally according to plan) (Mackenzie).

In assessing any administrator/manager, the evaluation should be based primarily on whether he or she has fulfilled the responsibilities and duties of the post capably. *Those who are appraising the managerial efforts of another should be aware of the agreed-upon job description for the position.* In many cases this has been spelled out carefully and is available for all to examine. Thus, you are assessing administrative performance not so much on the basis of *your own personal idea* of how the job should be done, but more on what it is generally expected (i.e., the job description and existing institutional rules and regulations) that the manager executes to fulfill his or her duties and responsibilities.

Instructions (Specific)

In this Appraisal Guide for the Administrator/Manager, therefore, you will find twenty (20) questions covering different phases of a person's job performance. These questions were gleaned from various sources in the literature, with the questionnaire format itself adapted initially from a format developed by General Telephone System (n.d.).

Please place an "X" in the appropriate box before the adjective (Excellent, Good, Fair, Poor, X) that most nearly answers the question asked. You should do this by judging how adequately the administrator measures up to his or her present job responsibilities and duties. Thus, you should consider carefully what the job is, its degree of responsibility, its degree of authority, how it fits into the organization, and what kind of person is required. *If you don't know*, ask questions to get answers to aspects of the post you don't know or understand. If you really do not have enough information to answer a question accurately (and you can't locate the answer), indicate that you "cannot form a judgment based on experience" (X).

Understand that your response to this questionnaire will remain absolutely anonymous (no identifying numbers are included anywhere). *This puts unusual pressure upon you to be fair and ethical to the best of your ability (and conscience!).* The plan in using this appraisal form is to make two ratings available to all members of the faculty and staff: (1) the numerical

318

average from the *one* General Overall Rating requested at the end of the questionnaire (e.g., 3.3), and (2) the overall numerical average of the 20 individual items added together and averaged (e.g., 3, 4). This should suffice to let faculty and/or staff members know how the final, subjective, overall assessment each person offered
compares to the average evaluation of his or her peers determined in two ways (as explained above).

The administrator, however, would receive the results of the 20 item-by-item evaluations along with two overall assessments, the one determined from the overall subjective assessment and the other the overall averaging of the 20 individual-item averages. The manager would also receive a summary of any other comments offered in the open-ended section of each individual questionnaire.

Please place the completed questionnaire *unsigned* and *sealed* in the blank white envelope in the sealed carton provided in the administrator's office during regular office hours. The secretary on duty will check your name off on a roster indicating that you have "voted." This must be done before [say] June 15 at 1:30 p.m.

A tally and summary of the returns will be prepared subsequently by a committee of three determined by faculty/staff ballot, which in turn shall name its own chairperson at its first meeting prior to fulfilling its function. The results will remain confidential as to specifics, but the Executive Committee will be notified officially by the committee chairperson as to the two numerical averages as explained above. The Executive Committee will not see the synopsis of the final individual comments, nor any other results of the averages of specific categories within the appraisal guide. Within a month the committee chairperson shall shred all retruns in the presence of the administrator concerned.

> **Note:** Please consider it your professional responsibility to complete this evaluation and turn it in prior to the deadline established. To be fair to the administrator/manager, it is important that we obtain as close as possible to a 100% return. Thank you.

Keep in mind that an *Excellent* evaluation means an assessment ranging from 3.1 to 4.0, a Good ranges from 2.1 to 3.0, a Fair ranges from 1.1 to 2.0, and a Poor ranges from 0 to 1.0.

Name of Person Being Evaluated _____

I. Can the administrator get ideas across to other people?

( ) Excellent = Expresses self well in speech and writing
( ) Good = Generally good; has some minor problems
( ) Fair = Has difficulties in communicating ideas
( ) Poor = Lacks skill in communication; often misunderstood
( ) X = Cannot form a judgment based on experience

II. Can the manager determine priorities with the tasks to be performed?

( ) Excellent = Yes; puts first things first
( ) Good = Usually takes care of the most important items
( ) Fair = To a degree; quite often concentrates on secondary items
( ) Poor = No; frequently spends time on items of little importance
( ) X = Cannot form a judgment based on experience

III. What is administrator's knowledge of present responsibility?

( ) Excellent = Full working knowledge of all major items
( ) Good = Good overall knowledge with a few weak spots
( ) Fair = Satisfactory knowledge with some definite gaps
( ) Poor = Does not have adequate job knowledge
( ) X = Cannot form an judgment based on experience

IV. Is manager a creative thinker?

( ) Excellent = Yes; uses original thought to solve problems often
( ) Good = Yes; can generally modify old ideas to meet new problems
( ) Fair = Not usually; shows very little creative thought
( ) Poor = No; usually follows former pattern or regulation
( ) X = Cannot form a judgment based on experience

V. Does manager consistently seek to build strong associates?

( ) Excellent = Yes; encourages variety of experiences for
                associates and gives ample opportunity to "get your
                feet wet"
( ) Good =   Yes; most of the time staff members have varied assign-
                ments within the scope of their positions'
                responsibilities
( ) Fair = Somewhat; people are occasionally encouraged to accept
           new responsibilities or to volunteer for assignments
( ) Poor = No; assignments are far too rigid and tend to be
           stifling because the administrator dominates and holds
           people back

( ) X = Cannot form a judgment based on experience

VI. Can administrator accept criticism?

( ) Excellent = Takes fair criticism well; tries hard to improve
        thereafter
( ) Good = Accepts criticism favorably most of the time
( ) Fair = Not too well; is quite apt to resent it
( ) Poor = No; ignores it and often becomes quite disturbed
( ) X = Cannot form a judgment based on experience

VII. Is manager loyal to organizational policy once established?

( ) Excellent = Completely so, even when he/she disagrees
( ) Good = Will defend the organization's policy on most items
( ) Fair = Will often blame organization's policy for an unpopular
        procedure that manager must enforce
( ) Poor = Will enforce established policy only if he/she agrees
        with it
(...) X = Cannot form a judgment based on experience

VIII. Has manager gained acceptance and "worn well" with staff?

( ) Excellent = Yes, the longer he/she is on the job, the greater
        the acceptance by the staff
( ) Good = Yes, he/she gets along very well most of the time
( ) Fair = Quite average; does have problems on a continuing basis
( ) Poor = Below average; has caused continuing irritation to a
        fair number of people
(..) X. Cannot form a judgment based on experience

IX. Is the administrator a self-starter with initiative?

( ) Excellent = Yes; needs no urging to "get going" by
        himself/herself
( ) Good = Generally good; occasionally needs prodding or
        encouragement
( ) Fair = Often slow to get moving on own initiative
( ) Poor = Will react usually only if pressure is brought to bear
( ) X = Cannot form a judgment based on experience

X. Does manager systematically plan and complete work on schedule?

( ) Excellent = Consistently well organized and on schedule
( ) Good = Yes, typically plans well and generally on schedule
( ) Fair = Impression is created that forward planning is average;

there is often rushing to meet deadlines

( ) Poor = A poor planner typically; often far behind in work
schedule

( ) X = Cannot form a judgment based on experience

XI. How well does manager combine theoretical and practical ideas?

( ) Excellent = Combines both very effectively

( ) Good = Quite well, with occasional overemphasis one way
or the other

( ) Fair = Average; there is some inability to preserve a balance
on occasion

( ) Poor = Often significant overemphasis in one direction or the
other

( ) X = Cannot form a judgment based on experience

XII. Does manager control his/her anger?

( ) Excellent = Maintains firm self-control
( ) Good = Almost always; on occasion gets excited
( ) Fair = Fairly well; needs to exercise more self-control
( ) Poor = Apt to blow up at any given moment
( ) X = Cannot form a judgment based on experience

XIII. Does administrator make a good initial impression?

( ) Excellent = Yes; people like him/her at once
( ) Good = People take to him quite soon
( ) Fair = So-so; sometimes creates an unfavorable impression
( ) Poor = Generally makes a poor first impression
( ) X = Cannot form a judgment based on experience

XIV. How well does manager understand the organization's general
policies and procedures?

( ) Excellent = Full working knowledge of most major items
( ) Good = Quite good overall knowledge; has some weak spots
( ) Fair = Present knowledge is just enough to get the job done
( ) Poor = Needs considerable amount of study and/or training to
develop adequate knowledge
( ) X = Cannot form a judgment based on experience

XV. Is manager open-minded in considering new ideas?

( ) Excellent = Freely accepts new ideas for consideration

322

( ) Good = Quite open-minded; occasionally seeks to avoid an idea
because of source
( ) Fair = Somewhat open-minded, but has some problems here
( ) Poor = Considers new ideas if they are his own (or he "co-opts"
them from someone else); otherwise forget it!
( ) X = Cannot form a judgment based on experience

XVI. Is administrator honest and above board in dealing with people?

( ) Excellent = Completely honest, dependable, and reliable
( ) Good = Typically honest and dependable
( ) Fair = Fairly good; occasionally has problems here
( ) Poor = Quite unreliable; often gives concern
( ) X = Cannot form a judgment based on experience

XVII. Does manager follow the organizational channels?

( ) Excellent = Carefully follows proper channels in his/her work
( ) Good = Usually goes through proper channels
( ) Fair = Quite often; occasionally takes "short cuts"
( ) Poor = Tends to create tensions quite often because he/she does
not follow organizational channels
( ) X = Cannot form a judgment based on experience

XVIII. How fast and sound a thinker is he/she?

( ) Excellent = Has a "rapid" mind that quickly develops sound
thoughts and progressions
( ) Good = Quite fast; typically does well in this regard
( ) Fair = Pretty good; occasionally makes leaps to conclusions
( ) Poor = You can hear the wheels grinding, and the response is
usually not on the beam
( ) X = Cannot form a judgment based on experience

XIX. How capable is the manager in imparting knowledge to others?

( ) Excellent = An excellent teacher; imparts knowledge effectively
( ) Good = A good teacher; generally most satisfactory
( ) Fair = Fairly good, but has some weaknesses
( ) Poor = Does a poor teaching job
( ) X = Cannot form a judgment based on experience

XX. Is administrator willing to work along with the decision-making
process operative within the organization?

( ) Excellent = Yes, in all regards

( ) Good = Generally he/she is, with occasional lapses
( ) Fair = Quite well, but the process is often painful to him/her
( ) Poor = Not really; participatory democracy would give him/her
       an ulcer
( ) X = Cannot form a judgment based on experience

General Overall Rating

Everything considered. this person should receive the following rating for the administrative/managerial work he/she is currently carrying out within the organization:

( ) Excellent

( ) Good

( ) Fair

( ) Poor

(...) X = Everything considered, including my limited experience and understanding of the situation, I don't believe my *overall* opinion should be taken into consideration.

    Thank you for completing this questionnaire. If there is anything else you would like to say, please write it immediately below.

_____

_____

_____

_____

_____